True Canadian Stories of the Great Lakes

Mark Bourrie

National Library of Canada Cataloguing in Publication

Bourrie, Mark, 1957–
    True Canadian stories of the Great Lakes / Mark Bourrie.

Includes all material from the author's Ninety fathoms down.
Includes bibliographical references.
ISBN 1-55267-381-2

    1. Shipwrecks—Great Lakes—History. 2. Great Lakes—History.
I. Title. II. Title: Ninety fathoms down.

G525.B683 2004   971.3   C2004-902437-X

This collection produced for Prospero Books.

All of the stories in this collection with the exception of "The Heroine of Long Point," "Alone on the Bridge" and "Always Trust Your Accountant" first appeared in the collection titled *Ninety Fathoms Down* by Mark Bourrie, Hounslow Press, 1995.

Key Porter Books Limited
Six Adelaide Street East
Tenth Floor
Toronto, Ontario
Canada M5C 1H6
www.keyporter.com

Electronic formatting: Jean Lightfoot Peters

Printed and bound in Canada

05 06 07 08 5 4 3 2

For Marion, Maia, and the Bear,
and for Ernie, who could always tell them
better than I could.

Contents

Preface

I don't like boats.

It's not that I'm afraid of being on one when it sinks. I've been out in a Lake Erie summer gale and some frightening Georgian Bay fall weather. My own mortality doesn't come into it. It's just that I get grossly seasick. I have a lot of hard-earned respect for the people who ride submarines to the wreck of the *Edmund Fitzgerald* or spend their summers combing the lakes for even more mysterious wrecks. I stay on shore, however, unless I absolutely have to leave it, and when I do travel on water, I'm in a state of misery.

Sometimes I did it anyway. Some of the research for this book has required me to live with aquatic motion sickness long enough to get a grasp of what it's like to sail on the Great Lakes and to have been tossed around in some rough weather. Otherwise, I would only have been able to imagine situations that are hard enough to describe, let alone conjure up. For many people, riding on boats would have been the fun part of writing this book. I prefer seeing the great ships of the Great Lakes from shore, and in photos from the files of archives and museums.

I think I first became aware of the tragedies and adventures of the Great Lakes when I was ten years old. One day, I learned that many of the adults in my father's family were orphans, raised by their uncles and aunts. A storm on Lake Erie had taken the *Sand Merchant*, a ship on which several of my grandfather's cousins had worked. Soon after the disaster, the children's mothers had died. Not only had these children lost their fathers, but they had to live with the verdict of U.S. investigators who said their dads were to blame for the loss of the *Sand Merchant*.

At the time that I heard about the *Sand Merchant* disaster, I lived at Craigleith, a village on Georgian Bay that isn't far from the site of the wreck of the *Mary Ward*, the subject of one of the chapters in this book. My friends and I picked up pieces of cast-up wood and metal junk from the shore near the wreck site and kept it, thinking it was part of the ship's skeleton. Maybe it was, since the wreck of the *Mary Ward* is constantly being chewed up by the huge ice mountains along Georgian Bay that were winter castles for the children who lived along the shore. When I was in my early twenties, I dove on the wreck of the *Mary Ward* on a calm afternoon far different from the one that November day in 1872 when some of the ship's terrified crew and passengers took to a lifeboat and were drowned. Two years later, I was at Batchewana Bay on Lake Superior when an American search team found the wreck of the *Edmund Fitzgerald*.

Through those years, I lived in places with water at the end of the main street: Collingwood, Midland, Thunder Bay, Toronto, and Hamilton. As I grew older, the towns changed. The grain elevators in many of those towns were torn down or abandoned, left as empty towers guarding harbours that have no ships. The big lake boats didn't sail into the small town ports as often, and the focus of many of the Great Lakes towns shifted inland. These days, it's hard to believe that some harbours, like Midland's, were once literally jammed with ships in the winter. The crews who lived on them in the idle months turned the lakefronts into small towns, using horses and sleds to get from ship to ship to visit. Even just over a decade ago, the horn blasts from lake freighters added to the party noises of New

Year's Eve in the small Great Lakes ports. Now those places have become much too quiet.

Much of the ships' business has been lost to the Mississippi barge operators or the West Coast ports. Until the 1960s, the bulk of our grain exports were to Europe. Now, along with the majority of Canada's off-continent exports, most of the Prairies' grain goes to Asia. Big freighters still carry iron ore from the west shore of Lake Superior to Hamilton and the steel mills of the U.S. lakefronts, but unless you live along the connecting rivers and canals, in a place like Port Colborne, Sarnia or Windsor, you are unlikely to see anything like the kind of traffic there was on the lakes in the 1960s. Because of this decline, the towns on the shores along the Great Lakes are going through a quiet, sad revolution. Each town, as it loses its original purpose, has to search out new reasons for being.

Collingwood, for example, was founded in the 1850s as the northern terminal of a railway line. Grain elevators were built, a shipyard was established, fishing boats began working from the harbour. Within a generation, the land was cleared around the town. The fruit and vegetables grown in the town's hinterland were processed and canned in a factory next to the shipyard. During the two world wars, Collingwood built ships for the dangerous North Atlantic runs and provided men for the navy and the merchant marine. In peacetime, lake freighters were side-launched into Georgian Bay in spectacular celebrations that drew people for hundreds of miles. Life in the community was dramatic. Ships and men were lost, small disasters happened in the shipyards, but people made a decent living and the town proudly competed with similar communities along the lakes.

By the 1960s, things began to change. The cannery was the first to go. Fortunately, many of the people who worked there got jobs in a new auto-parts plant. The cannery company sold its downtown land for a new Woolworth's. In the 1970s, the shipyard began to show signs of trouble. Contracts came in more slowly than they ever had. By the early 1980s, a strike and the lack of customers for Collingwood's ships made the future of the ship-yard appear very grim. Collingwood no longer competed with its neighbouring towns, because those places had lost their shipyards years before, and their ports had become unimportant. Instead, it was competing with shipbuilding towns in Asia. Another part of the problem was quality. The boats built on the lakes were just too good. Collingwood and the Great Lakes shipyards on the U.S. side of the border made ships that are still used fifty years after they were launched.

In 1987, the Canadian government "rationalized" the eastern Canadian shipbuilding industry. Collingwood's shipyard was closed and 1,200 people lost their jobs. For a couple of years, the area enjoyed a recreational real-estate boom. By the time the 1989 reces-sion settled in, however, there was an overabundance of condominiums near the town's ski hills. Billboards went up on the highways around the town to advertise "two for one" condo sales.

Things got worse when one local auto-parts plant closed, and other factories in the town cut staff. By the end of the 1989-91 reces-sion, unemployment was a constant problem in the community and it had lost its link to the Great Lakes. The harbour was cleaned up and a proposal was made to the town council for a marina and com-mercial complex on the old shipyard property that would change the look and the ambience of the community, for better or worse, for-ever. The town had been remade. With new fast-food restaurants and strip malls going up, it began to resemble the homogenous commu-nities of middle America. The future will probably be better for

Collingwood, but it will be a different place, its heritage kept in a museum near the tranquil lake shore.

As I wrote earlier, I don't like riding on boats, but I do love the people who worked, and still work, on the Great Lakes. The lakes seem to strengthen people, make them more interesting and broaden their minds. A drunk can be tiresome, but give him fifty years' experience as a Great Lakes sailor, and your ordinary drunk can become a sage, filled with stories of adventure in exotic and dangerous places. My grandfather had the great thirst and some brains besides. He could tell stories of the lakes for hours: tales of storms, shipwrecks, interesting fellow sailors, scandalous port people. Maybe most sailors spend fairly long and tedious days at their posts, but adventure comes their way often enough for a real culture to have taken shape on the Great Lakes. I've been lucky enough to hear some of the stories.

In all the years that the lake towns and cities have been evolving, Canada has been gripped with angst about its culture. Does English-speaking Canada have a culture at all? Those who know little about Canada's past and its geography say no. They drive through a place like Collingwood, see the familiar hamburger restaurants, the closed Woolworth's store that's now a bargain shop, the theatre showing the mass-market movies, and mistake the veneer of TV-land for the culture of a 150-year-old community. Lost are the stories of the native people, the mariners, the farmers, the oil workers in forgotten petroleum fields, the shipbuilders. The big ships and the gala launches survive only in quaint old photographs.

Ports like Collingwood would still be in business if people could make money building ships and handling grain. Times have changed and Collingwood is no longer a useful freight port. Canada's taxpayers won't pay subsidies to prolong the life of a dying harbour. The people of the town have made the best of the situation and will probably recover from the revolutionary change to their community. Some will stay and prosper. Others will move away. All of them will relegate Collingwood's shipping days to history, and, within a generation or two, to mythology and trivialization. And Collingwood is just an example of something happening along all of the Great Lakes coasts. Other towns, on both side of the lakes, are living with the same kind of change. Fortunately, in most places, there are a few local historians who keep stories, photos, and scrap books, hoping that someone will come along who shows interest in their history.

This book was written to be part of the canon of Canadian Great Lakes history. Much of the body of the Great Lakes documentation hasn't been written yet. It begins with the arrival of the native people before the end of the last ice age, continues with their evolution into farmers and townspeople, and moves on to the time of the first native contact with Europeans. The horrendous wars that occurred along the Great Lakes shores have been written about, but the stories of the desperate fights between native nations for dominance and survival in the seventeenth century are no longer in vogue.

Very little written material exists about the French colonization along the lakes and the early fur trade. There are books about the War of 1812, but anyone trying to find a well-written, properly researched book about the first settlement of southern Ontario will be disappointed. Nor is there a high quality marine history of the Canadian side of the Great Lakes. As far as this century goes, there has never been a comprehensive social history of the changes that have taken place in Ontario. It seems that Ontario is seen as a static place, one that is far less interesting than the rest of Canada or other places in the world. I hope this book will help erode that myth by making Canadians realize that the people of the Great Lakes are part of a great adventure. They have a destiny that is rooted in their past and continues on—if they choose to know themselves as they really are.

Introduction

Nearly 500 million years ago, the Great Lakes basin was sea bottom, part of a shallow arm of a tropical ocean that was bordered by the lifeless hills of an early continent. In the Ordovician period of geologic time, the equator ran north to south through present-day Winnipeg and the place that is now Lake Huron lay at the latitude of Peru. The closest land to this region was the Canadian Shield, which, in those days, was a range of mountains with some peaks higher than Mount Everest.

Life was certainly simple when the rocks that underlie the lakes were laid down. The most complex animals were trilobites, buglike creatures that swam in the warm waters, crawled along the bottom or buried themselves in the mud. Nautiloids, related to modern squid and octopus, shot their cone-shaped tails through the warm waters using a form of jet propulsion.

Over time, the continents shifted and the sea receded, rolled back in, and receded again. In southwestern Ontario, huge, lifeless tidal flats were buried under new sediments to create wealth for people in salt-mining towns along Lake Huron. Animals trapped in the sediments became the raw material for North America's first oil fields, which were developed near Collingwood and at Petrolia in the 1850s.

About 200 million years ago, the land rose high enough for the seas to retreat for good. The ocean sediments, now rock, were cut by rivers that flowed through dry country. Bays along the shores of the Great Lakes, such as Owen Sound, are often hundred-million-year-old river valleys. At least twenty times in five great ice ages, mile-thick glaciers spread southward and ground the rocks into sand and stones. The glaciers obliterated the great river valleys and buried the old desert landscape, except for the Niagara Escarpment and the flat-topped mesas of the north shore of Lake Superior. At the end of the last glaciation, nearly all of the land was under the waters of great glacial fresh-water seas.

By the time that the land began rising from the water, people had arrived. They followed the giant mammals that lived on the plains and in the scrubby sub-arctic forests that began to grow in the lakes basin: huge beaver, gigantic bears, mammoths, elk, bison. The people, descended from hunters of northern Asia, used lances pointed with eight-centimetre flint and obsidian blades. Their distinctive spearheads, which were simple but effective weapons against the large post-glacial animals, have been found throughout North America. Man's weapons, combined with the climate changes that had caused the demise of the glaciers, doomed most of the ice-age mammals. Within a few thousand years of the arrival of people on this continent, most of the great herds of animals were gone. The horse and mammoth were lost to North America. The camels were slaughtered, as were millions of great horned bison. Only the buffalo was left in its giant herds, destined to be destroyed by the coming of European civilization.

The lake levels rose and fell dramatically in the first few thousand years after the retreat of the glaciers. Meltwater from the glaciers covered the land for a few millennia and helped to smooth the rough edges of the hills. Sometimes, shifts in the retreating ice allowed much of the water in the lakes basin to flow out. When that happened, lake levels became much lower than they are today.

People lived on the shores of these ancient freshwater seas. Archaeologists find traces of their camps on fossil beaches. The land resembled the countryside of the Northwest Territories when people first hunted and fished along the shore of the glacial lakes seven thousand years ago. Nomadic hunters could net the fish of Lake Algonquin or travel to the Ottawa Valley to kill seals and whales in the saltwater Champlain Sea. As the glaciers receded and the climate changed, so did the people who lived in the Great Lakes region. They became more settled, following a routine that took them from camp to camp as the seasons changed. At better fishing spots, people sometimes built wooden weirs, fencelike fish traps, that have survived four thousand years.

Centuries later, the first real villages were built on the edges of marshes and streams within sight of Georgian Bay. Southward from Sault Ste. Marie, the forests were broken by corn fields and towns. Settled people invented complex forms of government and law, created alliances and waged war against each other. The most powerful nations were the Huron and Petun on Georgian Bay, the Neutral in the Niagara and Grand River regions, the Erie on the south shore of the lake that was named after them, and the Five Nations of the Iroquois, who lived south of Lake Ontario. By the time the Europeans arrived, the Huron Confederacy was the most powerful group of people in northeastern North America. Only the Iroquois could challenge its power.

The native people had their own story of the creation of the Great Lakes which shows the link between the Indians and the lakes they lived on. In their creation stories, the great seas that covered the land after the ice age figure prominently, along with the struggle and turmoil of a world in dramatic change.

In the Huron creation story, a young man and a young woman lived in the sky, secluded by their parents, at opposite ends of a longhouse. To prevent them from making love, their parents had surrounded them with cattail down, which would show any trace of disturbance. The parents hoped that, by keeping them chaste, the children would be endowed with special powers. Each day, however, when the others had left to go about their daily tasks, the girl went to the man's end of the house to groom his hair.

The girl became pregnant and gave birth to a baby girl named Aataentsic. This child later married a great chief, who rewarded her people by showering them with corn. The chief grew ill and began to believe his new wife had been unfaithful. To punish her, he uprooted a tree, creating an opening in the sky. He pushed his wife down the hole, and she fell from the sky toward the endless water below.

Aataentsic was seen falling by the turtle and by the other animals that swam in the waters. The turtle moved so that the woman landed upon its back. The beavers and muskrats made earth for her to live on by diving down into the water and bringing up muck and silt which they piled on the turtle's back.

Another great native nation of the Lakes, the Ojibwe, told a story of the creation of the world which could only be repeated in the winter. In the summer, the animal spirits mentioned in the tale could hear their names being spoken and take offence.

Nanabozho, a manito, or great spirit, who worked hard to help the Ojibwe people, was fathered by the wind. In the form of a rabbit, he stole fire from neighbouring people and gave it to his grandmother, with whom he lived. Nanabozho fought with his brother, named Flint, and finally killed him with the help and advice of a woodpecker. He waged fierce warfare against the vicious beings who lived under the surface of the lakes.

One day, Nanabozho met an old toad woman in the woods who carried a load of basswood on her back and sang medicine songs. Nanabozho learned from her that she was on her way to cure the wounded manitos of the water, so Nanabozho killed her, stripped off her skin, and dove into the water. He swam to the camp of the water manito wearing her hide as a disguise. When he arrived at the camp of the water manito, Nanabozho was able to get close enough to kill him, thus releasing a great deluge upon the earth that drowned every creature that could not swim.

A kingfisher warned Nanabozho to make a raft to escape the flood, which the bird said would cover the world. After the deluge had come and, finally, subsided, Nanabozho decided to create a new earth. He told the beaver, loon, muskrat, and otter, who were swimming near the raft, to dive down and gather a piece of the old earth. The muskrat succeeded while the others failed. Nanabozho shaped the earth in the manner of a muskrat house upon the water. He blew upon the earth to expand it to its proper size. Nanabozho named the animals, created laws, placed trees, lakes, and mountains on the landscape and created men and women.

The world filled with the people who had been created by Nanabozho. The Ojibwe kept his memory alive in their camps by recounting his adventures. On the rock cliffs of the Ojibwe homeland, at places like Agawa and Nipigon on Lake Superior, Ojibwe people recorded the mythology of their world. When writing came to the Ojibwe, they carefully wrote down the story of their creation and have preserved it so that it will never be forgotten.

When French fur traders arrived on the Great Lakes in the first years of the seventeenth century, the world of the natives turned upside down. Within two generations, war and disease destroyed the old homelands.

The Huron bartered their corn for furs to trade with the French for axes, knives, copper pots, tools, and guns. The Iroquois trapped animals themselves, traded with other tribes, or attacked their enemies and stole pelts. Throughout the 1640s, these fur wars took the Iroquois farther into what are now the northern regions of Ontario, Michigan, Wisconsin, and even farther west.

In the late 1630s, the Iroquois began exterminating neighbouring tribes and taking over their hunting and trading territories. Guns were the key to Iroquois success, not because of their killing power, which, in the days of flintlock muskets was not much better than steel-tipped arrows, but because of their psychological shock. At first, the authorities in the French, Dutch, and English trading colonies opposed the sale of guns to their trading partners. Bootleg firearms were sold, however, from ships on the St. Lawrence and by the English and Dutch below Lake Ontario. Old-style challenges to fight outside of villages were replaced with dawn attacks, in which large numbers of warriors rushed villages, pillaged and burned longhouses, and returned with long lines of prisoners. By 1650, the Huron had fled to Quebec and the western Great Lakes, and nearly all of the rest of the region's natives were on the run. For the next twenty-five years, the Iroquois were a constant threat to the peace of the Great Lakes.

During the next century, the lakes were used as the waterways to the west. The French and their native allies preferred to travel by canoe, and few ships sailed the Great Lakes until Britain's conquest of Canada in 1759. Very quickly, English merchant ships were built at places like Kingston, Niagara and Detroit. The American Revolution brought new military tensions to the lakes, and more warships. The War of 1812 story of the schooner *Nancy*, told fairly early in this book, shows how important the naval struggle was to Canada's survival during that conflict.

Just as the War of 1812 ended, steamboats started showing up on the waterways of England and North America. The steam revolution took place as colonists spread the frontier from the St. Lawrence Lowlands into the Great Lakes basin. As Ontario grew, so did the states on the other side of the lakes. By the 1830s, when Canadian rebels were trying to bring democracy to Upper Canada, cities were taking shape on the American side. Cities and people meant commerce and the need for more ships, better ports and railways. The 1850s and 1860s saw the creation of most of the cities and towns we know today on the Ontario side of the lakes.

The great days of lake navigation came in the years before World War I and slowly petered out until the opening of the St. Lawrence Seaway in the 1950s. There were several reasons for the decline in lake boat traffic. After the *Noronic* fire in Toronto harbour in 1949, most of the passenger ships went to the scrapyard, instead of being refitted with modern fire-safety systems. Airplanes had taken most of their business, anyway. For people who wanted to see something when they travelled, the new Trans-Canada Highway was a lure that took money out of the pockets of the ship companies.

Once the passenger fleet was gone, most people on the Great Lakes were separated from the waterways they lived on. The slow decline in shipbuilding and freight traffic has been almost invisible to them. They have rarely been electrified by the old dramas of the Great Lakes. Ship disasters are far rarer than they used to be. Before

World War II, there was, on average, a major shipwreck at least once a year. After the war, as better navigation and safety systems were installed on the ships, wrecks and sinkings became much less frequent. At most, they happen every fifteen years, on average.

To understand the lakes' stories, you must realize a few facts about the lakes themselves. They truly are huge bodies of water. Lake Superior is the largest freshwater body in the world. On a map, its north coast appears to be a haven of small harbours, and there seem to be many little towns along the shore. In fact, only one of the little towns on the north shore, Marathon, is even on the water. The rest are a kilometre or two inland. Ships travelling from Thunder Bay to the Soo sail far from the wilderness coast on a freshwater sea that is capable of as much violence as any of the world's oceans. Even now, after more than two centuries of navigation, new shoals are being found in Superior. One unmarked submerged ridge may have claimed the *Edmund Fitzgerald*, the lakes' newest and most famous wreck.

Lake Huron is barely smaller than Lake Superior, with the added hazard that north winds pushing down the lakes can move for more than two hundred kilometres across open water almost every month of the year. Storms on Lake Huron and Georgian Bay are at least as powerful as those on Lake Superior. There are few harbours on the Canadian side of Lake Huron, so when a cyclone like the Great Storm of 1913 hits, there's nowhere to run.

Lake Michigan's weather and geography is little better for navigators and it's a much busier body of water than the other two large northern lakes. It's been the scene of some strange accidents. The people who died in the worst disaster on the lakes, the capsizing of the cruise ship *Eastland* at a Chicago dock on July 24, 1915, never even left the pier. At least 830 people were killed when the ship, loaded with factory workers on a company picnic, rolled over. Many other ships have gone down on Lake Michigan, accounting for the loss of thousands of lives on a lake that seems to many people to be the home of just bass-fishing boats and summer yachts.

Lake Erie, the southernmost of the Great Lakes, gets gusts of warm air from the southwest, carrying moisture and heat from the Gulf of Mexico. These winds often collide with arctic air, blasting the people and ships along the north and east shores with heaping drifts of snow and terrible flooding. The prevailing winds can push the level of Lake Erie up by as much as two metres in a few hours, remarkable indeed on a lake with an average depth of less than fifteen metres. The shallow water creates powerful, choppy waves that move close together and can cause a ship to be torn apart from its ends and sides and battered on the bottom of the lake at the same time.

Lake Ontario, the less travelled of the southern lakes, is known to sailors for its deadly squalls. Two U.S. War of 1812 schooners were sunk together off Hamilton by a squall, a sharp blast of wind at the edge of a thunderstorm cell. The *Speedy*, which took with it much of early Canada's aristocracy, was also lost in a Lake Ontario storm. Most of the truly terrible disasters on Lake Ontario, however, such as the *Noronic*'s have been caused by fire.

For nearly four hundred years, people have written down the stories of the Great Lakes, leaving us with a half-forgotten legacy of stories of tragedy, courage, greed, negligence, and bravery. The lakes bring out the virtues of people, as well as their follies. In the beginning years of modern Canada, they were the scene of the cruellest struggle in Canada's history, when the first little ship on the Great Lakes failed to save thousands of people who became refugees in their own homeland in a terrible war over beaver pelts.

For in their interflowing aggregate, those grand freshwater seas of ours—Erie, and Ontario, and Huron, and Superior, and Michigan—possess an ocean-like expansiveness, with many of the ocean's noblest traits; with many of its rimmed varieties of races and climes. They contain round archipelagoes of romantic isles, even as the Polynesian waters do; in large part, are shored by two great contrasting nations, as the Atlantic is...they have heard the thunderings of naval victories...for leagues and leagues are flanked by ancient and unentered forests, where the gaunt pines stand like serried lines of kings in Gothic genealogies; those same woods hiding wild Afric beasts of prey, and silken creatures whose exported furs give robes to Tartar emperors; they mirror the paved capitals of Buffalo and Cleveland, as well as Winnebago villages; they float alike the full-rigged merchant ship, the armed cruiser of the State, the steamer and the beach canoe; they are swept by Borean and dismasting blasts as direful as any that lash the salted wave; they know what shipwrecks are, for out of sight of land, however inland, they have drowned full many a midnight ship with all its shrieking crew.

Herman Melville
Moby Dick, 1851

Chapter One

The Little Boat
of Charity

The Huron Feast of the Dead was an important part of the ritual life of the agricultural people of Ontario.
(CONTEMPORARY FRENCH ENGRAVING)

In the first half of the seventeenth century, as little villages of French settlers were founded in Quebec, Jesuit missionaries set out to build a new, Christian, native country in the Great Lakes basin. They chose the Huron country to be the place where they would labour to build this new nation of Roman Catholic farmers. The Huron were already settled people, living in villages with as many as five thousand people. They were the wealthiest, most organized Indian nation that the French had met so far. The Huron were willing to let the Jesuit missionaries into their country to help keep their trade alliance with the French.

After about ten years of living among the Huron in their villages, the Jesuit missionaries on southern Georgian Bay decided to build their own settlement, Sainte Marie, on land they bought from the Hurons near the modern-day town of Midland. A church and a mission house were built in the middle of a fortified courtyard on the Wye River. Around the central mission were outbuildings where blacksmiths, carpenters, and leather workers plied their trades. Farm animals were brought from Quebec along the tortuous canoe route that led up the St. Lawrence and Ottawa rivers, through the Mattawa River, Lake Nipissing, and the French River to Georgian Bay.

The Hurons lived near the shore of Georgian Bay but preferred to build their villages a few kilometres back from the coast. To reach the native communities, the Jesuits walked the trails of the Huron country or travelled in a small sailboat they built at Sainte Marie in the 1640s. Called a shallop, it was the first European-style boat to sail the Great Lakes. It was probably a small, open sloop, rigged with sails fore and aft. Similar boats, descended from the style used by the Vikings, had been built for hundreds of years in Normandy, which was the home of most of the French priests and workers at Sainte Marie.

The sloop was used for carrying people and supplies along the shore of Georgian Bay, which was a natural highway to the native tribes to the west. In later years, missionaries from Sainte Marie were carried to even more remote places, such as Manitoulin Island and the parts of the upper Great Lakes where Lake Michigan, Lake Superior, and Lake Huron come together. It was much easier to use the breezes of Georgian Bay to push a boat along than to depend on the Huron birch bark canoes, which were perfect for travelling on rivers and portaging, but were so light that they were dangerous on the open Great Lakes.

With the arrival of French, Dutch, and English colonists along the Atlantic coast in the early 1600s, traditions of native warfare changed and the eastern part of this continent became a very dangerous place to be. Instead of fighting over past wrongs and old quarrels, the natives of the Great Lakes region began waging war for fur trade territory and for trade routes to the nomadic hunters of the west and the Canadian Shield. In the days before the Europeans, war had been something of a bloodless, ritual game, but during the first years of the fur trade, it became a bloody struggle of ambushes and massacres.

In 1644, the governor of New France sent twenty-two French soldiers to winter at Sainte Marie to protect the Hurons and the priests from the Iroquois. He had originally planned to send these troops to Huron villages, but the Jesuits were afraid the soldiers would corrupt the Hurons with their poor morals. In 1647, more soldiers and a small cannon were dispatched to the mission. The Jesuits' little sloop probably sailed up Georgian Bay to the mouth of the French River to meet the soldiers and their heavy burden of weapons.

Even with the French soldiers, the Hurons were losing the war with the Iroquois. Part of the reason for the failure lay in the presence in their country of the French, especially the missionaries. In their zeal to convert the Huron, the French had destroyed the native traditions and government. Families and communities were torn apart over religion. Christians were encouraged to stop taking part in community celebrations and rituals. By the middle of the seventeenth century, the Huron were divided and demoralized. The Iroquois have been painted as heartless conquerors. The beaver wars were brutal and bloody, but in many ways the victors were trying to save their native traditions. Historians often argue over the reasons behind the Iroquois attack on the Huron. Perhaps they defeated them simply because it was finally possible, after centuries of war. The Iroquois tried to establish peace, on their terms, throughout the Great Lakes and Ohio River valley. Until the American Revolution, they were the dominant native power east of the Mississippi River, obeying no one, not even the colonizing Europeans.

In the early summer of 1648, the worst blow so far fell on the Hurons. Teanaostaiae, the largest town in the Huron country, fell to the Iroquois. The attack came after sunrise of July 4, when most of the Huron men were away hunting or trading in Quebec.

The Iroquois climbed over the fortifications and ran through the town, killing people and setting fire to the houses. The fires spread through the longhouses and ignited the little village church, where Jesuit priest Antoine Daniel was killed. The captured people were used by the Iroquois to carry off the loot, mainly furs, from the town. Of the two thousand people who were in Teanaostaiae at the time of the attack, seven hundred were estimated by the Jesuits to have been killed.

Panic struck the country. Many people began seeking refuge in the village on Christian Island, which was considered safer than mainland towns because it was about six kilometres offshore in Georgian Bay.

In the fall of 1648, an army of about one thousand Iroquois, well equipped with guns and ammunition, crossed Lake Ontario and spent the winter in the forests southeast of the Huron country, moving slowly north so that they arrived in the Georgian Bay area in the early spring. In the early morning of March 16, 1649, the Iroquois struck at St. Ignace, a village of about four hundred people southeast of Sainte Marie. The raiders reconnoitred the town in the dark. At a weak spot in the town's stockade, the Iroquois broke through shortly before dawn and took St. Ignace by surprise. Nearly all of the Hurons were captured without much fighting. Only ten Iroquois died in the attack. Later that day, they captured the Huron village of St. Louis, after a short fight with the men of the village. Two Jesuit priests, Jean de Brebeuf and Gabriel Lalemant, were captured at St. Louis, forced to march to St. Ignace, and were tortured to death by traditionalist Hurons who had joined the Iroquois. Over the next couple of days, there were battles in the area of Sainte Marie. The Hurons inflicted some casualties on their tormentors, but the Iroquois had succeeded in their mission. The Hurons knew they could no longer defend their homeland.

Within two weeks, fifteen Huron villages were abandoned. People fled north to the small lakes and islands of the Canadian Shield, or to the Tobacco Nation who lived between Georgian Bay and the Niagara Escarpment. Christianity had split the Hurons. Most of the traditionalists, who had opposed the European culture, moved west or joined tribes that hadn't been converted. More than six thousand Hurons, nearly all of them Christians who had given up many native traditions, went to Sainte Marie, now the strongest fortification in the country. The Huron villages were burned so they would not be used as forts by the Iroquois.

The Jesuits' mission was an obvious target for the Iroquois, who were expected to send more warriors to the Huron country in the summer. Fearful that Sainte Marie would bear the full brunt of the next Iroquois attack, the priests decided to burn the fort and travel with the Huron in their flight. The Jesuits had to choose whether to follow the Hurons who had moved north or west, or to go to the village of Charity on Christian Island, which was flooded with refugees. The Jesuits wanted to create a new Christian Huron country on Manitoulin Island, hoping they could preach not only to the Huron, but to nomadic people living nearby. They also expected to be able to use the island to maintain the Huron's trading role as middlemen between the upper Great Lakes nations and the French.

The Huron headmen knew that Manitoulin Island was unfit for growing corn, which was the crop the Huron relied on, because the soil was poor and the island was too far north for the climate to be dependable. The issue of the future of the Huron country was settled at a spring meeting at the mission house at Sainte Marie. For three hours, the chiefs spoke to the Jesuits and presented them with ten large collars made of beads. This gift was given to persuade the Jesuits to stay with them on Christian Island and to try to take away some of the grief for the loss of the missionaries at St. Ignace.

The Jesuits needed a great deal of persuasion. Already, the situation on Christian Island was becoming grim. In late May, after the panic, thousands of Hurons, many of them widowed women, children, and elderly people, had arrived on Christian Island. The people already living there were starving, trying to live on acorns, and on Otsa, a bitter root. Hurons who were unable to gather nuts or roots were barely surviving on wild leeks baked in ashes or on small amounts of smoked fish.

All that spring, the Jesuits' boat searched the Georgian Bay shore, looking for natives with food for sale. Outside the Huron country there had been little warfare so far, so some of the Algonkian nomads in the Canadian Shield had acorns, fish, and even some extra corn for sale. The people living in the Beaver Valley, across Georgian Bay, also had extra food, so the Jesuits bartered for supplies to help the Huron through the winter. The food was loaded into the sloop and taken to Sainte Marie, where it was put under heavy guard. Within a few weeks, however, the boat and its precious cargos of food were on the move again, this time to the people struggling to survive on Christian Island.

On June 14, 1649, the Jesuits put Sainte Marie to the torch. The destruction of the fort, its churches, hospitals, and Indian dwellings, along with its fields and tradesmen's lodgings, was a heartbreak to the priests: "We even applied the torch to the work of our own hands, lest the sacred House should furnish shelter to our impious enemy; and thus in a single day, and almost in a moment, we saw consumed our work of nearly ten years, which had given us hope that we could produce the necessities of life, and thus maintain ourselves in this country without the aid of France. But God has willed otherwise; our home is now laid waste, and poor Penates forsaken. We have been compelled to journey elsewhere, and, in the land of our exile, to seek a new place of banishment."

The Jesuits loaded their little shallop and some barges with their men, livestock, tools, weapons, and the rest of their belongings. Iroquois raiders lurked on the mainland and attacked Christian families who had followed the Jesuits by walking on the trails along the shore of Georgian Bay. The little sailboat made its way past the places where the towns of Midland and Penetanguishene would be built two centuries later, just offshore of the seemingly tranquil forests and empty fields that had once been the Huron homeland.

The new fort that the Jesuits built on Christian Island was encircled with a stone wall. Armed with a small iron cannon and protected by the soldiers and armed labourers, it was a strong military deterrent to an attack on the nearby Huron villages that were being built.

"These grand forests, which, since the Creation of the world, had not been felled by the hand of any man, received us as guests, while the ground furnished to us, without digging, the stone and cement we needed for fortifying ourselves against our enemies," Paul Ragueneau, leader of the Jesuit missions in Huronia, wrote. "In consequence, thank God, we found ourselves very well protected, having built a small fort according to military rules, which, therefore, could be easily defended, and would fear neither the fire, the undermining, nor the escalade [ladders] of the Iroquois. Moreover, we set to work to fortify the village of the Hurons, which was adjacent to our place of abode. We erected for them bastions, which defended its approaches, intending to put at their disposal the strength, the arms, and the courage of our Frenchmen. These would most willingly have hazarded their lives in a defense so reasonable and so Christian, the village being truly Christian, and the foundation of the Christian church that is dispersed throughout these regions."

The main Huron town had nearly one hundred longhouses, and smaller villages were scattered over the southern part of the island. The hardest work was clearing the forest and preparing it for cultivation. The Jesuits had saved ten chickens, a pair of pigs, two bulls, and two cows, along with several tonnes of corn. Ragueneau makes it quite clear in the *Relations* that this corn was to be used primarily to feed the priests and their French helpers and for attracting Hurons to the Christian faith.

The Hurons had poor luck with the small fields they planted on Christian Island that summer. A dry spell lasted so long that they lost all hope of a harvest and begged the Jesuits to pray for rain. With no food on the island and the Iroquois on the mainland, the Huron were starving. The little shallop, along with Huron canoes, travelled along the shores to the north, picking up more acorns and dried fish through the fall.

As the winter of 1649-1650 settled in, the famine deepened. The weakened people began to suffer from diseases that spread through the village, especially among the children. To make the misery worse, the precipitation that the Hurons had needed so badly in the summer finally arrived as a heavy blanket of snow that covered the ground more than a metre deep.

"Then it was that we were compelled to behold dying skeletons eking out a miserable life, feeding even on the excrements and refuse of nature," Ragueneau wrote. "The acorn was to them, for the most part, what the choicest viands are in France. Even carrion dug up, the remains of foxes and dogs, excited no horror; and they even devoured one another, but this in secret; for although among the Hurons, ere the faith had given them more light than they possessed in infidelity, would have considered that they were not committing any sin in eating their enemies, any more than in killing them, yet I can truly say that they regard with no less horror the eating of their fellow-countrymen than would be felt in France at eating human flesh. But necessity had no longer law; and famished teeth ceased to discern the nature of what they ate. Mothers fed upon their children;

brothers on their brothers; while children recognized no longer, in a corpse, with whom, while he lived, they had called Father."

Rather than starve on the island, some Hurons began, as early as the summer of 1649, to slip over to the mainland in their canoes to look for food, even though throughout the autumn false rumours spread of a larger enemy force heading toward Christian Island. Soldiers and workmen watched over the priests and the starving Hurons while those Frenchmen who did sleep at night kept their weapons nearby.

The calamities that had shattered the lives of the Hurons were seen as a boon by the priests, who had found an opportunity to spread Christianity. They believed the harvest of souls on Christian Island was superior to any inroads they had made on the Hurons while they were still a strong, healthy nation. Sadly, they mistook the troubles of a once proud people as an opportunity from God to collect souls. The Jesuits recorded acts of religious fervour by people desperate for food and emotionally shattered by the horror around them. Mothers with sick and starving children were said to have thanked God that their children were dying as Christians. The church was filled night and day with worshippers, sometimes ten or twelve times before nine o'clock in the morning. In the evening, a bell would be rung to call the Hurons to church again, and similar crowds would come for the evening Mass. It was a grotesque mockery of real faith by a people whose world had been destroyed.

Some Hurons sold their only possessions, the clothes on their backs, for a meal of acorns. Knowing they were to die, others refused to part with their clothing, as they did not wish to be buried naked. Frenchmen helped lay out and bury people whose relatives were too hungry or sick to do the work. Some asked to be buried alive so their clothing would not be stolen.

" 'Ah!,' they say to us, 'I entreat thee, my brother, bury me now, at once; for my life is over; and thou seest plainly that I am among the dead. Now, what I fear is this, that, if I should die before being buried, other poor people, as destitute as I am, may rob me of these rags to cover my nakedness, to put upon themselves. It will be a consolation to me, on going down to the grave, to know that, after my death, my body will not suffer that humiliation, of which I have had a horror all my life.' "

The Jesuits cut copper cooking pots into round coins, which they stamped and gave out to the sick and the hungriest people. At noon, all of the people who received one of these coins lined up in front of the fort. Some were given a few of the acorns or some of the dried fish that had been brought to Christian Island in the Jesuits' boat.

"Hunger is an inexorable tyrant, one who never says, 'It is enough;' who never grants a truce; who devours all that is given him, repays himself in human blood and rends our bowels, ourselves without the power to escape his rage, or to flee from his sight, all blind though he be," Ragueneau wrote.

In the early weeks of March, people from the island began walking across the ice to the mainland to look for acorns on the bare southern slopes of the hills just inland from the shore. One large group of hungry people, mostly women and children, set out across the strait between Christian Island and the mainland to look for food.

"Hardly had these good Christians left our sight than the ice melted under their feet. Some were drowned in the depths; others, more fortunate, extricated themselves, though benumbed with a deadly cold. It was a most cruel death to the poor old men, women and children, to give up their souls on these snows, without help or succour,—not, however, without consolation from him whom they adored in their hearts, and who could never die therein. An old Christian woman, aged sixty years, who had passed the whole night lying on the ice, was found on the following morning, full of life. She was asked who preserved her. 'I called out,' she replied, 'from time to time, JESOUS TAITEUR, Jesus have pity on me. At that same moment, I felt myself quite warm. The cold again seizing on me, some time after, I renewed my prayer, and my body again recovered its warmth. I passed the whole night in that way, and cheerfully awaited my death.' This poor woman could recall but those two words of her prayers. She recovered, for that time; but since then has fallen into the hands of the enemies, and has thus met the termination of her miseries," Ragueneau wrote.

More than three hundred people died that day. It was the worst recorded disaster on Georgian Bay. However, the people of Christian Island were so desperate that the tragedy hardly changed life in the stricken village at all. And things were about to get worse.

The Hurons on the island were just beginning to harvest the new supplies of food from the spring fishing and the exposed acorns when the Iroquois arrived back in force. On March 25, they began their attack on the Huron's mainland camp and, within two days, had killed all of the people who had crossed the ice in the winter and spring. One hundred people were murdered in one place, fifty in another, and families that had deliberately travelled to isolated places were systematically hunted down. Still, there were people on the island who were prepared to risk death or captivity to escape the horror of famine.

Shortly before Easter, another party of Hurons decided to try to evade the Iroquois and find food. On Easter Sunday, the Jesuits held a Mass for them, and, the next day, they left the island, naming the Jesuits as their heirs and leaving behind their property. A few days later, the news arrived back on Christian Island that they had been captured. Eight days later, another group set out and met the same fate.

Soon afterwards, the survivors on the island learned that two more Iroquois war parties were on the way. These warriors sealed the fate of the Huron nation in its old homeland. Two elderly chiefs went to Father Ragueneau and told him that the Hurons were leaving the island. Some chose to go westward, but the majority wanted to move to Quebec. The Jesuits agreed, and a few days later, the priests loaded their small ship one last time to flee from southern Georgian Bay. Along with a canoe flotilla of Huron survivors, it headed toward the French River, the first leg in the overland route to Quebec. Somewhere near the mouth of the French River, the Jesuits abandoned their little boat forever. Whether they burned it or allowed it to rot, they never said. Few people have bothered to search for the first European water craft on the Great Lakes, and marine histories rarely even mention its existence.

Behind the Jesuits lay the ruins of the Huron homeland and five thousand bodies of famine victims on Christian Island. Never in Canada's history have so many people suffered such misery as the Hurons in their last few years as a nation. For more than a century, their country was a cursed place and people avoided it whenever possible.

Chapter Two

The *Griffin*

The Griffin *on her maiden voyage to Green Bay.*
(Canadian Steamship Lines Archives)

René Robert Cavalier de La Salle was a man whose vision and ability was not matched by his luck. He was a gambler, a man who took chances that bordered on recklessness. La Salle arrived in Canada in his mid-twenties and started a feudal estate at a place that he named La Chine. This was an interesting choice of both name and location for La Salle's investment of much of his life savings and inheritances: La Chine, China, was about as close to the Iroquois homeland as La Salle could get. He couldn't have found tougher people to have as enemies. Then he pushed even further inland, building a post and estate at the site of Kingston, Ontario, a short hop across Lake Ontario for any Iroquois war party that didn't have the time or energy to go down to New France. It's a wonder he survived in Canada as long as he did, but it would be a Frenchman, not an Iroquois, who would eventually put a bullet in his back.

Perhaps not surprisingly, La Salle was to have more trouble with his own people than with the native people. The Iroquois seemed to respect La Salle's vision. They caused him no trouble as he built a few small boats to carry furs across Lake Ontario in 1673. In a sense, La Salle had the same grandeur as the Iroquois leaders, and there was a place for them in his great schemes. La Salle and his patron, Count Frontenac, Quebec's governor, had made trade easier for the Iroquois while at the same time skimming off for themselves much of the fur business that had been going to Montreal. It was only a matter of time, they hoped, before they would be able to pay off the creditors that hounded them. The bill collectors would just have to wait until La Salle's ships came in.

La Salle got greedy when he decided to build a post at Niagara, in a place that had only recently been conquered by the Iroquois. The new French fort cut off part of the Iroquois war-and-trade route to the west and skimmed furs from Iroquois traders the same way that Fort Frontenac, at Kingston, had bled furs from the Montreal merchants. Then La Salle went to work building ships.

The completion of an armed ship to collect furs from the west would have put the canoe-bound Iroquois out of the fur business. At the same time, La Salle could have happily sailed past the rival French traders and the Jesuit priests who hated him. The new ship wasn't to be the first sailing vessel on the Great Lakes. The Jesuits at their mission on southern Georgian Bay had travelled in their shallop, and La Salle himself had built boats on Lake Ontario. The *Griffin* was to be the first full-sized ship, a vessel capable of long voyages far from land or in hostile waters. There would be five cannon on board, more than the entire total on the Great Lakes up to that time.

By 1675, when the work at Niagara began causing consternation to the Iroquois, La Salle had been bitten by a very expensive exploration bug. The recent discovery of the Mississippi seemed to change La Salle's whole vision of the world. He realized there were huge new lands to exploit in the west that would feed into his Great Lakes operations. Up to the time that the Mississippi was found, the French view of central North America seemed limited to the fertile land of the southern Great Lakes and the rocky wilderness of the Canadian Shield to the north. The Mississippi and its tributaries were a great untapped source of wealth. La Salle decided he would go after those riches with ships.

In the winter of 1675, La Salle and a group of hired men began building the ship at a creek mouth near the site of what is now Buffalo, New York. She was the *Griffin*, a brigantine that had the capacity to carry a rich load of furs through Lake Michigan, Lake Huron, and Lake Erie. While the ship was under construction, guards had to be posted around the clock to protect her from the Iroquois, who were determined to wreck or burn the vessel. La

Salle himself drove the huge spike that joined the sternpost, the rear support that held the rudder, to the great beam of oak that was the *Griffin*'s keel. The ship's name, portrayed at bow and stern by carvings of the mythical flying monster, was taken from the coat of arms of Count Frontenac. "This Griffin will soar over the ravens," La Salle said in a joke that was made at the expense of the black-robed Jesuits.

The *Griffin* (Griffon in French) was a well-fitted-out sailing ship, made of rather green oak from trees that were cut down and sawn near the building site. She was about twenty metres long, the size of a large sailing yacht. On board, at least upbound, was a fairly skilled crew, two Recollet friars, and La Salle himself.

All they needed was a chart.

On today's maps, the Great Lakes look like waterways that are sheltered and safe. That appearance is deceiving. The old desert mesas and glacial gravel bars hidden under the lakes are treacherous to sailors. The currents of the lakes can push a sailboat onto sand bars like Long Point and Point Pelee before crews have a chance to react. Then the lake's strong surf tears them apart. The connecting rivers, the Detroit and St. Clair, have their own traps. For someone who has no charts, challenging them is an act of arrogance. Then there are the storms. Summer squalls packing winds of a hundred kilometres an hour are common. In the fall, cold arctic air sweeps across warm water, becoming charged with gale-forced winds, rain, and snow. La Salle had never laid eyes on the upper lakes, nor had most members of his crew.

Not only did La Salle lack nautical charts of the lakes themselves, but the maps of the shorelines that had been drawn by earlier explorers were simply wrong. For example, two generations of French cartographers had drawn a large bay on the Lake Huron side of the base of the Bruce Peninsula. What is really there is a dangerous, unprotected shoreline of rocks and sand bars. Any ship depending on these maps that got into trouble along Manitoulin Island or the Bruce Peninsula would have made for this bay and been wrecked. If an explorer, a trader, or a native told a map maker about some island or bay that he had never seen, the artist drew it into his map, and subsequent cartographers copied the error. In fact, the Lake Huron ghost harbour doesn't disappear from maps until the end of the 1700s.

Before La Salle, no one had tried to map the shoals farther out in the lakes, simply because they had no ships to do so. They could get advice from natives, but few of the aboriginal people had been out of sight of land in their canoes and they had no need to take soundings for their small craft.

The wonder is that La Salle ever made it to Green Bay, on Lake Michigan, the *Griffin*'s first port of call.

The only eyewitness to write a description of the *Griffin*'s maiden voyage was a rather dubious character, a Recollet friar named Louis Hennepin. The European discovery of Niagara Falls has been credited to Hennepin, probably because Etienne Brule, who saw it first, was killed and eaten by the Huron before he could put the discovery in writing. The Jesuits, who were writing down the events of the time, had despised Brule's wild lifestyle. Hennepin wrote a description of the falls that has never been surpassed: readers back in Europe, where his books were best sellers, learned that the falls were fifteen kilometres wide and two hundred metres high. His ability to exaggerate natural wonders was surpassed only by his dislike of the Jesuit priests who ran most of the missions in New France.

Hennepin and La Salle became partners because of their mutual antipathies.

Despite Hennepin's artistic creativity in describing the wonders he saw in North America and the heroics he performed to see them, the story he wrote of the *Griffin*'s voyage has the ring of truth.

In the spring, Hennepin wrote, La Salle found he couldn't get the *Griffin* up the Niagara River into Lake Erie until the wind was in his favour. Rather than paying his rough gang of sailors and ship-builders to sit around, La Salle put them to work digging and planting a vegetable garden. They must have been less than pleased. They preferred to spend their time gathering wild leeks along the shore. These herbs, a relative of the lily, are tasty, but so powerful that the breath of someone who eats them is almost intolerable. By the time the *Griffin* had the wind with her, it was a foul wind indeed.

When the ship finally started moving up the Niagara River, most of the crewmen on board the *Griffin* had to walk along the river bank so the ship would be light enough to clear the rocks. Twelve of the crewmen trudged along the shore, pulling ropes to drag the *Griffin* through the current. Luc, a seven-foot-tall Danish sailor who was the ship's pilot, was sure the *Griffin* wouldn't make it into Lake Erie, but at last, when the ship was in calm water, her crewmen fired off their guns and the five cannon aboard, and celebrated Mass.

On shore, members of an Iroquois war party and their Sioux pris-oners watched in amazement and dismay as the *Griffin* made ready to sail. Some of the Iroquois left immediately for New York to tell their Dutch and English trading partners about the ship. Many of the Iroquois had seen ships before, at Montreal and farther down the St. Lawrence River. Some bigoted non-native writers have patron-ized the Iroquois with talk about "big canoes," but by the late 1600s, the Iroquois had no primitive illusions about ships and no "cargo cult" ideas about European technology. They knew exactly how much effort would be needed to overwhelm the *Griffin*, kill its crew and toss its weaponry into the lake. For now, they just didn't have the manpower to do the job. They fully understood what the *Griffin* could mean to their trade and their military control of the Great Lakes. Eventually, given the chance, they would have fixed the ship for good.

On August 7, the *Griffin*'s crew and passengers finally went aboard and began their trip. In all, Hennepin wrote, there were thirty-four men, including himself and another Recollet friar. The *Griffin* sailed west-southwest and travelled one hundred kilometres the first night. The next day, it sailed past Long Point and Point Pelee, clearing the hazardous strait between the southern tip of mainland Canada and Pelee Island. This, in itself, was an achievement. Many bigger, stronger ships carrying accurate charts were to be lost in this Lake Erie ship graveyard. To the southwest, the *Griffin*'s crew could see the Bass Islands on what is now the Ohio side of Lake Erie.

Along the route, Hennepin had visions of the future of the lakes. At Chippewa Creek, where the *Griffin* was built, he believed a settlement could grow into an important town. He was right. The Buffalo-Niagara area now has more than a million people. As he sailed the Detroit River, he saw that its banks were fertile meadows. He realized that a city on the waterway could be a great trading port, one that would serve a huge area of prosperous farms. Hennepin told La Salle his ideas, but the fur trader, a man who was famous as a visionary, thought the priest was too ambitious. As they passed the future site of Detroit, La Salle said their fortunes were to be made inland, putting the natives to work gathering furs. These lakes, he told the priest, were just a highway to the west, something to pass through. They would never amount to much, he said.

Hennepin let La Salle have the last word, but he didn't change his mind about the Detroit River country:

"The forests are chiefly made up of walnut trees, chestnut trees, plum trees and pear trees, loaded with their own fruit and vines. There is also an abundance of timber fit for building, so that those who shall be so happy as to inhabit that noble country, cannot but remember with gratitude those who have discovered the way, by venturing to sail upon an unknown lake for about one hundred leagues (five hundred kilometres). That charming strait lies between 40 and 41 degrees northern latitude.

"I had often advised M. La Salle to make a settlement upon the strait between Lake Erie and Ontario, where the fishery is more plentiful... but M. La Salle, and the adventurers who were with him, would not harken to my advice, and told me they would make no settlement within one hundred leagues of their fort, lest other Europeans should get before them into the country they were going to discover. That was their pretence, but I soon observed that their intention was to buy all of the furs and skins of the remotest Savages, who, as they thought, did not know their value, and so enrich themselves in one single voyage.

"I endeavoured also to persuade him to make a settlement upon this charming strait... M. La Salle would by no means harken to my advice, and wondered at my proposal, considering the great passion I had a few months before for the discovery of a new country."

By taking a pass on Hennepin's suggestion, La Salle missed out on the opportunity to be the founder of Detroit. Instead, Antoine de

La Motte Cadillac built the first fort there twenty-five years later. Perhaps, if La Salle had listened to Hennepin, rich and powerful people would be riding in La Salle limousines today and Cadillac cars would be the stuff of trivia.

The *Griffin* sailed across Lake St. Clair, and, with some hauling by its crew and careful depth soundings, made its way up the St. Clair River to the upper lakes. So far, the worst that had happened to the *Griffin* was a few groundings on sand bars. When they reached Lake Huron, the men aboard the *Griffin* began their education in the power of the Great Lakes.

Lake Huron was the body of water that the French knew best. Traders, explorers, and missionaries had been canoeing along its shore for almost seventy years. The part of Lake Huron they had travelled on the most, however, was Georgian Bay, not the open lake to the west. The *Griffin* sailed just off the Michigan shore, nearly running aground on rocks several times. A storm that began August 26 intensified just after the *Griffin* passed the mouth of Saginaw Bay. The crew took down the ship's main sail and let her run at the mercy of the wind.

La Salle thought the *Griffin* was finished. Hennepin wrote that most of the crew and passengers were ready to make their peace with God:

"Therefore, everybody fell upon his knees to say his prayers, and prepare himself for death, except our pilot (Luc the Dane), whom we could never oblige to pray, and he did nothing at all except to curse and swear against M. La Salle, who, as he said, had brought him thither to make him perish in a nasty lake, and lose the glory that he had acquired by his long and happy navigations on the Ocean."

La Salle's luck hadn't run out. The August storms on the lake usually aren't as powerful as those that come in the fall. Gradually, the wind calmed, and the *Griffin* hoisted sail. The next morning they reached Michilimackinac, where Lake Michigan joins Lake Huron.

The Huron and Ottawa who lived at Michilimackinac were allies of the French and enemies of the Iroquois. They shared, however, the Iroquois' feelings about the *Griffin*. In the years since they had been driven out of their rich Georgian Bay homeland, the Huron had been living as traders on the upper lakes. The Ottawa made their living transporting furs down the river named in their honour to Montreal. The *Griffin* threatened to put all of them out of work.

La Salle, dressed in a scarlet cloak decorated with gold lace, accompanied by sailors carrying guns, visited the leaders of the natives while some Ottawas came aboard the *Griffin* carrying gifts of whitefish and trout. La Salle had sent men ahead to stay with the Huron that summer and, when the ship arrived, they took the side of the natives, who considered the *Griffin* to be a menace to the fur trade. The presents that La Salle had given the native leaders had been wasted. The mood in Michilimackinac was turning ugly, so La Salle and his crew went back aboard the *Griffin* and sailed on into Lake Michigan for about two hundred kilometres, to a camp of Pottawatomis.

Their chief was a friend of Governor Frontenac, and the natives were not opposed to the presence of the *Griffin*. For four days, while the *Griffin*, anchored just offshore, rode out a storm, La Salle and his men feasted, traded and watched native dancers. While he was with the Pottawatomis, La Salle traded enough furs to fill the *Griffin*'s hold and he decided to send her back to Niagara, with a crew of only five men. He and the rest of his entourage would stay on Lake Michigan and prepare for an expedition to the Mississippi.

On September 18, the *Griffin* hoisted sail and fired a salute from her cannon. That was the last the French saw of her.

"Though the wind was favourable, it was never known what course they steered or how they perished, for after all the enquiries we have been able to make, we could never learn anything else but the following particulars," Hennepin wrote.

"The ship came to an anchor to the north of the Lake of the Illinois [Michigan] where she was seen by some Savages, who told us that they advised our men to sail along the Coast, and not towards the middle of the Lake, because of the sands that make navigation dangerous when there is any high wind. Our pilot, as I have said before, was dissatisfied, and would steer as he pleased, without harkening to the advice of the Savages, who, generally speaking, have more sense than the Europeans think at first. But the ship was hardly a league from the coast, when it was tossed up by a violent storm in such a manner that our men were never heard of since, and it is supposed that the ship struck upon a sand and was there buried."

So, what happened to the *Griffin*?

Like Hennepin, La Salle had no doubt. He didn't, however, believe the priest's story that the ship had disappeared at the junction of Lake Michigan and Lake Huron. La Salle was sure, for the rest of his life, that the *Griffin*'s crew had stolen the furs on board and had scuttled her. Playing detective, there are a few clues that suggest La Salle may have been right. First, there were rumours among the natives west of Lake Michigan that several Frenchmen who had been travelling down the Mississippi had been taken prisoner and that one of them was a giant matching Luc the Dane's description. Supposedly, they were all dead by the time La Salle passed by on his own expedition down the Mississippi.

There are several holes in that scenario, not the least of which is that the Mississippi valley was about the last place a handful of fugitive French sailors with a cargo of stolen furs would have wanted to be in the winter of 1676. For one thing, there were no reliable maps of the area, and these men, heavily weighed down with furs, would have had to struggle to find their way. There was also a war going on: the Iroquois were attacking the Illinois tribe. And where were they supposed to have been going? There were no European settlements along the Mississippi. It would be years before New Orleans was founded. A cargo of furs would have been worthless with no buyers and no likelihood of transportation from the Gulf of Mexico. The most the *Griffin*'s crew could have hoped for would be to hook up with the Spanish, who were French allies at the time. Maybe they would have been friendly, maybe not. In those days, allegiances changed hourly, and force counted more in transactions in the wilderness than honour or national alliances.

The alternative for the hijacked-fur scenario is for the crew to have made their way to the English post at Fort Albany. Many French traders had skipped off to their rivals by travelling through Iroquois territory, and La Salle was later to be betrayed by employees who did exactly that. Yet, for these five men, including a giant, to have made their way back to Lake Erie, scuttled the *Griffin* and made it overland through, or past, all of the territories of the Five Nations of the Iroquois, would have been quite a feat. At best, they would have been relieved of their burden of furs and been killed or kept as prisoners. It is almost unthinkable that the news of such an event wouldn't have travelled around the Great Lakes. The Iroquois would have had no reason to keep it a secret.

A similar theory holds that the *Griffin* was attacked by natives and pillaged. Her crew were supposed to have been killed and the ship was said to have been scuttled. This lays blame on people for something they certainly didn't do. The evidence points entirely the other way. Had the natives of the upper lakes, allies of the French, committed the crime, they would have been obliged to get rid of a large cargo of furs and to have hidden anything of value that was stolen from La Salle's ship. They would also have been burdened with keeping the attack on the ship secret from their families and their trading partners, and they would have lied to the French. Such a secret could never have been kept. There is simply no proof at all, either in documents of French traders showing a one-year fur glut or in the oral historical record of the Great Lakes natives, of such an attack. And, again, if the *Griffin* had been taken by natives who were enemies of the French, why would they have kept their victory a secret?

What evidence there is still points to the ship going down in the area where Lake Michigan and Lake Huron join. Over the past century, many hulks have been said to have been La Salle's ship. Two wrecks, one near Tobermory and the other on Manitoulin Island at the junction of Lake Huron and the north channel of Georgian Bay, are said to be the most promising. The tales surrounding the Manitoulin wreck would seem to clinch the site as the place where La Salle's ship foundered. First, there is a claim that the skeletons of six men dressed in French clothes were found in a Manitoulin Island cave, along with French coins and brass buttons. One of the skeletons is claimed to have belonged to a huge man. These coins, skulls and buttons, however, are all supposed to be lost. No one seems to know the whereabouts of the cave. There is a wreck in the area, but nothing proves it is the *Griffin*. There isn't much left of the ship, whatever it is. The Niagara Escarpment, of which Manitoulin Island is a part, abounds with treasure-in-cave folklore. In the Collingwood area, people have talked for years about caves with native pots and weapons, but none have been found by archaeologists.

The Tobermory wreck is even less complete than the Manitoulin site. Again, it may be the *Griffin*, but it could also be an old schooner or fishing boat that was left to rot or that foundered. The Great Lakes are dotted with the hulls of boats that were allowed to sink or went down without loss of life and were forgotten.

So let's look at the clues we have. They are the ones presented to La Salle after they were fished out of Lake Huron or Lake Michigan: a hatch cover, some pants, a bundle of furs. They sound like the sort of debris that is often cast up after shipwrecks. The natives said they were found in the northern part of Lake Michigan. The prevailing wind, especially in fall storms, comes from the northwest. All things being normal, if they turned up downwind of the *Griffin*'s sinking, she went down somewhere between the end of Green Bay and the junction of Michigan and Huron.

That would mean the old priest, that master of creative writing, was right when he said the *Griffin* was lost just as she slipped out of sight of the main native settlements at the lake junction. Her little crew never had much of a chance to get lucky twice on the lakes. Upbound, they had barely made it. Downbound, they hardly got out of port before their journey ended.

Chapter Three

Revenge of the *Nancy*

The schooner Nancy *was attacked at Wasaga Beach by a US naval force.*
(Huronia Historical Parks Archives)

The War of 1812 was more a series of naval skirmishes than a struggle between land armies. A quick glance at a map of Ontario shows why. There is no place between Cornwall, on the St. Lawrence River, and the Pigeon River, west of Lake Superior, where the border can be crossed on foot, except maybe in the winter. The waterways were both a barrier and a highway. The navy that controlled the lakes could transport soldiers and supplies to their enemy's shore, and could maintain the web of communications between isolated forts at the strategic places where the Great Lakes join each other.

At the beginning of the war, both sides had only a few merchant schooners on the lakes, so, during the two years of struggle, they raced to build fleets that would give them the upper hand. Every conceivable vessel was pressed into service, along with obsolete old cannon, elderly fur trappers and anyone or anything that could add strength to the fleets.

In September, 1813, the naval stalemate on the lakes above Niagara Falls was finally broken when Commodore Oliver Hazard Perry defeated a British fleet on Lake Erie. Perry's victory hadn't come cheaply. His flagship, the *Lawrence*, was shot out from under him, so he fled to the brig *Niagara*, carrying a flag with the slogan of Perry's dead colleague Captain Lawrence: "Don't Give Up the Ship." Perry's success on Lake Erie ensured that the Americans could strike at will at the British forts along the four Great Lakes above Niagara Falls. Soon after the Battle of Lake Erie, they began trying to pick off the best British posts on the upper Lakes: Fort William, which controlled most of the western fur trade, Michilimackinac, where Lake Michigan joins Lake Huron, and Sault Ste. Marie, where the Northwest Company had built a primitive canal to join Lake Superior to Lake Huron. The capture of those places would have put Upper Canada's western frontier at Niagara. In the peace talks that followed the war, it is unlikely that British negotiators would have been able to hang onto the Canadian sides of Lake Erie and Lake Huron, and they could possibly have lost the prairies and the Canadian fur-trade country as far north as the Hudson Bay lowlands.

The crew of one small ship helped make the difference.

In the summer of 1789, a small, independent fur trading company based in Montreal paid for the construction of a schooner at the little town of Detroit, which was still in British hands. The *Nancy*, as she was to be christened, was considered by her owners to be well built and had the capacity to carry 350 barrels of provisions. Her figurehead, a woman wearing a plumed hat and gaily coloured clothes, was carved in New York City.

By the turn of the century, Forsyth Richardson and Company, the fur traders who owned the *Nancy*, had merged with the much larger Northwest Company. As part of the Northwest Company, the *Nancy* became a pawn in the continent-wide struggle with Hudson's Bay Company for control of the fur trade in northern North America. At the beginning of the War of 1812, she was berthed at Moy, on the present site of Windsor, Ontario.

Good luck on the *Nancy*'s part had kept her out of the Battle of Lake Erie. She was on her way down from Lake Huron to Detroit and had just entered Lake St. Clair when she was raked by American cannon fire. The *Nancy* managed to escape up the St. Clair River with her rigging shot up and one man badly scorched by the enemy's cannonade. For nearly a year, the *Nancy* was a fugitive. She was also the last link in an overland supply route that brought desperately needed food through the small lakes and rivers of southern Ontario to Georgian Bay. Voyageurs hauled food, cannonballs and gunpowder northward from York in canoes and small, flat-bottom boats, hoisting the supplies on their backs to cross long portages. At the mouth of the Nottawasaga River, the *Nancy* picked up the supplies. She carried them to the besieged fort at Michilimackinac, the key that unlocked Lake Michigan, Lake Superior, and British and American possessions beyond. By the summer of 1814, Michilimackinac was the fort U.S. generals and admirals coveted more than any other place in Canada.

In the spring of 1814, more than four hundred British soldiers and sailors were able to slip through the U.S. naval blockade at Michilimackinac. They arrived at the fort with enough cannon and supplies to get through the summer but unless more food made it past the American fleet, the garrison would not survive through the next winter. South of the British post, Britain's native allies in Michigan, Illinois, and Wisconsin were being attacked, so there was no hope of help from them. More than one thousand U.S. soldiers, backed by artillery, were heading north from Detroit toward the strategic fort.

The arrival at Michilimackinac of this powerful American army, backed by naval superiority, caused a panic among British and Canadian forces. The *Nancy* was no match for any of the American ships. In the middle of July, Royal Navy lieutenant Miller Worsley accompanied by a few sailors and some allied native warriors had waited for the *Nancy* at the Nottawasaga River and had loaded her with supplies before word of the American assault on Michilimackinac reached southern Georgian Bay. The *Nancy* was far from the action but similar supply ships nearer to the battlefield, the *Mink* on Lake Huron and the *Perseverance* at Sault Ste. Marie, were quickly captured by the Americans. A talkative member of the *Mink*'s crew told the Americans that the *Nancy* was probably somewhere on Georgian Bay.

On August 1, 1814, the *Nancy*'s crew and Worsley's men got word from a messenger to hide their ship in the sluggish mouth of the Nottawasaga River. For the last ten kilometres of its long, slow route across southern Ontario, the Nottawasaga flows through a deep estuary, parallel to Georgian Bay. Only a small, tree-covered sand spit, now the site of the resort town of Wasaga Beach, separates the Nottawasaga River from the lake.

The *Nancy* hid behind that tree-covered sand spit while her crew built a blockhouse on the high bank of the land side of the river, on the side away from the lake. The effort was almost hopeless, since the thirty-two-member ragtag collection of navy regulars, native warriors, and fur traders protecting the *Nancy* had only three small cannon. All they could hope for was luck.

At first, luck let them down. On August 13, three American ships, the *Niagara*, the *Tigress*, and the *Scorpion* arrived at the Nottawasaga River looking for the *Nancy*. The *Niagara* was the largest of the three U.S. ships, but the *Tigress* and the *Scorpion* were heavily armed and quite capable of destroying the *Nancy* on their own. Like the *Niagara*, the *Tigress* and *Scorpion* had been part of Perry's line of battle at Put-In-Bay. There were more than three hundred soldiers on board the American ships along with several field guns, howitzers, and the cannon of the American vessels. For the men cramped aboard the three U.S. ships, the Nottawasaga River mouth must have been an inviting place. Crystal clear water lapped against pine-covered sand dunes. The American soldiers went ashore on the sand spit to stretch their legs and set up a camp for the night when they spotted the *Nancy*'s masts through the trees. The Americans went back to their ships and got ready to fight the *Nancy*.

The twenty-three-year-old lieutenant who commanded the *Nancy* was a child of the Napoleonic Wars. He was born in 1791 on the Isle of Wight and had joined the navy when he was twelve. He had seen action as a boy at Trafalgar and Copenhagen, along with several less famous naval battles. Worsley passed his lieutenant's exam in October, 1810, and received his commission a year later, when he was already in Canada.

The young officer had seen Eastern Canada the hard way, walking overland from Halifax to Kingston in the winter of 1812-13. In May, 1814, he fought at the bitter assault on the U.S. fort at Oswego, New York. Then, within a few days, he was sent into the bush to the part of North America that was then called "The Northwest."

Worsley, who had no illusions about the fighting power of his three small cannon and his band of sailors, decided to stay and fight. The Americans opened the battle the next day by sailing close to shore and trying to blast the British ship by firing across the sand spit. The dunes and white pines, however, proved to be enough protection for the *Nancy*. British cannon in the blockhouse fired back at the Americans but didn't hit anything.

That afternoon, the American troops, under the command of Lieutenant-Colonel George Croghan, landed on the spit and set up their heavy artillery only a few hundred metres from the *Nancy*. Now there was no hope for the Canadian ship. With cannon balls landing closer to the *Nancy* with each volley, Worsley decided to blow up his ship rather than let her be captured. His men hammered spikes into the touch-holes of their cannon to make them useless to the enemy, then took the last of their gunpowder into the hold of the ship. They made a crude fuse with the powder from the blockhouse to the *Nancy*, but before they could light it, an exploding American shell blew up the little fort. The fire ignited the line of gunpowder and, a second later, the *Nancy* blew up, and what was left of her began to burn. The British had planned to take all of the cargo off the *Nancy* before scuttling her, but it was lost, along with an unlucky sailor who was near the ship when she blew up.

Croghan, the commander of the American soldiers, described the destruction of the *Nancy* in a letter to his commanding officer:

"My first impression on seeing the explosion was that the enemy, after having spiked his guns, set fire to the magazine itself, but on examination it was found to have been occasioned by the bursting of our shells, which, firing some combustible material near the magazine, gave the enemy but barely time to escape before the explosion took place. The Commodore secured and brought off the guns, which were mounted within the block-house (two 24-pound carronades and one long six-pounder) together with some round shot, grape and canister. The enemy will feel severely the loss of the *Nancy*, her cargo consisting (at the time of her being set on fire) of several hundred barrels of provisions intended as a six-month supply of food."

The only loss to the Americans was one soldier who was wounded by a native sniper who had been hiding in the trees near the U.S. artillery.

In a letter to his father, written about two months after the Nottawasaga River attack, Worsley talked about the desperate fight. He somewhat exaggerated the casualties to his men and the distance he had to walk to safety:

"The enemy's force consisted of a 20-gun brig and three schooners mounting each a long 24-pounder with 450 soldiers. I, however, contended with them for my vessel from 9 A.M. until 4 P.M. with my three guns, 24 seamen and ten Indians. Finding my

little crew were falling all around me, I immediately formed a resolution to blow it [the *Nancy*] up, which I did, and made my escape
with the rest of my little crew through the woods to the great aston-
ishment of the enemy.

"We walked that night with our wounded and dying 36 miles
before we came to any house. We lost everything we had except
what we stood upright in. On my arrival at this house, which had
stores, etc. for the Island Michilimackinac, which Island I had to
supply with stores and provisions, I waited two days and then made
my mind up to go to it in open boats, the distance of 380 miles."

The commander of the American fleet, Captain Albert Sinclair,
took some pity on the *Nancy*'s brave men and ordered his crew and
soldiers not to chase them. The Americans salvaged the three spiked
cannon and a couple of small boats from the *Nancy*'s wreck site and
picked through the rubble of the blown-up blockhouse before heading back to their ships. Worsley and his men rowed up the
Nottawasaga to the British base of Schooner Town, where there
were another hundred barrels of supplies the Americans didn't know
about. By not hunting down the *Nancy*'s men, the Americans made
one of their biggest blunders of the War of 1812. Compounding their
mistake was their decision to send the *Niagara* back down to Lake
Erie, along with most of the soldiers on board the three U.S. ships.
The Americans thought the *Tigress* and *Scorpion* could hunt down
any fur-trade canoes that tried to run the blockade. They hadn't considered Worsley's thirst for revenge for the loss of his little schooner,
which was now a smouldering hulk lying partially submerged on the
bottom of the Nottawasaga River.

The *Tigress* and *Scorpion* stayed for a few days in the lower part
of Georgian Bay mapping the shoreline, then headed north to the

junction of Lake Huron and Lake Michigan. The Americans didn't know they were being followed. Worsley's gallant little force loaded two boats and a canoe at Schooner Town, upstream on the Nottawasaga, then set off toward Georgian Bay. The Americans had cut down trees across the mouth of the river, but the Canadians and British quickly hauled them out of the way. Then they made for open water and a 550-kilometre trip across Georgian Bay and Lake Huron to the besieged post of Michilimackinac.

Most yacht captains today would never try to tackle the open waters of the Great Lakes in heavily loaded open boats. Worsley's men rowed an amazing one hundred kilometres a day into the prevailing winds. During the trip, a fierce northwest gale blew into their faces. The storm nearly sank the *Niagara* as she made her way south in Lake Huron on the far side of the Bruce Peninsula and forced the *Tigress* and *Scorpion* to flee the relatively unprotected waters of Nottawasaga Bay.

At St. Joseph's Island, near Sault Ste Marie, Worsley learned that the *Tigress* and *Scorpion* had appeared at the north end of Lake Huron only a couple of days before the arrival of his little fleet of rowboats. They were guarding the main passage between St. Joseph's Island and Michilimackinac. Not wanting to be hammered by the ships' guns again, Worsley hid his supplies in a little bay on the island; then, along with the other twenty-five men under his command, he travelled in one large fur-trade freight canoe to Michilimackinac. On a moonless night, they passed within one hundred metres of one of the American ships, so close they could hear the enemy talking. The other ship lay about fifteen miles away. On September 1, Worsley arrived at Michilimackinac, eager to cash in on his luck. He began looking for volunteers to avenge the loss of the *Nancy*.

The entire British fleet on the upper Great Lakes was put at Worsley's disposal. It wasn't much. Worsley was given four row-boats, one of them armed with a six-pound gun. One of the other rowboats carried a three-pounder. The attackers were a hodge-podge of British regulars, soldiers of the Royal Newfoundland Regiment led by Lieutenant Albert Bulger, Canadian militia, and about two hundred native warriors who were expected to fight native soldiers who had joined the Americans. In all, there were about eighty British and Canadian raiders under Worsley's command. The natives were headed by their own chiefs and by four British civil servants.

The little armada travelled about thirty-five miles, arriving on September 2 near the last place where Worsley had seen the American blockaders. The main bulk of the attackers landed on St. Joseph's Island and waited while scouts searched for the *Tigress* and the *Scorpion*. Within a few hours, the *Tigress* was spotted about five or six miles away. Worsley and his men decided to wait until nine o'clock to attack. By then, it would have been dark for more than an hour and most of the Americans would have gone to sleep.

Ninety-two men set out after the U.S. ship just as the sun was going down. Most of the native warriors stayed behind, but three of their chiefs were taken in the British rowboats. For three hours, the little flotilla rowed quietly toward the *Tigress* and her crew of twenty-eight men. At about nine o'clock, when the *Tigress* could just barely be seen looming in the inky darkness, the four little war-ships split up so that they could take the American crew by surprise from both sides of their ship. Worsley's boat was only a few yards away from the *Tigress* before the dozing sentries finally saw it.

The Americans demanded to know who was out there.

Worsley and his men didn't answer.

Within a few seconds, the sound of an American cannon cut the summer air and the night erupted in flashes of musket fire from both sides. Fortunately for everyone concerned, no one fired with much accuracy in that darkness. Worsley and his men swarmed over the side, killing four officers aboard the ship and driving the rest of the crew into the *Tigress*'s hold. The American sailors fired up through the ship's deck, killing one of Worsley's men and wounding seven others including Bulger, the commander of the Newfoundland troops. After a few threats, the shooting stopped. Worsley had lost two sailors to American gunfire, and eight of the Canadians and British were wounded. The fighting had lasted five minutes.

After Worsley rummaged the *Tigress*'s papers and learned the name of the ship, the American prisoners were taken out from the hold and loaded onto the rowboats. Some of the Newfoundland soldiers took them back to Michilimackinac, while Worsley and most of the men under his command stayed behind on the *Tigress*. The Americans arrived in the enemy fort dressed only in their underwear, since Worsley's men demanded their uniforms.

A canoe was sent out to scout for the *Scorpion*. Within a few hours, the second American ship was spotted coming toward the *Tigress*. Worsley and his men kept their cool. They put on the clothes of the American officers and men. Those who didn't get enemy uniforms went down into the hold of the *Tigress*. Then they hauled aboard the small cannon from their rowboats and set them up on the *Tigress*'s deck. For about six hours, Worsley and his men waited for the *Scorpion* to tack closer. They left the American flag flying on the *Tigress* and prayed the *Scorpion* hadn't heard the noise of the battle carrying across the still waters of the north channel of Lake Huron.

Worsley was lucky. Not only was the *Scorpion* unaware of the

Tigress's change of ownership, she was also unready for battle. She only had two cannon working, and one of them was on a carriage that was so decrepit that the gun was almost useless. Also, the ships had no way of communicating with each other. The *Scorpion* sailed to within a couple of miles of the *Tigress*, then dropped anchor. Lieutenant Daniel Turner, his five officers, and the *Scorpion*'s crew of thirty-one sailors and soldiers spent the last few hours of darkness sleeping on their ship.

At dawn, Worsley's men hoisted their anchor and raised the jib on the *Tigress*. They slowly sailed toward the *Scorpion*, with only a small number of sailors visible on the *Tigress*'s deck. A few soldiers who couldn't fit in the hold stayed on the *Tigress*'s deck, covered in overcoats. On the *Scorpion*, a gunner kept watch and a few sailors were up early scrubbing the deck. No one suspected trouble.

When the *Tigress* was only about a dozen yards from the *Scorpion*, the British twenty-four-pound gun blasted a hole into the *Scorpion*'s hull. The shot was the signal for the attackers hidden in the *Tigress*'s hold to rush up on deck. The soldiers who had been hiding under the coats tossed them aside and leapt to attack. The boarders raked the deck of the *Scorpion* with a volley of musket fire, killing two men. That was the extent of the fighting. The *Scorpion*'s crew were now prisoners and would soon join their colleagues at Michilimackinac.

Worsley's attack changed the balance of power on Lake Huron. The two ships, newly renamed *Confiance* and *Surprise*, sailed to the Nottawasaga River, past the site of the *Nancy*'s wreck, to pick up the supplies that were needed at Michilimackinac. They returned in October with enough supplies to last the people in the fort for the rest of the war, which was to end a few months later.

News of the loss of the two blockaders was carried to the Americans in late October by four members of the *Tigress*'s crew, who escaped while they were being taken to prison in Kingston. In those days, there were different rules for officers and men. The sailors rotted in jail until the end of hostilities. The American officers were paroled, on condition that they promise not to fight in the war again.

Captain Sinclair of the *Niagara* wrote to his superiors of the "mortifying" loss of the *Tigress* and *Scorpion* and tried to put the blame on Lieutenant Turner. Sinclair said the *Scorpion* could have defended herself better, especially since the crew of the American ship had been handpicked by Turner himself. Also, Sinclair claimed he had warned Turner that the British at Michilimackinac were desperate enough to launch an attack on the *Tigress* and *Scorpion* in an attempt to break the siege.

An American naval inquiry held on the deck of the man-of-war *Independence* in Boston harbour exonerated all the officers on board the two captured ships:

"After they [Worsley's men] were discovered, every exertion was made by Lieutenant Champlin [master of the *Tigress*] to defend his schooner that bravery and skill could suggest, and not until all of the officers were cut down, did the overwhelming numbers of the enemy prevail. The enemy thus having captured and having mounted on her their 6 and 3-pounders, and having placed on board a complement of between seventy and one hundred men, remained at St. Joseph's until the 5th of September. On the evening of that day, the court find that the *Scorpion* returned from cruising off French River, and came to an anchor within five miles of the *Tigress* without any information having been received or suspicion entertained by Lieutenant Turner of her capture. At the dawn of the next day, it appears that the gunner having charge of the watch passed word to the sailing master that the *Tigress* was bearing down under American colours. In a few minutes after, she ran alongside the *Scorpion*, fired, boarded her and carried her.

"It appears to this court that the loss of the *Scorpion* is in a great measure to be attributed to the want of signals, and owing to this deficiency, no suspicions were excited as to the character of the *Tigress*, and from some of the English and men on board her being dressed in the clothing of her former officers and men, and the remainder of her crew being concealed, a surprise was effected which precluded the possibility of defence.

"The court are therefore of the opinion from the whole testimony that the conduct of Lieutenant Turner was that of a discreet and vigilant officer.

Wm C. Aylwin, John Shaw,
Judge Advocate President.

Approved,
B. W. Crowninshield."

Worsley's feat of capturing two U.S. Navy ships would not be repeated by any enemy of the United States during the country's war with Mexico, the Civil War, the Spanish-American War, World War I, World War II, the Korean War, or any of the invasions, occupations, or skirmishes that the United States was to become involved in for 154 years. The next time a U.S. Navy ship would be hauled into an enemy port was in 1968, when the North Koreans captured the U.S.S. *Pueblo*, a spy ship operating off the Asian coast.

For the rest of the war, Worsley commanded his two captured ships, with the impressive title of Commander of Naval Forces at Michilimackinac. His letter to his father makes it clear that he was delighted with both his new fame and the two ships. In October, 1815, he was given command of the brig *Star*, a much larger boat than either of his two captured ships. A year later, with the end of the worldwide hostilities of the Napoleonic Wars and the War of 1812, he was laid off. Worsley returned to the Isle of Wight to live as a young gentleman. There, he was given a job as an inspector of boat safety. He finally felt secure enough to be married. In 1820, he exchanged vows with Joanna Evered, the daughter of a Bristol doctor. She was left a widow with three small children when Worsley died in 1835.

The *Confiance* and *Surprise* were tied up at Amherstburg when the war ended. Along with most of the warships on both sides of the lakes, they were left to rot at their moorings. The *Niagara* met a similar fate at an American base on Lake Erie.

The ghost of the *Niagara* lived on, however, and was given a new home in a reconstructed version of Perry's famous ship. Timbers from the original *Niagara* were salvaged and built into the walls of the new replica, which is operated by the Pennsylvania Historical Society as a sail-training vessel.

The *Nancy* settled onto the bottom of the Nottawasaga River. Sand carried down the stream collected around the wreck, creating an island. Anything of value was removed from the schooner in the last century, including the ship's figurehead. It was stored in a barn owned by William Wilson on the Penetanguishene Road, north of

Barrie, Ontario, until, early in the twentieth century, a tenant at the farm used it for firewood.

In 1928, the *Nancy*'s hull was raised and put on display on the island she created. Seven years earlier, a twenty-four-pound cannon ball from the *Niagara* had been found on the river bank where the blockhouse had once stood. In July, 1994, the mayor of Wasaga Beach and the captain of the *Niagara* met on the bridge of an American Coast Guard training ship anchored at the mouth of the Nottawasaga River. In deeper water, the *Niagara* waited as a little ceremony took place to end the saga of the *Nancy*.

The last time the *Niagara* was at his town, "it wasn't particularly welcome," Wasaga Beach mayor Walter Borthwick said as he presented the salvaged twenty-four-pound cannon ball, which had been mounted on a wooden stand. Walter Rybka, captain of the *Niagara*, said the old cannon ball will have a place of honour in a new museum in Pennsylvania which will be devoted to War of 1812 naval history.

"This is the only cannon ball that is known to have been fired by the *Niagara*. To us, it is a very important artifact," he said. "When we were told last March that we were getting the cannon ball, one of my staff asked me, 'What speed do they intend to send it back?'"

The real legacy of the *Nancy* lies in the present border between the United States and Canada. Michilimackinac was given to the Americans, but Canada and the United States might not be sharing the upper Great Lakes today if Worsley hadn't snatched the *Tigress* and *Scorpion* from the Americans and changed the fortunes of the Canadians and British on the upper lakes.

Chapter Four

The "Coffin Ship"
Atlantic

The collision of the Atlantic *and the* Ogdensburg *was one of the worst disasters on the Great Lakes, with as many as 350 people lost on the wreck.*
(CONTEMPORARY NEWSPAPER ENGRAVING.)

At the bottom of Lake Erie, not far from the tip of Long Point, a sophisticated security system protects the wreck of the *Atlantic*, a paddle-wheel steamer which sank in 1852. The computerized alarm uses the same technology as cellular phones to detect any movement on the steamer *Atlantic*. If anyone enters the invisible grid of radio signals that blankets the wreck, an alarm sounds at a nearby Ontario Provincial Police station and a patrol boat is sent to the wreck site immediately. Already, unauthorized divers have been arrested and charged under Canada's criminal code and the Ontario Heritage Act.

What is so valuable that the Ontario government is willing to pay for one of the best security systems in the world to protect it? Probably not much. The *Atlantic* was an immigrant ship, carrying hundreds of people who wanted to be farmers in the American Midwest. In fact, the Ontario government believes the security system is protecting a wreck that possesses some archaeological value, rather than wealth as a sunken-treasure ship.

A group of California divers and promoters disagrees, however. They say the *Atlantic* has $60 million in old gold and silver coins aboard and that the treasure is theirs. The ship, they argue, was American. They have a U.S. court order saying they have legally bought the rights to it and everything on board. They want the Ontario government to stand aside and let them bring the *Atlantic* and its coins to the surface, nearly 150 years after she went to the bottom.

In its day, the *Atlantic* was one of the better ships on the Great Lakes. With a length of about eighty metres, she wasn't particularly large but she was fast. The *Atlantic* had set several speed records on the lucrative Buffalo to Detroit run in the four years since she was launched at Newport, Michigan. Her cabin passengers, about 150 during the busy summer months, travelled in modest style. With just those passengers, the *Atlantic* would have been a commercial success. The flood of immigrants, who needed transportation to the western parts of the lakes, guaranteed the *Atlantic*'s owners a windfall.

Certainly, the timing of the *Atlantic*'s owners had been fortuitous. In the middle of the last century, Europe was a good place to leave. Beginning in 1845, a series of crop failures, financial collapses and revolutions sparked a wave of immigration to North America. That year, the Irish potato crop was stricken with blight, a mould that destroyed entire fields and even ruined the potatoes that were in storage. It spread from the eastern seaboard of North America to the Isle of Wight, turning up in Ireland just before that summer's harvest. Within weeks, entire counties lost all of their crops. Since most Irish families relied entirely on the potato, the effects were devastating. Ireland was a tenant society in which farm families lived on the produce from their potato plots while growing wheat to pay their rents. The failure of the potato crop meant the expulsion of millions of tenants by their landlords. Displaced by their cruel landownership system and one of history's worst famines, more than one million of Ireland's six million people left their country. Back home, a third of the population died before the potato crops revived in 1850.

Grain and potato crops had failed in parts of England and Europe as well. In 1847, financial markets collapsed, and in the spring of 1848, revolutionaries in Paris overthrew the government of King Louis Philippe. The revolution spread to Austria, Italy, and Germany, with flare-ups in much of the rest of Europe. In most countries, the old order was restored with brutal repression. Karl Marx and Frederick Engels tried to inspire working people with their Communist Manifesto, published in 1848. Some farmers and labourers, however, decided that their future was abroad, far from the troubles in the streets, in the new booming heartland of North America.

Immigrants who survived the harrowing and disgusting "coffin ships" of the Atlantic immigrant trade usually reached land at Quebec City or New York. The healthy and smart ones kept going. New York was a warren of slums, ruled by gangs that stole what little the immigrants had, before putting them to work at starvation wages. In Quebec, Irish immigrants were kept in quarantine in a festering "hospital" at Grosse Isle, where more than six thousand people died of typhoid fever during the potato famine years. Nearly as many perished in another camp just outside of Montreal.

The lucky ones made it to the Great Lakes. In the 1840s, Buffalo was the jumping-off point for most immigrants heading west. The railways to the plains hadn't been built yet, but there was still good, cheap land in the Great Lakes region. The last leg of the terrible immigration voyage took newcomers from Buffalo to Detroit or Chicago, where the better-off people bought farms sight unseen from land agents and the poorer ones set out for the frontier, hoping to get hired as farm labourers. Within a couple of generations, most became prosperous settlers and had all but erased from their minds and their family histories the horrors of the trip to the interior.

The story of the *Atlantic* fits into the pattern of exploitation and suffering that immigrants faced as they tried to get to the frontier. Something quite criminal happened on the afternoon of August 19, 1852. The *Atlantic* left Buffalo on her regular run, with every cabin filled and with about 250 Irish and European immigrants crowded below her decks and scattered in the open air on the top decks. Captain J. Byron Pettey had heard there was a large number of Norwegian immigrants waiting at Erie, Pennsylvania, for any ship that would take them west. They hoped to reach Detroit, then walk inland to the new farming areas that were opening up in the fertile forests of southern Michigan.

The *Atlantic* arrived at Erie in the dark and loaded just over half of the Norwegians aboard. About seventy lucky but enraged Norwegians were left on the Erie dock. There was no way in which any more people could be jammed onto the overloaded ship, even by the lax safety standards of those times.

The ship's purser collected as much cash as he could. He didn't keep a list of passengers, so no one knew how many people were aboard the *Atlantic*, but she left Erie with at least six hundred people crowded on a boat that carried about two hundred people comfortably. Baggage was stacked in huge piles all over the deck. People jammed the ship, looking for a place where they could stretch out. They ended up on narrow walkways, sleeping over the hurricane deck that covered the bridge, and on the roof of the *Atlantic*'s cabin. Eventually, the ship entered the open waters of Lake Erie, her giant paddle wheel beating a steady rhythm, and people started getting used to the cramped conditions. They expected to be in Detroit the next afternoon.

At 2:00 A.M. that Friday, the *Atlantic* was still in the east end of Lake Erie, steaming along the busy steamer track near the centre of the lake. Her three-storey paddlewheel dug through the warm water, while her bow cut through fog that formed when warm, moist air rising from the lake hit the cooler night air that had settled over it. Below deck, the steerage passengers were warm and dry, unlike the men crowded on the deck. Some immigrants slept on makeshift beds. Others tried to get rest by sleeping on the trunks that were stacked all over the deck. Between the noise made by all these people, the sound of the engine and wheel, and the smoke from the *Atlantic*'s two twenty-metre smokestacks, the cabin passengers weren't getting much sleep either. On the bridge, the

Atlantic's tired officers squinted to see their way through the fog.

Coming the other way, the steamer *Ogdensburg* was blinded by the same banks of mist. She was a freighter heading toward Buffalo. The *Ogdensburg* was a propeller-driven ship about the same size as the *Atlantic*. She was moving toward the *Atlantic* from the passenger ship's left side.

The people crowded aboard the *Atlantic* felt the ship shudder as the *Ogdensburg* cut into her side. The hull of the *Atlantic* offered little resistance to the freighter, which buried her bow in the *Atlantic*'s baggage room. The people on deck were horrified to see part of the *Ogdensburg*'s bridge towering over them. The whole scene was accompanied by the terrifying noise of ripping metal and snapping wood, the shouts of the half-panicked sailors and the screams of frightened passengers.

It was a night for mistakes. At this point in the collision, no one had been hurt, and the *Ogdensburg* was almost undamaged. If people had stayed calm, taken stock of the situation and used some sense, there wouldn't have been a disaster. Instead of evacuating the *Atlantic*'s passengers to the *Ogdensburg*, however, the crews of both ships focused on the damage to their vessels. Once the *Ogdensburg*'s crew was sure their boat was still seaworthy, they put the engines in reverse and backed out of the punctured *Atlantic*.

Once free of the passenger steamer, the *Ogdensburg* resumed her course.

Good sense doesn't seem to have prevailed on Lake Erie that night. The *Atlantic*'s engines were still working, the paddlewheel was turning, but water poured through the hole left by the *Ogdensburg*'s hull. Later, the *Atlantic*'s officers claimed they were trying to run for shore, but nothing was done to alert passengers that the ship was in danger. Most had been reassured when the *Ogdensburg* steamed away after the collision. Within a few minutes, however, the water flowing below the *Atlantic*'s decks flooded into the boiler room, extinguishing the fires. When the engines stopped in a cloud of smoke and steam, the passengers finally realized the danger.

Showing some rather primitive survival instincts, a mob of men from the *Atlantic*'s deck tried to launch an overcrowded lifeboat from the ship's starboard side. The boat was so crowded and the men lowering it were so incapable that the bow of the lifeboat was allowed to drop, and the men inside tumbled into the lake. At about the same time, Captain Pettey tumbled into another lifeboat, landing on his head. He staggered from the boat, suffering from a concussion, and sat out the rest of the night's terrors in a daze.

No one took over the captain's authority. As the bow of the *Atlantic* settled into the calm waters of Lake Erie, people aboard the *Atlantic* could see that the fog was lifting. While the water was warm and still, and the night was placid, the scene around the *Atlantic* wasn't. Mobs of people tried to get on deck from below. People were jumping into the lake clinging to pieces of baggage or dove overboard to try to swim to shore, about ten kilometres away.

In the midst of the panic, one of the *Atlantic*'s big smokestacks crashed down on the deck, hurting a few passengers and adding to the terror. Few people noticed that the ship had almost stopped sinking once her bow and midsection had gone under. The stern section of the *Atlantic* floated on a giant bubble of trapped air, while around her, more than three hundred people were drowned in Lake Erie. The 250 people who stayed aboard the *Atlantic* screamed and panicked, adding to the noise made by the people in the water. The terrible sound drifted across the lake.

About four kilometres away, the *Ogdensburg* had stopped again to take stock of her damage. Once her engines shut down, the crew of the *Ogdensburg* could hear the awful shrieks coming from the *Atlantic*. Finally, after a night of utter stupidity on their part, they realized that the passenger ship was in trouble, and they turned back toward the wreck site.

Ten minutes later, they reached the half-submerged *Atlantic* with its crowd of frightened people clinging to its stern. The *Ogdensburg* pulled alongside and its crew began helping people cross from one ship to the other. They tried to rescue the people in the water but, for at least 250 of them, the *Ogdensburg* had arrived too late. Their bodies had sunk into the lake or mingled with the wreckage and baggage that floated around the doomed ship. A short time after the last passengers were taken from the *Atlantic*, the trapped air in the stern finally began to escape and the *Atlantic* sank in about fifty metres of water off Long Point, in Canadian waters.

After spending about an hour at the wreck site recovering some survivors from among the debris, the *Ogdensburg* steamed toward Erie, Pennsylvania, the closest U.S. port.

In Erie, the enraged, grieving survivors held a protest meeting to denounce the incompetence of the *Atlantic*'s captain. Little was done to recover the bodies or search for any belongings that might have eased the lot of the now penniless survivors. Within a few weeks, the immigrants left Erie to try to pick up the pieces of their lives somewhere else.

The *Atlantic* settled into the thick mud on the bottom of the lake. She was upright, undamaged except for the hole in her hull, and the cold water of the lake has preserved her. In the next century, about one hundred other wrecks joined her in eastern Lake Erie, and, except for the terrible loss of life that makes the *Atlantic* the fifth-worst marine disaster on the Great Lakes, she was just another tragedy in a time when overloaded "coffin ships" plied the Atlantic Ocean and the Great Lakes. Only the geography of the wreck makes her Canadian but the location of the sinking has played an important role in the controversy that now surrounds the *Atlantic*.

If there was a huge treasure on board, John Green would have liked to have heard about it. Green was a Canadian-born diver who lost his health trying to salvage the *Atlantic* in the years just after she sank. He was twenty-six years old when the *Atlantic* went down.

Green was born in Montreal, but when he was still a child, his family moved to the New York side of the St. Lawrence River. While still a schoolboy, he made his first commercial dive, recovering a box of soap bars and a clock that a thief had thrown into the Oswego River. As a teenager, he made money salvaging freight that had spilled in Oswego harbour and hauling cannon and other weapons off a War of 1812 wreck. Before his mid-twenties, Green never dove with an air link to the surface. In deeper, colder water, however, he sometimes wore a primitive wetsuit made of three old sweaters.

During the same summer that the *Atlantic* was sunk, Green was aboard the paddlewheeler *Oswego* when it was rammed and sunk by the steamship *America*. Green had relatives on board the *Oswego*, so he spent weeks living on shore nearby, swimming out to the wreck every day to try to recover their bodies. Commercial divers working on a nearby shipwreck met Green and liked him. They showed him how to dive with "armour," brass diving bells linked to the surface with a rubber hose.

That fall, Green was hired by American Express to try to salvage the *Atlantic*'s purser's safe and some money known to be in a nearby cabin. The expedition was a failure. On the first dive, just below the thirty-metre mark, the air pump broke. The people working the pumps quickly hauled Green back to the surface. He fixed the machine and went down again. On the second dive, he found himself in the *Atlantic*'s smokestack. Again, the surface crew hauled him back up. The third time, he reached the *Atlantic*'s deck. As he felt his way along, his air hose broke. Again, he was hauled to the surface. His employers decided that was enough and everyone went back to Buffalo.

In 1855, Green was back at the wreck site after some salvage work on other vessels and a stint in the Caribbean. This time he was on his own, without the backing of any company. His surface ship was an old schooner, the *Yorktown*. Eighteen people worked on his surface crew. On his first dive, he reached the deck of the *Atlantic*, which was now covered with about twenty centimetres of mud. After five days, he found the purser's cabin, where the safe was. Green tied a line to the railing, just outside the cabin, and went up to the surface for a hearty lunch. In an hour or so, he was back down on the deck of the *Atlantic*, feeling around for the small safe and hauling it out a window onto the deck. Then he went back to the surface for a hook and rope to haul the safe to the surface.

As Green sat resting on the *Yorktown*, a horrible pain tore into his chest and he lost all feeling in the lower part of his body. He had a near-fatal case of the bends. The *Yorktown* set off immediately for Port Dover, Ontario, to get Green to a hospital. There was nothing the doctors could do, so they sent Green to a clinic in Buffalo. After five months, Green was able to move around with crutches. By the next summer, Green was able to walk, but only with great difficulty.

He went back to the *Atlantic* on July 1. When he reached the wreck site, he found his line to the purser's cabin was gone. In extreme pain, Green went down to the *Atlantic*'s deck and found the safe was missing, too. So was the money in the cabin next door.

Back in Buffalo, diver Elliot Harrington and his crew were counting the money for which Green had risked his life. Harrington was an inventor who had taken the design of the diving bell and had improved it, making it into a sort of diving armour. Harrington had heard about Green's calamity and had gone out to the wreck in June. Within a few days. he had found the safe still lying on the deck where Green left it.

Harrington had felt his way along the *Atlantic*'s deck, using a steel bar to smash windows and doors. When he found the safe, he attached it to cables that were pulled by a steam engine aboard his salvage boat. The steam engine applied too much force to the safe and the strongbox went flying, giving Harrington a glancing blow. Had the safe hit him straight on, it probably would have killed him. As it was, Harrington had to be hauled to the surface to recover. On the next dive, the strong box was reattached to the cables, Harrington got out of the way, and soon the safe was brought to the surface and the lucky divers began dividing the swag. They let the newspapers know about their good fortune, and word of their luck reached officials of the American Express Company.

The $36,700 taken from the *Atlantic* was a fortune in a time when many people were happy to work for a dollar a day. American Express went to court, demanding its money. Eventually, the case was settled, with the money being split between the company and the salvagers. Each of the four people who worked on Harrington's salvage project ended up with a little less than $2,000, enough money to buy a small ship or a good-sized farm in those days but much less than a full share of the salvaged money. They could have made as much money with a lot less risk.

Later, Harrington worked for the Union in the Civil War. He tried to raise the *Merrimac*, the first Confederate ironclad, and salvaged ships that the South had sunk at the entrance to Charleston harbour. He explored the bottom of the Confederate naval fortifications at Charleston, walking on the ocean floor to find ways for Union ships to pass through the heavy chain barriers that the Confederates had lain at strategic places. After the war, he became an inventor but never made any money.

Neither Green nor Harrington lived to be old men. Green's case of the bends caused him to be an invalid for the rest of his life, while Harrington died of cancer in 1879, when he was fifty-five years old.

After Harrington's salvage work, no one bothered to take more from the *Atlantic*. There were easier pickings for looters on wrecks in shallower water: bells, compasses, clocks, and other valuable artifacts that could be pulled up from wrecks that are more accessible with snorkel and Scuba equipment. Most historians believe that the only money to be found aboard the ship would have been the immigrants' savings, much of which would have been paper money, now long gone, or coins scattered among the wreckage.

In the spring of 1991, the California divers, operating under the name Mar-Dive, found the wreck of the *Atlantic*. They made an agreement with an Ohio company that claimed it owned salvage rights to the wreck, and applied in a California U.S. Circuit Court for an order confirming Mar-Dive's rights to salvage the ship. Ontario, however, has a heritage law that prevents the looting of archaeological sites, including shipwrecks. Provincial officials said they would not allow the looting of the *Atlantic*, and said they would prosecute Mar-Dive if artifacts were taken from the *Atlantic* without a license. As well, they said the U.S. court had no jurisdiction over Canadian territory, even if it is under Lake Erie's waters. Punishment under the Ontario Heritage Act can be as stiff as a $250,000 fine and a year in jail, but the law's real effectiveness comes from the power it gives Ontario's courts. Judges can order any salvage to stop and jail anyone who defies their order by handing down jail terms and fines for contempt of court.

The summer after the wreck was found, historical preservation and education officials in New York State and Pennsylvania came down on the side of the Ontario government. Oren Lehman, commissioner of the New York State office of Parks, Recreation and Historical Preservation, gave the beleaguered Ontario heritage workers a boost when he said: "The importance and need to protect both artifacts and historic sites, such as those on the *Atlantic* are in no way diminished because they are buried beneath water rather than land. Uncontrolled commercial salvage of this site would unquestionably compromise the qualities which make it significant, and would deprive the citizens of both the United States and Canada of a unique source of information regarding our marine heritage."

His colleague, Thomas Sobol, New York's commissioner of education, said his department would not have granted an archaeological salvage license for the *Atlantic* if it had been in New York's water.

"Our heritage is not for sale," he said.

The fight over the *Atlantic* wreck's future drags on. Since the first opposition from government officials surfaced, backers of the salvage operation have fought a media campaign for support of the stripping of the *Atlantic*. Stories in U.S. newspapers, especially in Los Angeles, have hyped the *Atlantic* wreck as being a gold-rich piece of Americana. Estimates were given to the press that there is more than $60 million in gold coins aboard the ship and that it is so miraculously preserved that it can be taken from the lake bottom and displayed across North America as a sort of mid-nineteenth century time capsule.

In 1991, Steve Morgan, head of Mar-Dive, told Los Angeles reporters: "We're not going to be kicked around. This is a U.S. vessel. We own the ship and have a treaty protecting our rights to it. To allow her to lay there on the bottom [of Lake Erie] and rot is not doing anyone a service."

The salvagers portrayed the ship as a luxury liner, its spacious hull filled with six hundred rich passengers, many of them packing gold-filled safes. The artifacts that were displayed at the Los Angeles press conference told a different story: a Norwegian cheese box, some old shoes, an ordinary snuff box, and some crockery— these were the belongings of ordinary people who didn't have much in 1852 and who don't even have a grave now. The electronic detection system protects their resting place until the courts or the reality of salvage economics decide whether their baggage, their belongings, and the shiny parts of the boat that took them to the bottom will be laid out on an auctioneer's table.

Chapter Five

The Heroine of
Long Point

Abigail Becker in later years, wearing her gold medal.
(NORFOLK COUNTY HISTORIC SOCIETY ARCHIVES)

A bigail Becker was never very lucky with men. A wise woman knows when to reel them in and when to throw them back. More than once, Lake Erie tossed good men on Abigail's doorstep, but she always just gave them a cup of warm tea and sent them on their way.

Abigail was The Angel of Long Point, a heroine still famous along the lakes. She was a celebrity in the fifty years between her greatest rescue and her death. Men tipped their hats to her, ships blew their whistles when they passed her home, even a prince came to visit, but, in the end, she stayed with her shiftless husband and raised his brood in a wind-rattled driftwood shack while her man wandered the woods and drank.

Abigail Becker was the first-born child of a family of United Empire Loyalists, the Jacksons. They settled in Norfolk County, in farming country where land was cheap and very good. Abigail was an attractive woman with bright eyes and a demure smile. For some unknown reason, in 1848, at the age of seventeen, she married a local widower, Jeremiah Becker. Becker was twice Abigail's age, a widower and failed farmer with five children. He was a trapper and sometime-fisherman, rarely home and never solvent. He did make it back to the family cabin often enough to father five boys and three girls with Abigail, thus giving her a brood of thirteen kids to raise in a shanty hidden among the forlorn dunes of Long Point.

There are quite a few "ships' graveyards" in the world. The most famous are Long Point, Sable Island and Cape Cod. These places have the same things in common: placid-looking waters sheltered by islands or long spits of land, treacherous currents and sandbars. Long Point cuts almost half way into Lake Erie. The west side (where most of the wrecks are) is dune country. Marshes cut in from the east side, in some places almost bisecting the point, especially near its base. The point has had a lighthouse at its tip since the early 19th century, but that hasn't stopped dozens of schooners, tugs, barges and steamers from being wrecked around the point. It's now one of the more popular diving places in the Great Lakes, though many of the wrecks have dangerous tangles of nets lost by fishermen operating out of Port Rowan, Port Dover and Wheatley.

Long Point is a 40-kilometre-long land of sand dunes, marshes, wild animals and even stranger people. For instance, Dr. John Troyer, the first permanent settler on the point, was a self-proclaimed witch doctor. If he had any medical training, Dr. Troyer never used it. Instead, he contrived spells, engaged in black magic, hid from the locals and from witches he believed stalked him in the lightless gloom of stormy nights. He was not always successful at dodging these witches, nor could his own powers prevent them from periodically turning him into a swamp animal. Abigail Becker would probably have preferred the company of a paediatrician, but in those pre-Medicare days, an impoverished family took what help they could get. Long Point folks, by and large, trusted Dr. Troyer's diagnoses and cures, and his medical tools are still preserved in a local museum. The only other neighbour close to the Beckers by land was some 20 kilometres away.

Twice in the early years of her marriage, Abigail Becker helped members of crews of ships that ran aground on Long Point.

The first time Abigail helped a ship's crew, a band of half-frozen sailors arrived at her shack and told her their ship was stranded on a sand bar. Their cook, the only woman aboard, had drowned on the ship. Abigail gave the shaken sailors a hot meal, helped them dry their clothes, and sent them on to Port Rowan, the closest town.

Several years later, four exhausted, half-frozen sailors wandered out of a winter storm and knocked at the door of Becker's shack. Their ship had foundered among Long Point's sandbars. All six of the crew had made it to shore, but two of the men were so badly frozen that they hadn't been able to walk. Abigail wrapped the men in blankets, stoked up her stove, and left her children to make tea for the shivering men. Then, with two of her sons, she went into the storm, carrying a lantern, to look for the two lost men. When, at last, Abigail came upon the sailors, neither man had the strength to get on his feet. She knew the men would die if they stayed on the beach, so she and the boys dragged the men back to the cabin.

On the stormy afternoon of November 24, 1854, 23-year-old Abigail was, again, home alone with her small children. Needing a bucket of water, she pushed herself through the wind and filled it in the surf of Lake Erie. A kilometre offshore, the three-masted grain-carrier *Conductor*, carrying a load from Amherstburg, Ontario, to its home port of Buffalo, New York, was caught in the storm and jammed into a sandbar. The ship had been driven across one reef and now lay nearly on her side. If the storm continued, the waves would tear the ship apart. The men aboard the ship had tied themselves to the ship's mast. They believed no one was nearby, and that they had no chance of rescue. Then, when they had pretty much given up hope, they saw Abigail Becker standing on top of a sand dune, waving to them.

Abigail had a problem: even if she came up with a plan to rescue the sailors, there was little she could do, since she couldn't swim. Becker went back to her cabin and bundled up her oldest children. "We will go down on the beach at once and see if they will come ashore," she told the children and led them to the beach. They gathered a large pile of driftwood, set it alight as a signal, and waved to the crew of the *Conductor* to jump into the water and try to swim towards her.

The first man to make the leap was the *Conductor*'s captain, Robert Hackett. "If we stay here, we will be lost," he told his men.

"I will go first; if I get to shore safely, the rest can follow." He pulled off his heavy coat and boots, then jumped into the surf, pushing his way through the waves and the undertow, and came close enough to shore that Abigail could wade in and fish him out. She set him ashore near the fire. Her stepson, Edward, a boy with a crippled leg, tried to wade in and pull the *Conductor*'s first mate, John Jerome, from the waves. Abigail had to drag both of them out of the lake. Five more crewmen followed, arriving on shore in varying states of unconsciousness and exposure, but the ship's cook, another non-swimmer, stayed behind. Fearing the *Conductor* would be torn apart, he tied himself to the rigging. By the time the last man came ashore, darkness had fallen. The sailors and the Beckers went back to the family cabin, where some of the rest of the children had made a large fire.

Abigail gave the men some of her clothes to keep warm, wrapped them in blankets and took them back to her cabin. The sailors dried out their clothes and paper money, found a place to lie on the floor and went to sleep. Through the night, Abigail worried about the cook, still helpless among the *Conductor*'s torn sails and ragged rigging.

She was up early the next morning, pouring tea for the sailors who had slept on her floor. By mid-morning, she had helped gather enough wood for a raft. The storm waves had settled somewhat, and the sailors from the *Conductor* were able to make it back to the ship to fetch their cook, now unconscious and half-dead on the wrecked vessel. He arrived at the Becker shanty with feet that were very badly damaged from frostbite. After a few days at Abigail's home, most of the *Conductor*'s crew walked to the closest village, Port Rowan, and found passage to Buffalo. The cook stayed behind to be nursed for three weeks by Abigail and her children. Word of Abigail's courage and kindness soon spread in the city and along the lakes.

Very soon, Abigail "Mother" Becker was famous among Great Lakes sailors. In some ways, this fame would rescue Abigail from her lakefront shack, but, in the catty atmosphere of small-town 19th century southern Ontario, it would also generate nasty rumours. E.P. Dorr, a local captain, pushed her cause. A banquet was given in her honour in Buffalo, at which she was given a purse of $500, most of it contributed by sailors. Later, Queen Victoria wrote Abigail a letter praising her courage and enclosed a gift of £50. In 1860, the Queen's son Edward, Prince of Wales, visited Abigail while on a cross-country tour and presented her with a cash gift before heading out duck hunting on Long Point. And the Governor-General sent a belated congratulatory letter in the 1890s.

The Life Saving Benevolent Association of New York wished to recognize the young heroine. President Joseph Walker wrote Captain Dorr: "The giving of our medal is confined to the saving of American life. If you will find that there was an American life saved from on board *Schooner Conductor*, Abigail shall have our best medal." Captain Dorr learned that Jerome, the first mate, and a crew member were, in fact, American seamen.

Two and a half years after the rescue, Abigail was invited to Buffalo, where she was presented with a large gold medal portraying her heroism. The gold medal is inscribed: "Presented in May, 1857, to Abigail Becker of Long Point, Lake Erie, Canada West, for extraordinary resolution, humanity and courage in rescuing from impending death the crew of the schooner *Conductor* lost November 1854." On the reverse is engraved a vessel foundering in the breakers, a beach on which a fire is burning with people near it, and, in the background, the Becker cabin among the dunes of Long Point.

The ugly business of money now surfaced. Some $550 was raised from the sailors on the Great Lakes and sent by the Life Saving Benevolent Society to the collector of customs at Port Rowan. He wouldn't hand it over. Abigail had to "go to law" to collect it, and, after court fees, got the sum, minus $15. She invested the money in a fifty-acre farm in the Seventh Concession of Walsingham Township, north of Port Rowan. Neighbours spread stories that Abigail was a miser, that she had been given a thousand dollars or more, that she secretly owned land throughout the area.

Rumours of her wealth brought conmen and sleazy writers to the farm. At the time of the *Conductor* rescue, few newspapers had noted Abigail Becker's courage, but through the last half of the 19th century, her tale was written up, in story and verse, many times. An account of her struggle was a chapter in the school readers used across Ontario, and strangers came to the farm to take Abigail's picture with her gold medal. None of this fame helped the Beckers make ends meet and, as the years went by, the stories of her heroism became somewhat scrambled. Near the end of Abigail's life, one of her daughters, with the help of a local clergyman, wrote a short book to set the record straight.

An infusion of money could not turn Jeremiah Becker, now pushing fifty, into an industrious man. Abigail had to take in laundry and do odd jobs off the farm to make ends meet and pay for livestock. It didn't help that the family had terrible luck with animals. One cow died from drinking sour tree sap; another was killed by lightning. Abigail was beset with other bad luck: she broke her toes and arm when a horse bolted and knocked her to the floor of the barn (she set the breaks herself); another time, she tumbled from the hay mow, nearly breaking her skull.

John Backus, owner of the local grist-mill, later said the Beckers tried to pay for his services with her gold medal. He refused to accept it, but kept it in pawn for his fees. He held it in his safe for years, believing, if he hurried to give it back, the Beckers would offer it to another local merchant with less scruples. During those years, Abigail is said to have saved a man and a child who had fallen down a well. But, while she gained fame for her rescues, she could not save a son who drowned in Lake Erie while fishing near Port Rowan.

Not long afterwards, Jeremiah was back in the bush. Abigail was left to farm the small family holding, work for cash and raise the children. One winter, after Jeremiah Becker returned to his trapline on Long Point, a vicious storm came up, one so powerful that it threatened to tear the shack apart. Jeremiah loaded his gear into a trunk and began dragging it to the nearest house, which, with an infusion of settlers into Long Point, was just six kilometres away. It was a mistake: the shanty survived, but, some three months after Jeremiah had fled the storm, his frozen body was found sitting on a log.

Despite her size—Abigail was a tall woman, and, by middle age, weighed about 100 kilograms—and her impressive family commitments, she soon found another husband, Henry Rohrer. He was a more productive husband than Jeremiah Becker, and, in the last years of her life, she was finally free of money problems. It helped that some of the kids had finally left home. In all, she raised nineteen children before dying peacefully on her farm in 1905, at the age of seventy-four.

She left behind two proud possessions: the gold medal (which she had redeemed from the miller) and the trunk given to her by the first mate of the *Conductor*. It had survived three wrecks and had spent fifty years on land, the most tangible reminder of that frightening time.

The community took up a collection for a monument, but, instead, used it to pay for a ward in the Norfolk General Hospital. Years later, the Ontario government put up a plaque to the Heroine of Long Point with these words:

THE HEROINE OF LONG POINT

In November 1854 the schooner Conductor *was wrecked off this shore during one of Lake Erie's many violent storms. Jeremiah Becker, who resided nearby, was away on the mainland but his courageous wife, Abigail, risked her life by repeatedly entering the water while assisting the exhausted seamen to reach land. The eight sailors were housed and fed in her cabin until they recovered from their ordeal. In recognition of her heroism she received a letter of commendation from Queen Victoria, several financial awards, and a gold medal from the Life Saving Benevolent Association of New York.*

Long Point is now an Ontario Provincial Park, busy in the summer with campers who share the long spit of land with large herds of deer. Bird watchers come in the fall to see the migration of water-fowl and songbirds. There are still a few cottages in the area, but the Becker shack is long gone. Maybe it was torn down, or, perhaps, it lies buried in one of the ever-shifting sand dunes. But Abigail Becker is not forgotten. Along with the plaque, she's commemorated in the museums around Long Point, in the stories of Great Lakes sailors, and in the chivalry of the captains who still remember to sound their whistles when they pass the place that was the home of Mother Becker.

Chapter Six

Politicians in Peril

Sir John A. MacDonald aboard the Ploughboy *when it came close
to being wrecked on the Georgian Bay.*
(NATIONAL ARCHIVES OF CANADA)

Many Canadians would enjoy the prospect of seeing their
more powerful political leaders on a leaking ship in dangerous seas. Although this is unlikely to happen with the
present bumper crop of busy federal and provincial parliamentari-

ans, there have been two occasions when the Great Lakes have toyed with the rulers of Canada.

In October, 1804, the Provincial Marine, the arm of the Royal Navy that patrolled the Great Lakes, was in sad shape. Many of its ships had been bought second-hand or had been quickly built out of newly-cut wood that cracked under the sun and rotted under water. The sailors on the ships were not exactly the cream of the Royal Navy. During the Napoleonic Wars, one British commander had described his men as "the scum of the earth, enlisted for drink." The Provincial Marine, for the most part, was the scum of the scum. In those days, however, before a decent road system had been hacked out of the forests of Canada, the Marine provided the only way for important people in the colony to get around.

George Cowan would never have considered himself important. He was a fur trader running a little post near Coldwater, Ontario, about thirty kilometres west of modern-day Orillia. Cowan traded with all of the native bands living in central Ontario. His customers travelled the Kawartha waterways from Lake Ontario to Georgian Bay. At the end of the canoe route, Cowan had built a fine trading post which was called The Chimneys because of its towering masonry. He was prospering despite being caught between the Hudson's Bay Company and the North West Company in their fight for control of Canada's fur trade.

Cowan's mastery of the Ojibwe language helped him earn his fortune. Most of the native people in what is now Ontario still spoke their original languages and didn't know any English. Cowan's linguistic skills also made him useful to the colonial authorities at the treaty meetings whose purpose was to "unburden" the natives of their ownership of the most fertile part of Canada.

In the fall of 1804, Cowan had found another use for his Ojibwe skills. A native named Ogetonicut had killed a York merchant in revenge for the killing of one of his relatives by a white man. He was following the tradition of Ojibwe law, but when Ogetonicut killed John Sharpe in the marshes around one of the Kawartha Lakes, he hadn't sought the backing of his tribe's leaders. To keep the peace, they decided to hand the killer over to the authorities at York, today's Toronto.

Instead of letting the case fester into a dispute between the Ojibwe and English, Peter Hunter, the colony's governor, decided to have the case tried as soon as possible. Ogetonicut was shackled to the floor in the hold of the Provincial Marine schooner *Speedy*, near her bow, and the twenty-metre ship headed for Newcastle, the settlement that was the district capital for the region where the crime was committed.

In those days, murder was quite unusual in Ontario. British administrators had the decency to try native offenders under the same laws and in the same courts as whites, unlike the Americans, who refused to treat natives as citizens with rights. In most of the United States, natives accused of murder were shot or lynched. Because the trader's murder was a capital crime, senior members of the government, the Supreme Court, and the legal profession would be involved in the trial. Cowan was needed as an interpreter.

In the evening of October 8, 1804, Cowan walked across the gangplank onto the deck of the *Speedy*. The schooner's condition made a mockery of her name. A sailor stayed below decks working a bilge pump, and she creaked with each wave that jostled her. Thomas Cochrane, justice of the Court of King's Bench; Robert Gray, solicitor general of Upper Canada; Angus Mcdonnell, treas-

urer of the Law Society of Upper Canada; and John Fiske, high
bailiff of York, along with several prominent merchants and members of the colonial legislature, also boarded the ship.

Cochrane, the judge, was something of a prodigy. He was only
twenty-nine years old. The colonial administration expected
Cochrane to go far in the new province. The solicitor general, Gray,
was one of the colony's brightest young men. He had already built
up a substantial fortune, including 200 acres of cleared land, which
he left in his will to his black slave, John Baker. Mcdonnell was the
brother of the Earl of Selkirk, a wealthy, eccentric Scottish aristocrat
who founded the first real colony in Manitoba.

Lieutenant Thomas Paxton, commander of the *Speedy*, knew she
wasn't much of a ship. On an earlier trip, her top mast had fallen off
in a fairly light wind. The ship leaked so badly that some of her
cargo had been damaged. Sailors risked long prison terms or whip-
ping by deserting her, using small boats at Kingston to escape to the
States. Paxton's own career was an obvious dead end. He was paid
in pocket change and had been promoted only once in the past
seventeen years. Each time something bad had happened to the
Speedy, he had been blamed.

Off Oshawa, Ojibwes had met the boat in their canoes and had
tried to come aboard but Paxton had turned them away. The *Speedy*
was already overcrowded. If they were to go to Newcastle for the
trial, they would have to make the trip in their own boats. Two white
traders in the Ojibwe canoes were witnesses in the trial and might
have talked their way aboard the *Speedy*. They found the canoes
were faster than the schooner, so they stayed with the Indians. It was
a very wise choice.

That night, the *Speedy* was trying to find her way to Presqu'île in a light snowstorm which had suddenly moved in from the northeast. Paxton ordered the ship's gun to be fired, hoping that someone on shore would light a lantern or set a fire to guide the ship in. People on shore realized what Paxton was trying to do and lit a bonfire. Paxton tried to tack towards the fire but his vessel was so heavy with water that she couldn't be steered. Possibly, the *Speedy* slammed into a small uncharted shoal named Devil's Horseback and broke into pieces, or else she simply fell apart in the wind.

An eyewitness wrote:

"The vessel was seen a few miles from her defined port on the evening of the 8th, when the wind began to blow strongly against her. The gale becoming violent, the vessel was seen bearing away. The whole night was dreadfully tempestuous and the schooner was supposed to have foundered, as she was never heard of more. The binnacle, topmasts and hencoops (holding chickens in the cargo hold) were picked up on the opposite side of the lake."

No one survived the *Speedy*'s loss. Because the wreck wasn't found for years, there was speculation over her fate. Nasty talk circulated in the colony that Ogetonicut's mother had put some kind of curse on the *Speedy* but the ship's problems were obviously more earthly. People speculated about the existence of Devil's Horseback shoal. No one seems to have been able to find it. Gone with the *Speedy* was much of the cream of the new colony's establishment, many of her most important merchants, and Cowan, a popular, decent man who probably wished he had stayed in his secure little fort in the woods.

In the next half century, the politicians who travelled on the Great Lakes were treated kindly by them. The near-loss of one ship and its large cargo of politicians, however, nearly made up for the luck of all of the office-holders who had travelled on ships since the time of the *Speedy*.

In the years leading up to Confederation in 1867, Canada's most powerful and popular politician was John A. Macdonald, a Scotland-born lawyer whose political network stretched from the west end of the Great Lakes to the Maritimes. Every politician in British North America was either his friend or his enemy, or, quite often, both. The Canadas, as Quebec and Ontario were called at the time, were in a constant state of turmoil as alliances between the politicians of Upper and Lower Canada were forged and broken, and governments sometimes lasted only a day.

The wheels of politics were greased with patronage, graft, and mutual back scratching. B.W. Smith, sheriff of Simcoe County, was a minor functionary who wanted to court favour with some of the country's grander politicians. In those days, sheriffs were regional patronage dispensers as well as organizers of hangings and glorified bill collectors. Such people were necessary cogs in the political system, so when Smith wanted to organize a Great Lakes cruise, he was able to get Canada's most powerful politicians to come.

The ship that Smith chartered was the *Ploughboy*, an old side wheeler which had recently come north to Lake Huron from Port Stanley. The *Ploughboy* had long ago paid for herself with years of hard work. She was an antiquated boat, but fairly comfortable, so when Macdonald and many of his colleagues boarded her in Collingwood on June 30, 1859, for a trip to Sault Ste. Marie, everything seemed fine.

Along with Macdonald were three other cabinet ministers, several members of the colonial legislature, and the Speaker of the House. They sat on deck as the ship sailed up the nearly uninhabited shore of Georgian Bay, stopped at Owen Sound to stretch their legs and see the town, and anchored at some of the more interesting places along the Bruce Peninsula. The next day, the *Ploughboy* paddled across the strait that separates Manitoulin Island from the mainland.

The most direct route from Tobermory to Sault Ste. Marie is along the west side of Manitoulin Island, but the east shore is more protected and is cut by beautiful bays. The white quartzite islands of the North Channel, which are seen as one approaches the Sault, are still popular with present-day summer boaters. The politicians looked forward to visiting that idyllic corner of Lake Huron.

Macdonald never got to see those islands, at least not on this trip. Near Lonely Island, the place where the steamer *Asia* would sink twenty-three years later, the *Ploughboy* ran into trouble. Her engine broke down. There was no way to fix it in this wilderness.

At first, no one seemed worried, but the politicians probably fumed because their schedule was ruined. The *Ploughboy* dropped her anchors, hoping a ship would come by and give her a tow. After a few wasted hours, B.W. Smith, the erstwhile host, rounded up a couple of crewmen to row him to Owen Sound to get help. The trip was about 125 kilometres, so the people left behind didn't expect to leave the *Ploughboy* soon.

As Smith prepared to go, the winds started rising. July gales are fairly uncommon on Georgian Bay, but this wind had the power to be fatal to the *Ploughboy* and her distinguished cargo. The ship's anchors didn't reach bottom. They did help slow her drifting as the ship moved toward the jagged cliffs of Lonely Island, but eventually the ship would be driven ashore unless there was a rescue.

Through that Saturday night, the sound of the waves breaking on the island's shore grew louder to the politicians on board as the

Ploughboy drifted. In the darkness, she was pushed more than twenty kilometres. The next morning, afraid they were about to drown, the politicians tried to decide who would pray. There was no minister on the *Ploughboy* nor anyone who seemed to be saintly. Each day, before Parliament sits, the Speaker of the House of Commons leads it in prayers. Therefore, the logical choice for a petitioner for divine intervention was Henry Smith, the Speaker.

Reading from the Anglican Book of Common Prayer, Smith's voice intoned over the waters of Georgian Bay:

"Thou, O Lord, that stillest the raging sea: hear us, and save us, that we perish not. O blessed saviour, that didst save thy disciples ready to perish in a storm: hear us, and save us, we beseech thee.

"O Lord, hear us.

"O Christ, hear us.

"Lord, have mercy upon us.

"Christ, have mercy upon us.

"Lord, have mercy upon us.

"God the Father, God the Son, God the Holy Ghost, have mercy upon us, save us now and evermore, Amen."

It was an impressive prayer and it had its effect, although the anchors took a while to finally catch on the rocks. The *Ploughboy* rode out the storm just metres away from Lonely Island's treacherous cliffs.

Meanwhile, Sheriff Smith had arrived in Owen Sound after a rather impressive workout by his oarsmen. By telegraph, he summoned the steamer *Canadian* from Collingwood, which arrived at Lonely Island the next day to take the *Ploughboy* in tow. When the two ships arrived back in Collingwood, the party of politicians caught the train to Toronto.

In a letter to his aunt Margaret, Macdonald showed he believed the *Ploughboy* trip was almost his undoing. "Hughy" in this letter is Macdonald's son, Hugh, who was living in Kingston with the rest of Macdonald's family. Loo is his aunt Louisa:

"Toronto, July 7, 1859

My dear Margaret,

You will see by the papers what a narrow escape we had. None of the party will again be nearer their graves until they have been placed in them. The people behaved well, the women heroically.

I am none the worse for the trip. The Governor General will be here to-night, and I hope, therefore, in a few days to get away to Kingston.

Love to Mamma, Hughy and Loo, not forgetting the Parson.

Yours always,
John A.

P.S. I sent you specimens of the letters of congratulation I got."

A month later, Macdonald finally got his vacation. Rather than risk another voyage on the Great Lakes, he took his tourist dollars south to the rocky coastline of Maine for a couple of weeks of sun-bathing. As for the *Ploughboy*, she burned at Detroit in 1876.

Chapter Seven

Spies and Rebels on the Lakes

The USS Michigan *was the target of the only Confederate naval action on the Great Lakes.*
(GREAT LAKES HISTORICAL MUSEUM)

On the morning of September 19, 1864, the steamer *Philo Parsons* was preparing to leave Detroit for a routine trip to Sandusky, Ohio, when two anxious men came aboard and asked Captain Atwood when the ship would be ready. He answered that his ship would cast off just after daylight. The men wanted to know if Atwood would take the *Parsons* across the river to Sandwich (now part of Windsor, Ontario) to pick up some extra passengers. The *Parsons* wasn't full, so Captain Atwood agreed. At about 8:00 A.M., the steamer, carrying about thirty American passengers and the two inquisitive men, drifted from her dock at the foot of Bates Street in Detroit, caught the river current and began making for the Canadian side of the river to pick up some rather strange passengers indeed.

At Sandwich, four or five more men got on board. Then, at Fort Malden in Amherstburg, Ontario, about a dozen more men walked onto the deck of the *Parsons*. They were scruffy looking men, carrying an old trunk tied with rope. Some of the Americans thought the men were draft dodgers trying to slip back into the United States, a rather common occurrence on the frontier during the U.S. Civil War. At Amherstburg, someone threw something off the ship. It was a note wrapped around a rock.

The suspicious passengers on the *Parsons* were Confederate military agents. There was a double agent among the spies, a man in the pay of the Canadian government. This was, for the South, the normal procedure in the underground war that went on in Canada during the Civil War. Double, even triple, agents riddled the Confederate spy apparatus, making it one of the great failures in the history of espionage.

Canada had a hard time with the Civil War. The British government was an obvious supporter of the South, while Canadians had stronger geographic and philosophical links with the North. Britain's policy was based on self-interest. Most of the cotton used in the factories of England came from the South. The Confederacy was selling bales of cotton below cost and using the money to buy guns and ships from Britain. Slavery had few supporters in Britain, which had freed those in bondage in the empire in 1832. The merchants of Great Britain, however, had control of the government and the textile industry was the largest British profit-maker. The British government came perilously close to being dragged into the Civil War during the early years, but after the Battle of Gettysburg in 1863, the outcome of the war was obvious and Britain stood aside. Instead, the United Kingdom loudly proclaimed neutrality while still paying low prices for its cotton. Fortunately for the Confederacy, Britain paid in gold.

Canadians didn't import much cotton, nor was there much support for the cause of slavery. Many Canadians volunteered for the Union armies as a chance for a little excitement or to take a stand against the institution of forced servitude. Canada had a free-trade agreement with the United States that could (and, eventually, would) be cancelled if the Union government became angry with Canada. Authorities in Ottawa, the new capital taking shape along the Rideau Canal, sensed the anger against Canada that was brewing in the northern states. As the war wound down, there were calls in the Union for an invasion of Canada, the last bit of work to complete the U.S. Manifest Destiny of controlling the western hemisphere.

Canada didn't want trouble. It would have preferred to stay out of the conflict to the south. The country was on its way to confederation and independence from Great Britain. It had its own legislature and civil service. And it had spies. Foreign policy was still, supposedly, in the hands of Great Britain, but the person who really ran Canada and its spies was Attorney General John A. Macdonald. The rock with the note was tossed on the Amherstburg dock by someone on his payroll and it had a message that would eventually find its way to him.

The *Parsons* steamed down the Detroit River and headed into Lake Erie. To the left, the spies on board could see the Canadian coast, with Point Pelee forming a line on the horizon. Ahead was an archipelago of flat limestone islands. Now, they are the playground for the Windsor-Detroit-Toledo area. Back then, they were wilderness.

Except for one. Johnson Island was a prison for 3,200 Confederate officers who had been shipped up to that isolated place to wait out the rest of the war. A treaty between Britain and Canada limits the number of warships on Lake Erie to one on each side, so only the U.S.S. *Michigan*, a destroyer-sized gunboat, kept the Confederates from leaving Johnson Island. By noon, the edge of the group of islands was within sight of the *Parsons*.

At their first stop in the islands, Captain Atwood left the *Parsons*. The first mate, a man named Campbell, was given the helm of the ship to finish a run that was supposed to be routine. The new commander, however, was getting worried about the scruffy passengers that had been picked up in Canada.

On deck, the strange group of passengers seemed a little more observant, a little more nervous, than the sort of people the crew of the *Parsons* was used to. When the islands came in sight, one of the spies asked Campbell to lend him a spyglass. In the ship's saloon, a group of regular passengers played cards. One of them muttered that the men on deck seemed like a strange bunch. A card player noted to Campbell that some of the men seemed suspicious. The bulge of revolvers was apparent under some jackets. Campbell told the card players that he had noticed some of the men picked up in Canada talked like Southerners.

Campbell walked out of the saloon and went down below to check on the boat's engines. He looked into the women's lounge and saw a couple of the strange passengers loading revolvers. The mate started to become scared.

While Campbell was below, the ship stopped at its first American destination, Kelleys Island. The suspicious men seemed to be grouping into squads, Campbell noted, but their leader told them to calm down. They weren't at the right place yet, he whispered. The *Parsons* left Kelleys Island after a few minutes and headed for Cedar Point, now one of the more exclusive resort areas in Ohio.

Campbell was just poking his head up the ship's staircase after a check in the boiler room when a shot rang out and someone screamed. He saw one of the Southerners, armed with a pistol and an axe, chasing the *Parsons*'s stoker, the crew member who tossed logs into the ship's fire-box.

"Go down below to the forward hatch, or I'll blow your brains out," the hijacker spy demanded. The stoker, however, got away and ran to the bridge, where he hoped the ship's officers would protect him.

Then the spy turned to Campbell and ordered him to go below and get the ship moving. Campbell just stood there, so the spy fired a shot between his legs. Fortunately, Campbell was a bit bowlegged and the man was a good shot.

Walter Ashley, the ship's pilot and co-owner, watched the action from the *Parsons*'s bridge:

"Five of the rebels were at the steps reaching to the lower decks, each armed with one or two revolvers and an axe. The passengers and crew had been thrust forward on the deck known as the 'promenade deck', where they were being examined singly to see if they had any weapons, and after the examination, they were taken aft to the cabin. This was about four o'clock. After this part of the program was concluded, they were all ordered down to the hold, excepting the ladies and children and a few elderly men, who were placed in the cabin."

The hijacked ship was then lightened. Much of the freight, including several large pieces of pig iron, was tossed onto the Cedar Point dock. Campbell was ordered to run the ship back to Amherstburg, but the fuel was getting low.

The men who captured the *Parsons* were a collection of amateur spies, soldiers of fortune, and scoundrels. John Yates Beall, a Virginian, was in charge of the operation. His second-in-command was a Scot, Bennett G. Burleigh, who was in it for the money. Burleigh had already been captured by the North aboard a ship that had tried to run the Union blockade of Confederate ports. He had escaped from jail and found his way to Canada, where he joined Beall's raiding group.

To the passengers on board the *Parsons*, the leader of the spies was a man called "The Colonel" by his colleagues. He, more than Beall and Burleigh, did the talking. The Colonel was told that the ship was running low on fuel. The closest place to get more was Put-in-Bay. The idea of heading to the site of Perry's victory in the War of 1812 wasn't appealing to the Colonel, so he talked with Beall and Burleigh and ordered the *Parsons* to Middle Bass Island. When they arrived, a couple of the rebels jumped off the boat and tied its lines to the dock.

Things started to go wrong. Four of the women hostages decided they'd had enough of the war for one day, so they left the cabin and jumped from the *Parsons*'s deck to the dock. One of the hijackers fired three shots at the women but none of them were hurt. They kept walking.

At about the same time, the hijackers found they had more serious problems. The little steamer *Island Queen*, which supplied the settlers in the Bass Islands, started coming toward the *Parsons* while the hijackers were still loading fuel on board. The Colonel told his men to try to look normal. Men in suits were rarely seen tossing firewood into the holds of lake boats, but the spies did their best to be inconspicuous. Their friends on the *Parsons* kept out of sight and told the hostages below deck to keep their mouths shut.

Three or four of the spies stayed at the front of the *Parsons* while the rest went to the cabin at the rear where the rest of the women, children, and elderly people were. The *Island Queen*, with Captain Orr of Sandusky in command, coasted into the dock. This part of the story should have been the end of it. The *Island Queen* had three hundred federal troops aboard. These soldiers were on an unauthorized picnic to kill some time before being discharged in Toledo.

Captain Orr called over to the *Parsons* to ask why she hadn't finished her run to Sandusky, but he didn't get an answer. When he turned to resume work on his ship, the rebels at the front of the *Parsons* rushed towards the *Island Queen*. Captain Orr had no clue of what was going on, but he knew the sight of trouble. He rang his engine room to go ahead. The *Island Queen* didn't have much acceleration and the rebels had no trouble catching up to it, rushing into the engine room and taking her crew hostage. It became obvious that the troops aboard the *Island Queen* weren't ready to fight without guns. They did everything the eighteen rebels told them to do.

The size of the crowd of hostages was becoming ridiculous, so everyone was ordered onto the wharf. Some of the soldiers who were reluctant to leave their ship were smacked on the head with the blunt side of a hatchet, but no one was seriously hurt. The non-commissioned officers, accepting their status as prisoners of war, promised the Confederates that they and their men would not try to leave the island for twenty-four hours, nor would they fight against the Confederacy again. The spies tied a tow line to the *Island Queen*, then left the Bass Islands in order to start, they hoped, the real fight. They hoisted the Confederate flag on the flagstaffs of their ships. It was the only time that the Stars and Bars fluttered over the Great Lakes on a Confederate vessel.

Elsewhere, the Canadian authorities were piecing the story together while the bewildered crew of the two hijacked ships sailed Lake Erie and the passengers sat on the Middle Bass Island dock, waiting for a boat to rescue them. The government's agents realized that the Colonel was a Confederate named Johnson. They also knew that he was a double agent. He was the man who had dropped the note on the dock at Amherstburg.

The Canadian authorities realized Confederates planned to take the *Michigan*, free the prisoners, and take them on the *Michigan* and the *Parsons* to attack Buffalo. More than twenty thousand other prisoners would be rescued from camps near Indianapolis, Indiana, and Columbus, Ohio. If the plan worked really well, rebels would be freed from prisoner-of-war camps in the Chicago area, too. They would attack the cities nearby, causing the Union to send troops north. Ohio provided fifteen percent of the Union's soldiers, so the Union army would not ignore the attack on one of its most important home states. The pressure would be taken off the Confederacy, the thinking went, and there would be a chance that the South could take the offensive again.

The whole operation was run out of Toronto by Colonel Jacob Thompson, a Southerner who had been secretary of the interior in the Buchanan administration. He arrived in Canada a few months before the Lake Erie raid, loaded with gold to buy guns and ships. He was an accredited diplomat, but he had secret orders from Confederate president Jefferson Davis: "Confiding special trust in your zeal, discretion and patriotism, I hereby direct you to proceed at once to Canada, there to carry out such instructions as you have received from me verbally, in such manner as shall seem most likely to conduce to the furtherance of the interests of the Confederacy which have been intrusted to you." Basically, he had been told to make as much trouble as possible without blowing his cover and ending up on a Union gallows. If all went well, Britain would be drawn into the war as an ally of the Confederacy.

The Johnson Island plot depended on the skills of a con man in Sandusky, Ohio, namely Charles H. Cole. Later, Cole would claim to be a Confederate major but he had never held a commission in any army. He had been cashiered from a Confederate regiment, so he looked for profit in the spy world. Cole's single greatest motivation seems to have come from the $4,000 in gold that Thompson had given him.

Cole had been living at the West House Hotel in Sandusky for a while, flamboyantly posing as a wealthy oil speculator from Pennsylvania. Some of the $4,000 of Thompson's money was used to grease the social wheels in northern Ohio. Cole ingratiated himself with Ensign James Hunter of the *Michigan* and sent cases of booze to the ship's crew. Possibly, if any of Cole's later dubious testimony can be believed, he had two cohorts among the *Michigan*'s crew and ten spies in the guard on Johnson Island. Cole had joined the Masons, and had, through the lodge, ingratiated himself with the officers of the *Michigan*. On the night of September 19, 1864, he had an invitation for dinner. The hijackings of the two smaller ships had been done with the idea that Major Cole would keep his date and single-handedly capture the *Michigan*.

Once the ships got within a few kilometres of Johnson Island, the *Parsons* dropped anchor. As darkness closed in, the hijackers waited for a light to be hung on the bridge of the *Michigan*, the signal that the officers had been knocked unconscious with laudanum, an opiate that Cole planned to slip into their wine. Cole had come aboard the *Michigan* on one of the ship's boats. As the Union sailors closed in on the *Michigan*, the officers on the ship leaned over the rail to welcome Cole aboard.

The plot seemed to be working as the officers sat down to dinner, but the Canadian government had telegraphed the Union authorities in Sandusky with details of Johnson's message. The Canadian warning was relayed to Johnson Island. It was taken to the *Michigan*, where the captain was away from the dinner table and told. When he went back into the wardroom, he pulled a gun on Cole. Two armed soldiers quickly joined the captain in the dining room.

On board the *Parsons*, Beall became worried. As the night wore on, there was no sign that the plot was working. He began to pace the *Parsons*'s bridge, wondering what to do. By midnight, he decided that the plot must have fallen apart. He panicked.

The first thing he did was scuttle the *Island Queen*. The hostages aboard that boat were brought onto the *Parsons*. The crew of the *Michigan*, still unaware that the *Parsons* and the *Island Queen* were held by rebels, watched as the *Island Queen* settled into about three metres of water. As the ship went down, the Confederate agents could be seen loading everything of value, including the piano, from the *Island Queen* to the *Parsons*. The captain of the *Michigan*, already shaken by his dinner experience with Cole, ordered his boilers to be fired up. By then, the *Parsons* was already steaming toward Canada.

Campbell, the *Parsons*'s mate, was ordered to steer for the mouth of the Detroit river and keep to the Canadian channel. It was becoming daylight when the spies reached Sandwich. The Americans were ordered onto the dock while the Confederate agents went through all of their baggage, looking for money. They tore apart the suitcases and even carted off the stolen piano. After an hour or so of pilfering, the hijackers fled. While the spies searched for valuables, Beall chopped holes in the hull of the *Parsons*, sinking her in about three metres of water. Until they began stealing, the men who hijacked the *Parsons* hadn't broken any laws in Canada. Now they risked robbery charges. Robbery was an offence that could leave them open to extradition and execution in the United States.

One of the first agents to be arrested was Burleigh. Canadian authorities picked him up within a couple of days of the raid and charged him with robbery. Union authorities filed extradition papers, causing a rift among Canadians, many of whom were Scots. Eventually, he was taken back to northern Ohio to face the charges. The jury couldn't reach a verdict. Sent back to jail to await a new trial, Burleigh escaped. He went back to Canada, but after the war he returned to the United States to work as a newspaper reporter in Houston. He spent the next fifty years as one of the world's most successful war correspondents, writing for Great Britain's largest newspapers under the name Bennett Burley.

Cole spent the rest of the war in jail, changing his story just about every time he was interrogated. His creativity has clouded the Johnson Island raid, leaving so many false or padded versions that it has been almost impossible for historians to piece the details together. After the Civil War ended, Cole was pardoned and allowed to resume his career as a con man. Whether he was a real spy or simply out for Thompson's $4,000 will probably remain a mystery.

Beall was the only one of the Johnson Island plotters to come to a bad end. The failure of the Lake Erie raid didn't deter him from making trouble at other places along the Canada-U.S. frontier. The next month, he tried to lead an attack against Cleveland. This time, the raiders used small boats in their assault, but the winds were against them. Two months later, he tried to derail an express train in Niagara Falls, New York, near the suspension bridge across the river. This time, the authorities caught him. He was tried for his various acts of terrorism and hanged at Governor's Island, New York, a few days before the end of the war.

The *Parsons* was eventually patched and raised, only to be destroyed in the Chicago fire of 1871.

Meanwhile, back in Toronto, spymaster Thompson kept the rebel cause alive. Macdonald knew what he was up to, but, unlike Beall, Thompson never ended up on a Union gallows. Through a Confederate sympathizer, Dr. James T. Bate, he bought the little steamer *Georgian*, which was headquartered in Windsor. The plan was to use it as a privateer to attack ships and cities along Lake Erie. Union spies quickly heard about the *Georgian* and asked Canadian authorities to keep close watch on the boat. So many Canadian agents lurked around the *Georgian* that the spymaster decided to unload the boat, and he reported back to Richmond that it was becoming difficult to be an effective rebel in Canada:

"The bane and curse of carrying out anything in this country is the surveillance under which we act. Detectives or those ready to give information stand at every street corner. Two or three cannot interchange ideas without a reporter."

In the last months of the war, the parliament of the United Canadas passed new laws to clamp down on Confederate spies. They were sent back across the border or jailed in Canada, along with Canadians who helped them. Thompson, who was becoming more worried that his whole operation might be shut down by Macdonald's people, decided on one last project. Since the South was just about defeated, he decided to make sure this one worked.

George Taylor Denison, a militia cavalryman, was the heir to one of Canada's most prominent families. For some reason, he chose to embrace the Confederacy's cause, just as he had been a true-blue Tory and a tireless campaign worker for Macdonald. Perhaps it was because of the anti-Americanism that ran through his United Empire Loyalist family, which had been expelled from the United States after the War of Independence. Denison feared the threats against Canada that were made by Union leaders. He thought the only way to preserve Canadian independence was by helping the South win the war. Denison met Thompson in November 1864, and threw all of his rather awesome energy into helping the spymaster with his projects. Denison harboured Confederate spies in his home, worked to free the men held in Canada after the *Michigan* plot, and went to work for Thompson as a front man for his pirating plans.

They heard the steamship *Georgian* was up for sale. On January 17, 1865, Denison took the train up to a port on Lake Erie and visited the ship. She had lots of power but was a little heavy with superstructure. The sailing season wouldn't begin for another three months, so there was plenty of time for shipbuilders to get the *Georgian* into shape. Denison bought the ship, using some of Thompson's money and some of his own. Union agents knew of the purchase almost immediately, and armed U.S. tugs shadowed the *Georgian*, in breach of the Canada-U.S. boundary treaty, as she sailed into Lake Huron, heading for Collingwood. The trip wasn't much of a secret. Reporters from the Toronto *Globe* followed the *Georgian* as she made her way north.

At the same time, a cannon was stolen from in front of a house in Guelph. Police, investigating the theft, uncovered a bomb factory in that town and learned that fugitive raider Beall was supposed to become the *Georgian*'s master. Two boxes marked "potatoes" but filled with grenades were intercepted by police as they were being shipped to the *Georgian*'s new home on Georgian Bay.

By late February, despite thorough work by the authorities, a crew had been put together and carpenters went to work in Collingwood ripping off the excess cabins. The head woodworker was Larry MacDonald, an almost famous Confederate who had fled to Canada after a well-publicized attempt to burn New York City.

Back in Toronto, Denison and his friends went to work making more hand grenades, home-made bombs and rifle cartridges. They bought some guns and other off-the-shelf weapons. Unfortunately for Denison, one of the bomb makers was an agent for the Canadian government.

On April 7, a week before the Civil War ended and a month before Lake Huron was safe for navigation, Macdonald's agents struck. They raided the *Georgian* at her Collingwood dock and handed her over to the town's custom agent. Denison wasn't arrested. He feigned indignation but the double agents began coming out of the woodwork. In court, the presence of the Confederate carpenter on the *Georgian* and the existence of the bomb factory in Denison's house became part of the record. The judges in Toronto and Simcoe County weren't convinced that Denison had been illegally relieved of his property. A few weeks later, the U.S. government filed suit for ownership of the *Georgian*. Along with all the other property of the Confederacy, the *Georgian* was claimed to be a spoil of war.

Partway through the final court case, arsonist-carpenter Larry MacDonald changed sides. Union lawyers had come to him in jail, promising to let him off the hook for his New York terrorism if he would help the U.S. government get control of the *Georgian*. The carpenter had already been ordered deported by a Canadian grand jury, and there was a good chance he would face the same fate as the unlucky Beall. After a couple of visits, the U.S. lawyers sweetened the pot with an offer of cash. Larry MacDonald was theirs.

Denison, bled dry by the cost of the ship, the weapons, and the lawyers, fought on. His loyalty to the Confederacy never wavered. He was already corresponding with Confederate ex-president Jefferson Davis and General Robert E. Lee. He threw himself into his legal case with the same zeal he had given to the South's lost cause.

The turncoat carpenter was out of jail quite quickly once he had reached his deal with the U.S. lawyers. He went to Denison and told him that the United States would pay him $2,000 and his legal costs if he admitted that the Confederacy was the real owner of the *Georgian*. Denison refused and turned to his old political friend, John A. Macdonald.

The Tory chieftain wasn't any help. All the years of working for the Conservatives, all the money handed over to the party since the Denisons had arrived in Canada in 1792, became insignificant when Macdonald told Denison the case should be settled in the courts. After pushing for Macdonald's help, Denison tried to run as a Tory in the Confederation election of 1867. Macdonald gave his blessing to another candidate and Denison's political career was over. Denison became so angry that he and several friends started a new political party, Canada First, which ultimately amounted to nothing.

In the weeks of the election campaign, Macdonald tried to keep Denison and his party from aiding the Liberals by hinting that he would help Denison out with his losses from the *Georgian*. He suggested Denison would be given a job with an impressive title: Assistant Adjutant General of Cavalry. Denison tried to get the promise in writing but the wily old politician backed off. A few weeks later Macdonald was Sir John A., Prime Minister of Canada. There was no job for Denison, no help in his legal problems, and the Canadian government was still listed as one of the parties suing Denison.

A House of Commons committee investigated the seizure of the *Georgian* in 1868 and said it was illegal. The witnesses against Denison were untrustworthy, they ruled. The committee recommended to Parliament that $4,359.50 be given to Denison to cover his legal fees, but Macdonald killed the idea. In spite, Denison went out to Manitoba in 1870 to support Louis Riel's first rebellion.

As the money poured out of Denison's bank account to cover the fees of the lawyers, Thompson, the spymaster, filed suit against his former espionage pupil. He wanted the money that he had put into the *Georgian*. This strange act of betrayal was more then Denison could bear, personally or financially. He declared bankruptcy in 1869.

For years, Denison tried to get his money from Macdonald. He went up to Algoma District in 1872 to run as a Liberal, using his support for the first Riel Rebellion as an election issue. Over the years, however, the Prime Minister used his considerable charm and his well-lubricated social skills to win Denison back. In their old age, the men were fairly close friends and Denison became one of the Prime Minister's key supporters in Toronto. Denison died in Toronto in 1925, a respected soldier, businessman, and military strategist who enthusiastically gave World War I soldiers advice on the science of war.

Thompson, the spymaster, had died forty years earlier in England's lake country. After Lee's surrender, Thompson had tried to get to Halifax by travelling through Maine. He had been stopped but not arrested. Someone very powerful had intervened. On April 14, 1865, Abraham Lincoln had deliberately allowed Thompson to escape. Politics is a small world. Lincoln had known and liked Thompson back in the 1850s, when Thompson was one of the most important men in Washington. The next evening, Lincoln kept a date to see "My American Cousin" at Ford's Theatre.

In the end, the real value of all the Confederate spying in Canada lay in the propaganda it created for the Union. In the summer and fall of 1864, a tough presidential election campaign was under way. In August, Abraham Lincoln had expected to lose. In the same month that Beall and Cole were carrying out their Johnson Island scheme, the Democrats adopted an election platform that called for peace talks and the granting of Confederate independence. By the end of September, however, Atlanta fell to Sherman, the Confederates were driven out of the Shenandoah Valley, and the naval base of Mobile, Alabama, was in possession of the Union. The border raids strengthened the position of those who called the Confederates traitors and terrorists. Democrats in states along the Great Lakes who favoured peace were arrested, newspapers were muzzled, and Republicans were elected.

The jittery politicians in Canada, fearful of the huge Union military machine that was soon to be idle, dropped their political differences, created a coalition government and set to work drafting the details of Confederation. Denison, Burleigh, Thompson, Cole, and Beall can't take much credit for the founding of modern Canada, but they deserve their small share.

Chapter Eight

Georgian Bay
Ghost Ships

All of the people aboard the Mary Ward *would have been rescued
if members of the crew had not panicked.*
(NATIONAL ARCHIVES OF CANADA)

The highway from Collingwood to Owen Sound runs
between the Niagara Escarpment and Georgian Bay. In the
winter, Highway 26 is crowded with skiers going to the
resorts around Craigleith, the first community northwest of

Collingwood. In the summer, a provincial campground about twelve kilometres from Collingwood is booked up through most of the summer. Campers visit the caves on the hill above, drive through the scenic valleys near Thornbury, and walk the beach.

But the beach here is like no other shoreline in Ontario. It is made of great sheets of shale that rise in steps from the water. The shoreline consists of bare rock which is wonderful for people who like to sunbathe without having to put up with the nuisances of sand. The only visible animal life on this shoreline are a few harmless little brown spiders that dash along the flat stone, running from one hiding spot to another. At least, that is how things seem at first, until you look down at the rock itself.

Probably, something will be looking back at you. Thousands of fossil trilobites are preserved in the Craigleith shale. They look like bugs, ranging in size from less than a centimetre to thirty or forty centimetres. Most are in pieces, but it isn't hard to find one with its legs, eyes, head, and tail intact. Collectors come from across North America to look for them.

This rock has other interesting properties. Bang on the surface of the bedrock and you'll find it to be as hard as cement. Pick up a piece of the loose rock and you can split it from its edges into sheets with a table knife. Once the rock breaks open, you can smell the petroleum inside. The shale is grey-black, but if you toss a piece into a fire it will burn for hours, leaving white shale behind. It is interesting stuff, and it didn't take settlers long to realize it had some value.

In the middle of the last century, most people could only think of two uses for oil: lubrication of the moving parts of equipment such as wagon axles, farm machinery, and steam engines, or illumination oil, used in lamps. In those days, most lubricating oil came from boiling down animals such as whales or dead livestock. Lamp oil was made from plants like hemp, flax, or olives.

Craigleith was the first place in Canada where people extracted oil from rocks. Since the oil shale is at the surface, there was no need to drill. After several experiments, including using an old musket as a makeshift lamp, oil workers found a way to get oil out of the rocks and they set to work quarrying it near what is now Craigleith Provincial Park.

"For some time it had been known that wherever the rock was exposed, it would burn, and that fires lighted along the creek would continue to burn, thus proving the presence of oil," a Craigleith pioneer later wrote. "Eventually, a company of Toronto and Collingwood capitalists was formed. A building, forty by one hundred feet, and also a large log building, which was used as a boarding house, were erected."

Big chunks of rock were chiselled at what is now Hidden Lake, a large, deep pond surrounded by ski condominiums. The rock was heated in a distilling machine which was able to collect about half of the petroleum in the shale. Since the Craigleith shale is about thirteen percent oil by weight, it was worth the effort. The refinery employed about a hundred people in its best years.

The oil that was extracted from the shale was a light crude which worked well in lamps and could be further reduced to make dense grease for lubrication. The distilling system, however, released more volatile compounds such as gasoline and benzene, which were ignited by the boiler's fires. Several times, the Craigleith oil works blew up, leaving workers seriously injured. The entire refining building burned down two years after it was built. The company rebuilt the factory with better ventilation so that the explosive gasses could escape.

Other bad luck dogged the oil works. The quarry was so deep that groundwater poured through the sides and had to be sucked up with big steam pumps. Workers were afraid the whole pit would fill with water. The Craigleith works were not a good place to work, but there weren't many decent jobs in the farm country around Craigleith during the recession of the 1850s.

By the early 1860s, the Craigleith oil shale experiment had another problem. This one proved to be too big to overcome. Oil wells had been drilled in the Petrolia area in southwestern Ontario. It is a lot cheaper to pump liquid oil from the ground than to quarry big chunks of shale and feed it into a distilling system. The Craigleith technology simply couldn't compete. By the time of Confederation, the workers at the Georgian Bay oil operation had gone home, the machinery had been left to rust, the pumps had stopped, and the quarry had filled with water. In the summer, algae turned the quarry pond an emerald green colour. The trees grew back, the employees looked for farm jobs or worked in the Collingwood shipyards, and the experiment was forgotten. Today, the oil shale could be used profitably but the local tourist trade would be ruined.

Maybe somewhere else the shale oil could be mined and processed. The same rock surfaces again near the Lake Ontario shore. The foundations of the Darlington nuclear power plant are anchored to it.

Many people living at Craigleith have believed that a shipwreck near the old oil shale works may have a link to the failed petroleum extraction experiment. About a kilometre offshore, the same oil shale that was mined in the 1850s is stacked up into a reef which, in low water, breaks the surface. It is a hazard to ships that can be avoided by navigating with the lighthouse on Nottawasaga Island at the entrance to Collingwood harbour. Only one full-sized ship has been claimed by the shoal, which is named after her victim, the *Mary Ward*.

In the late 1860s, Collingwood was losing much of its ship traffic to other ports and the town was settling into a decline. These were hard times for Canada. People who had lost their jobs were making their living as best they could in those days before welfare and unemployment insurance. In 1872, a group of business owners in Collingwood bought the steamship *Mary Ward* to help recover some of the lost business. Her owners took the train from Collingwood to Sarnia to pick up the new ship. Before they left Sarnia, they had the *Mary Ward* loaded with salt, hardware and, perhaps ominously, oil.

The *Mary Ward* was a fairly small ship, only about forty metres long, but she was well adapted for the Collingwood to Thunder Bay marine trade. Her hull was strong and deep, and she had comfortable cabins on deck. On November 24, she entered Georgian Bay, stopped at Owen Sound for a few hours, and headed toward Collingwood.

What happened next is one of the Great Lakes' great mysteries. The afternoon and evening were warm and calm. Visibility was excellent. Most of the *Mary Ward*'s crew were from Collingwood, so they knew the waters around the town better than they knew any other part of the Great Lakes. Steaming through the dark, however, they saw things that certainly shouldn't have been there.

Anyone sailing south along Georgian Bay towards Collingwood

at night simply needs to take his bearing off the Nottawasaga Island lighthouse. Yet, the night the *Mary Ward* went aground, there seemed to be at least two Nottawasaga Island lighthouses. Not suspecting anything at first, the *Mary Ward* steered towards the wrong one.

By 9:00 P.M., the *Mary Ward* was far off course and in very dangerous waters. She was about two kilometres from shore before anyone realized the trouble she was in. By that time, the *Mary Ward* would have been very lucky to have been able to find her way out of the maze of submerged shale cliffs she had wandered into.

If the suspicions of the ship's owners and many of the people who lived in the Collingwood area at the time are true, the *Mary Ward* was the victim of "wreckers," land-based pirates who lure a ship into dangerous waters, wait until the crew abandons her, then go to the beached craft to strip it clean. There are no other known cases of wreckers working in Great Lakes waters, but they have been common along ocean coasts, including Canada's Maritimes. There have also been a few cases in Canada of people derailing freight trains with the same malicious intent. The night the *Mary Ward* approached Collingwood would have been perfect for wreckers. Calm water would have allowed the frustrated crew to get off safely and would have made life easy for the scavengers lurking on shore with their bright lights. Some Great Lakes historians have suggested the *Mary Ward* wasn't chosen by accident. There may have been resentment in Craigleith about that cargo of Sarnia oil.

One local story gives hints that the demise of the *Mary Ward* and the fate of the oil shale works were linked. The old boarding house at the refinery site was supposedly occupied by fishermen. The night the *Mary Ward* sank, a lantern had been hung in the window, supposedly to help guide one of the fishing boats home. It must have been a powerful beacon to have outshone the Nottawasaga lighthouse.

Defenders of the reputation of the local people blamed faulty navigation for the loss of the *Mary Ward*. In another local legend, it was the light of a tavern that drew the *Mary Ward* to her doom. There have been polite suggestions in some marine history books that the captain was drunk or that the light of the saloon was a beacon to a thirst that could never be quenched. None of the passengers, however, complained about the sobriety of the *Mary Ward*'s master at the time.

The bright, flickering lights did their work. The *Mary Ward* passed the first line of shoals but ran aground on the second. Passengers heard the captain and crew curse after they felt the jolt of the ship's impact. For an hour or so, the captain tried to back off the shoal but the *Mary Ward* was stuck there for good. Once the initial shock and fear had worn off, the captain suggested the passengers and crew get some sleep. He would send a lifeboat to Collingwood to get help, and by the next day, if everything worked out, the *Mary Ward* would be towed off the shoal.

There were still enough lifeboats left on the *Mary Ward* to take all the passengers off, and the waves were so small that they didn't scare the passengers. The warm late-fall weather, which has caused so much false confidence in so many doomed sailors, lulled the *Mary Ward*'s passengers and crew back into their bunks. Meanwhile, two men set out for Collingwood in one of the ship's boats.

The *Mary Ward* was close enough to shore for the wreckers to hear the grinding of her hull on the shale reefs and the frustrating sound of her engine trying to generate enough power to pull her off the shoal. As the night wore on, fewer stars were visible. A bank of clouds rolled in from the west, over the Niagara Escarpment.

One passenger had decided not to take the captain's advice to retire for the night. He paced the deck instead, looked up at the sky, or leaned restlessly against the ship's rail. He had good reason to be nervous. Later, he wrote down the details of what he saw:

"Shortly after midnight, the wind suddenly shifted and heavy, black, swiftly moving clouds arose over the mountain and the stars soon disappeared. There was an ominous moaning in the rigging, the import of which I knew too well. There was an uncanny stillness. I shall never, as long as I live, forget the weird feeling of alarm and terror which came over me, nor shall I ever wholly forgive myself for not acting on the impulse I had to arouse everyone and tell them that a storm was about to break and that we had better get to land while there was still time. But I had no authority and being young, I was reluctant to exhibit any fear.

"After a little time, I did suggest to the watchman that he call the Captain. This he did and the Captain realized the danger at once and began blowing the *Mary Ward*'s whistle again frantically and calling all hands on deck. The storm increased in fury suddenly and by dawn huge breakers were sweeping over the stern. Had she not been so well built, she would have gone to pieces in a very short time but she held together despite the tremendous strain and pounding. In a few hours we were all hanging on for dear life and most of us had become reconciled to our fate. We were all soaking wet and cold."

The boat began to rock back and forth, scaring the passengers and crew. In the morning, eight of the passengers rebelled. They told the captain they were going ashore. The captain knew that help was on the way. He begged the passengers and a crewman who had joined them not to launch a lifeboat.

They did it anyway. The passengers hauled their baggage from below deck, loaded up the boat and climbed inside. Crew on board the *Mary Ward* lowered the boat into the churning water. The lifeboat was only a few hundred metres from the *Mary Ward* when it flipped over, drowning all nine people on board.

Meanwhile, help was coming from shore. Fishermen along the Craigleith coast, as well as a tug boat from Collingwood, took on the lake to rescue the people on the *Mary Ward*. The fishermen, using small sailing skiffs called Collingwood Smackers, picked their way through the dangerous shoals until they got to the stranded ship. At about the same time, the tug tried to find its way through the maze of shoals but could only stand by as the small sailboats performed the rescue. The government minted a special commemorative medal for bravery and gave it to the rescuers of the *Mary Ward*, some of whom, by accident or design, may have been responsible for her stranding in the first place.

After all this excitement and danger, it turned out that everyone could have stayed on the *Mary Ward* quite safely. She was a well-built boat that held together through the rest of the fall's storms and the ice of the next winter.

Almost as soon as the rescue drama was over, the salvagers got to work. Whether they were the people who lured the *Mary Ward* to shore is still one of the lake's mysteries. No one in the Craigleith area wanted to admit to a crime that would have meant a long prison term.

By the spring of 1873, all of the oil, salt, and hardware had been taken off. Three salvage companies tried to budge the *Mary Ward* from the shoal that summer, but they gave up by the fall. November gales began chewing the *Mary Ward* apart, and the winter of 1873-74 finished her. The upper parts of the ship became driftwood, the lower parts settled into the lake, and she is now one of the more popular and accessible wrecks in Georgian Bay cottage country.

The old boarding house at the oil works was abandoned after the *Mary Ward*'s sinking. For many years, it loomed over the lake. All its windows were broken and superstitious people said it was haunted. On still, warm days like the one when the *Mary Ward* was lost, the house seemed to float on the water. Only brave kids went anywhere near it. They poked through the collapsed refinery building and marvelled at its high chimney, which stood on the oil shale site for years. Eventually, the chimney fell down and the haunted house burned in a midnight fire. The only real reminder of those times is a plaque at the lakeshore and the name "*Mary Ward* Shoals" on the navigation charts.

The power of late November gales has generated another Georgian Bay mystery, a full-fledged psychic occurrence that left Collingwood whispering about strange happenings for more than a century. Ironically, it happened exactly seven years after the *Mary Ward* was lost. Maybe numerologists would make something of that.

In November, 1879, the little steamer *Waubuno* supplied the small towns and camps along the southeastern shore of Georgian Bay. There was an economic downturn in those years, as there was so often in the last century, so the *Waubuno* had to work hard for the business she got. Pressure was put on her captain by the ship's owners to keep to his schedule, no matter how bad the weather was.

It is worth a trip to the lonely shores of Georgian Bay to experience real wind and weather. Along miles of empty shoreline cottages, gales reshape the dunes each fall. Grey scudding clouds cover the sky, merging on the horizon with the silver waves. The wind whips the water into mountainous peaks, snatching the whitecaps and throwing the foam forward. On the shore, the waves break and roll up onto the sand or wash the edges of the Canadian Shield islands. These are the winds that shaped the pine trees of the Tom Thompson and Group of Seven paintings.

If you walk those shores, chances are you'll be alone. It is a primal experience, a moment with nature that is as hearty as good Scotch whisky. You need to make some adjustments. First, it is nearly impossible to stay warm. The wind cuts through layers of clothes, paralyses your face, and dries your eyes. You have to lean into it as you walk, using the fast air to support your body. What appears to be fog on the horizon suddenly rolls towards shore and engulfs you in snow. These snow squalls can leave ten centimetres of snow in only an hour. Within minutes, your clothes and hair are covered with flakes. Afterwards, sitting next to a fire or wood stove with a cup of hot chocolate or coffee, think about what it would be like to be out in one of those fall gales on a small steamboat. Then imagine it was night, the boat was crowded and obviously unsafe. You'll have a sense of the feelings of the people aboard the *Waubuno* and so many other ships that have been lost. It is impossible, however, to simulate the feeling of helplessness, of being trapped in an inescapable situation of danger, that those people experienced. There are limits to empathy.

The *Waubuno* sat in Collingwood harbour on the night of November 21, 1879, waiting for such a storm to pass. She had loaded a good cargo of freight and passengers at Collingwood and there was more to be picked up in Parry Sound. There was, however, an unease around the ship because of what had happened the night before. Dr. W.D. Doupe and his wife, whose name seemed unimportant to people at the time, were sleeping. Mrs. Doupe tossed and turned, fretfully trying to get comfortable on one of the *Waubuno*'s cabin beds. In the middle of the night, she woke up shrieking.

She was in a state of panic, loudly telling her husband of her dream that the *Waubuno* would be wrecked and all aboard her lost forever. She begged her husband to go to their new home, north of Parry Sound, by land or to find another boat. Dr. Doupe, who had just finished his medical training, had little use for his wife's psychic vision. Less scientific minds, however, were quick to spread the story to the rest of the *Waubuno*'s passengers and her crew. Before the ship left Collingwood harbour, the story had swept through the town, too.

Passengers stayed at the ship all that afternoon but, finally, they grew tired of waiting and went to hotels in the town; Mrs. Doupe's vision had convinced some of the *Waubuno*'s passengers to change their plans. At 4:00 A.M. the next day, when Captain Burkett of the *Waubuno* began rounding up his passengers by sending sailors to the hotels, many refused to go. Some said it was too early or the weather was too rough. Some said they believed Mrs. Doupe's prophecy and would sit this trip out.

Among those who didn't act on it were the Doupses themselves. They, along with eight other passengers and fourteen crew members, left Collingwood on the sidewheeler, which was loaded down with furniture, crates, and even a few cows.

They crossed the open water of southern Georgian Bay in the

dark, arriving in sight of Christian Island just after dawn. The keeper of the stone lighthouse at the southern tip of the island noted the *Waubuno* as she passed. His log shows there was no sign of trouble on the ship yet.

Past Christian Island, the *Waubuno* had to go through another fifty kilometres of open water to get to the east side of Georgian Bay, a place of Canadian Shield islands and hidden rocks. Today, it is one of the most popular vacation areas in Canada, but in 1879 it was almost uninhabited.

Just after the *Waubuno* left Christian Island, snow began to fall. By the time she neared the Muskoka shore, squalls had cut visibility to nothing.

Loggers near the mouth of the Moon River, one of the waterways through Muskoka, heard the *Waubuno*'s plaintive whistle as she cast about in the whitecaps and snow, looking for a safe anchorage. Yet they couldn't see the ship or anything else that was more than a few metres away. They didn't see the *Waubuno* tear out her bottom on a submerged granite shoal or watch as her hull sprawled among the islands. There was no time for the passengers to try to save themselves. Mrs. Doupe never had a chance to be congratulated on her soothsaying skills.

The *Magnettewan*, a competitor ship that had left Collingwood for Parry Sound at the same time, had stayed in the lee of Christian Island for forty hours riding out the blizzard. When the *Magnettewan* reached Parry Sound, her captain realized that the *Waubuno* would no longer share in the cargo business of Georgian Bay. The cargo that had been stacked on the dock for the *Waubuno* was still there. She was hopelessly overdue.

Tugs found floating wreckage of the *Waubuno* in the days after the ship was lost. All her life preservers washed ashore but not one body ever turned up. Eventually, the story of her loss was pieced together when the main part of her hull was located in the 1960s. Mrs. Doupe's name was forever linked with a ship from which she would have been very glad to walk away.

Chapter Nine

The *Asia*

Christie Anne Morrison survived the sinking of the Asia, *which foundered in the middle of Georgian Bay.*
(National Archives of Canada)

Collingwood harbour often seems to give fair warning to passengers who embark on doomed ships. Like the tiresome Mrs. Doupe on the *Waubuno*, Joseph Shippe was tipped off by a voice inside him that said the *Asia*, a small steamship that hauled freight and passengers on Georgian Bay, was a death trap. Shippe wasn't the kind of man who worried too much, but he had the good sense to act on this particular hunch, although Georgian Bay had to give him some prodding.

Shippe had travelled on the Great Lakes many times. There was, however, something about the *Asia* that he didn't like when he went aboard her in Collingwood on the afternoon of September 13, 1882. The ship was older than most on the lakes and she was heavily loaded with people, horses, and freight. The *Asia* was bound for the lumber camps at the French River with supplies that were supposed to keep the loggers fed and equipped through the winter. She was taking a circular route, from Collingwood up the east side of the Bruce Peninsula to Manitoulin Island, then across northern Georgian Bay. After finishing at French River, the *Asia* was scheduled to sail to Sault Ste. Marie. With the lumbermen's food, cooking pots, and tools stacked on the *Asia*'s deck were fourteen very nervous and unhappy draught horses.

Shippe was a butcher by trade, living in downtown Toronto. He knew nothing about the rules covering the loading of boats and the maintenance of lake vessels. He had very good survival instincts, however, and he watched the loading with some consternation. He didn't like the way the horses were tied at the bow of the *Asia*. The deck seemed too heavy with pressed hay, crates of cooking pots, and sacks of flour. There were too many people on the boat, he thought.

The company that owned the *Asia* had tried hard to get fall business. In those days, the Canadian National Exhibition was held in September, so the *Asia*'s owners cut fares to try to lure passengers from Toronto during this slow month. As well, supplies were taken to camps and small towns to keep them stocked for the winter.

Mariners on the Great Lakes know better than to overload their ships, especially near the fall equinox. This is a time of storms on the lakes. The ominous signs were there before the *Asia* left her berth, but the passengers and freight kept streaming aboard.

Shippe handed his ticket to the *Asia*'s purser and carried his luggage aboard. There were so many people on the ship that there were no chairs on which to sit. Most of the passengers had to ride on the open deck. It was nearly dusk and there was a bit of a wind. The trip was shaping up to be unpleasant. Shippe was wondering just how badly he wanted to go to Manitoulin Island.

The ship left Collingwood harbour, sailed along Nottawasaga Bay just off the *Mary Ward* shoal and reached Meaford after dark. At about 10:30 P.M., the *Asia* left Meaford and headed for Owen Sound, carrying even more people and freight. Shippe's second thoughts about the trip were starting to obsess him. Everything about this trip was terribly wrong:

"A mile out (from Meaford) the full force of the gale struck the boat, and she immediately began to roll and pitch about in a fearful manner, and every now and then, cracking sounds could be heard, as if she was being torn asunder. Most of the passengers got seasick, and many of them began to get frightened. I lay down on a barrel, as I began to feel a little sick myself, and almost immediately afterwards, a loud report was heard, as if the vessel had burst in two. I jumped up, and as the passengers got frightened, I and an old farmer from Osprey Township, to pacify them, began to laugh and joke and tell them that it was nothing unusual.

"The steamer continued to lurch and roll about in a tremendous way, the horses began to kick and plunge, and the cargo to roll. The deckhands were kept busy trying to brace up the boat by screwing tight the iron rods placed across her, and I heard one of them say they were no use, as they wouldn't hold firm. They afterwards broke altogether. It was an awful time, and I thought we would never get to Owen Sound."

At Owen Sound, Shippe didn't know what to do. He had paid his full fare to Manitoulin Island and the purser had made it very clear that the Northern Navigation Company, which owned the *Asia*, didn't give refunds.

The night was cold, so after pacing for a while Shippe went back on the *Asia*'s deck and stood near the smokestack, trying to get warm from the heat it radiated. He couldn't believe what he saw: more freight was being loaded onto the *Asia* and more passengers, too. Some people had finished their trip at Owen Sound, but far more people were taking their place.

Shippe watched quietly as a government inspector talked with Captain John Savage on the pier. Savage stood by the gangplank, only a few metres from where Shippe was standing. Obviously, the inspector wasn't thrilled by what he saw.

"What about this boat?" the inspector asked.

"I don't know," Captain Savage replied.

"Well," the inspector said in a strong voice, loud enough for Shippe to hear, "I know this about her, she won't be going out of here tonight. If she does, she won't reach French River."

"You toll her, and I'll risk her," Captain Savage said.

"Well, I'll toll her, but she'll never make French River. She's strained," the inspector replied.

Then the captain, the inspector, and Shippe watched four cows being led up the *Asia*'s gangway.

That was enough for Shippe. He gathered up his baggage, hooked up with his friend Bowes, the farmer from Osprey Township who had worked with him to prevent panic on the ship just a few hours before, and the two of them walked off the *Asia*. They found a hotel in Owen Sound that was still open and caught a train for Toronto the next morning. It was the smartest thing they ever did.

One of the people who got on while Shippe was leaving the *Asia* was a seventeen-year-old youth. Duncan Tinkiss went aboard the *Asia* at Owen Sound about midnight, with his uncle, James Tinkiss, just as she was about to sail. The Tinkiss family owned a hotel in Manitouwaning, on Manitoulin Island. Because there were no cabins available or even steerage space below deck, passengers slept in chairs on the deck or stretched out on the floor of the main cabin. Duncan and his uncle slept on cots as the boat sailed along the shore of the Bruce Peninsula.

In one of the ship's cabins was Christie Morrison, a sixteen-year-old Owen Sound girl who was travelling to northern Michigan to visit an aunt. She had missed the *Asia*'s sister ship, the *Northern Belle*, which had left Owen Sound earlier that day. Morrison expected to go the entire length of the *Asia*'s run, then switch at Sault Ste. Marie to another ship, which was to take her to Grand Marais. Her cousin, John MacDonald, was the ship's first mate, so maybe she felt a little more secure than the rest of the passengers when the *Asia* left the Owen Sound wharf just after midnight.

The *Asia* had the wind behind her as she sailed up Owen Sound's long harbour, but, when she turned northwest toward Manitoulin Island, she felt the full blast of the gale that raged that night. About fifteen kilometres up the peninsula, she stopped at Presque Isle, where she was loaded with cordwood fuel. The *Asia*'s crew lined up to pass the wood along and to load it into the hold. Captain Savage probably hoped the heavy wood would give the *Asia* a bit more stability.

Tied behind the *Asia*, as she left Presque Isle, was a small sailboat named the *Dreadnought*, a fishing smack as they were called on southern Georgian Bay. The *Asia* was towing it to the French River.

After leaving the refuelling stop, the *Asia* stayed well clear of the dangerous rocks and small islands along the shore of the Bruce Peninsula. She steered almost due north, toward Manitoulin Island, and morning found her in the most isolated part of Georgian Bay. The towering waves tossed the overloaded *Asia*, and Christie Morrison spent most of the night lying in her berth, grossly seasick. Dunc Tinkiss slept through most of the storm.

Tinkiss even managed to eat breakfast the next morning, but most of the other passengers were in no shape to dine. They lay on their berths, sat huddled in the chairs, or stood on the soaked deck of the *Asia*.

The storm came from the southwest, across the open water of Lake Huron and Georgian Bay. People who saw it compared the gale to a November storm, saying the frothing water looked like carded wool. On shore, trees were doubled over in the wind. Whitecaps towered over the ship. And the storm was getting worse. For a few moments, the people on board the *Asia* could see a speck of land, Lonely Island, but it offered no shelter. At about 9:00 A.M., the little fishing boat *Dreadnought* was cut loose and freight was tossed overboard. An hour later, the poor cows and horses tied up at the front of the boat were thrown over the side too.

Just before noon, the *Asia* lost her fight with the giant whitecaps. She didn't have the power to keep her bow into the waves. Instead, she was pitched sideways into the troughs between them. The crew had no control over the ship and Captain Savage knew she was doomed. He called to all the passengers to come on deck, but many were so seasick that they didn't care whether the ship sank or not. Soon, passengers realized that there was no doubt that the *Asia* was about to capsize or be torn to pieces. Some tried to find ways to save themselves.

"My uncle jumped up and said the boat was doomed," Tinkiss later testified. "Dishes and chairs were flying in every direction. We left the cabin and found difficulty in getting on deck, the ship was rolling so heavily. I got a life preserver and put it on. The boat went into the trough of the sea and would not obey her helm. She rolled heavily for about twenty minutes, when she was struck by a heavy sea and foundered, going down with the engine working, about half past eleven. The *Asia* was making for the French River, and had men, horses, and lumbermen's supplies for the shanties there.

"I saw three boats lowered. I was in the first boat, and about eight were with me at first. More got in until the boat was overloaded and turned over. Two people were hanging on to my life preserver, which got displaced and I threw it off. I then left the boat and swam to the captain's boat, which was nearby, and asked Mr. John McDougall, the purser, to help me in. He said it was but little use, but gave me his hand. When I got in, there were eighteen in the captain's boat, and by that time there was a large number in and clinging to the boat that I had left. I know nothing of the third boat. Our boat rolled over, and I remember missing poor John McDougall a few minutes after he helped pull me in. People were hanging onto the spars and other pieces of wreckage."

Dunc Tinkiss never saw his uncle again. Also among the dead were the father of a future premier of Ontario, George Henry, and members of the prominent Sparks family of Ottawa.

Christie Morrison was already in the captain's lifeboat. Her account of the *Asia* sinking is less dramatic than Tinkiss's, probably because she was in shock, but the horror of the disaster would hit her the next day:

"I saw people putting on life jackets," Morrison said. "I lay down, and I could not move if the boat were sinking. The boat rolled on her side and I thought it was sinking. I jumped up and ran into the adjoining stateroom. I then put on a life jacket and sat by the cabin door.

"Before I went into the stateroom, I asked the mate if there was great danger. He said there was a very heavy sea, but they had already thrown some of the horses overboard, and would throw all the freight they could, and that they were very heavily loaded. I could hear a great noise made by the horses. I had hopes the boat would be saved until I saw water coming into the cabin; I was on the upper side of the boat. She was now on her side, and I took hold of the rail, and slid down into the water and sank, and came up by the side of the captain's boat."

Within a few seconds, the *Asia* slid sideways under the water. Some of the passengers had climbed to the highest point of the ship, the hurricane deck, which detached as the *Asia* went under. For a few moments, the wooden structure kept them afloat, but the waves soon tore it to pieces.

The captain's lifeboat was one of three boats that had been launched from the *Asia*. All were filled with people, and more of the *Asia*'s passengers and crew bobbed in the wreckage. The ship was gone now, and the boats were being tossed in the same waves that had sunk the *Asia*. The people in the water moaned and screamed but there was nothing the people in the overloaded lifeboats could do to help them.

As Morrison settled into the captain's boat, the other two lifeboats capsized. They were righted but fewer people climbed back inside. Again, they were flipped by the waves. Again, fewer people climbed inside. The *Asia*'s lifeboats were death traps, without enough oars. People in the other two lifeboats paddled them with their hands and called to Captain Savage in his boat, demanding to know where the lifeboats' oars were. The boats began drifting apart in the waves, and as the other boats went out of sight, Morrison saw them flip three more times. No one was in them or holding their sides anymore.

Within half an hour, the moaning and screaming of the survivors in the water had stopped and the captain's lifeboat had drifted away from the *Asia*'s wreckage and bodies. Ninety-five people had died at the place where the *Asia* went down.

"As soon as I got in," Tinkiss later said, "I looked towards the wreck, where nothing was to be seen but a struggling mass of humanity, who were clinging to pieces of lumber and other wreckage, to prolong their lives even for a few seconds. I hope I shall never see such a sight again, and as our boat drifted out of sight I felt some relief at having such misery shut from our view. We were now drifting we knew not where, with no appearance of land in view, and our boat was continually turning over with every wave that struck us."

The lifeboat Tinkiss had climbed into was the only one with floatation tanks. The heavy steel boat was dangerous to anyone who was struck by it but each time it flipped, it was able to right itself. When Tinkiss and Morrison were pulled aboard, there were eighteen people. The first time the boat capsized, the two other women aboard were lost. Three more times the lifeboat capsized, spilling the people inside. Each time, fewer people were able to climb back inside. Morrison and Tinkiss escaped being tossed into Georgian Bay by holding ropes tied to the boat's bow and stern. One of the first to die was the cabin boy, who was unconscious and being held by one of the crewmen when he was swept away by a wave. A few minutes later, a deck hand who had inhaled water was coughing over the side of the lifeboat when suddenly he fell into Georgian Bay. He panicked and began swimming away. Tinkiss watched him for about one hundred metres. Then he was gone.

By nightfall, the storm had passed and the lake was becoming calm. Morrison and Tinkiss finally climbed into the lifeboat. With them were five men: the *Asia*'s captain, the ship's mate, two crewmen, and a passenger. The night was cold and the older men were wet and exhausted. Although they had two oars, no one had the strength to row. The wind was blowing from the west, pushing the drifting boat across the widest part of Georgian Bay. They were far from help, and the lifeboat was about to become a scene of horror.

At first, the older men tried to stay awake and cheerful by singing maudlin Victorian hymns and uplifting sailor songs, but within a few hours, exhaustion and exposure sapped their strength.

"None of the five men died until after dark," Morrison later said. "The mate got up on his knees and said he could see land, and this cheered us all. The captain seemed very sad, and seldom spoke. None had hats on and none coats but Tinkiss. I had neither hat nor shawl. We were all in water up to our knees, but the water was not up to the seats. If we had had a baling dish, we could have baled out the boat after the sea went down, but we had nothing to do it with.

"The men all died quietly. They seemed to go to sleep. The mate (her cousin, John MacDonald) put his head up to my face in the dark and asked if it was me. I said yes. My hair was flying around, and he seized it in his death grip and pulled down my head. I asked the captain, who was near, to release my hair. He did so, and the mate soon breathed his last. We saw a light, Byng Inlet, about dark. We could see it all night, but were drifting south. Shortly after the mate died, the captain laid his head down. I tried to rouse him, but he was dead. I think it was about midnight."

The captain died with his head cradled in Tinkiss's lap. For a while, he had been delirious and was giving orders to crewmen who were now dead. Tinkiss had tried to keep him awake and comforted, but when a wave toppled the youth onto the bodies in the bottom of the boat, Captain Savage began slipping away. He had lost hope when the wind had changed to an offshore breeze. Finally, with a sigh, he stopped breathing and was put in the bottom of the row boat with the other men. The two teenagers, each in different ends of the corpse-filled boat, stayed awake most of the night, looking for land.

"Mr. Tinkiss and I kept up a conversation. I was nervous and feared that Mr. Tinkiss would put his head down like the rest. I asked him to come to the bow, but he said we would balance the boat better by remaining where we were, and that he would not go to sleep."

Eventually, they fell asleep. When they woke up, they could see islands in the dawn light. They were in the archipelago of islands off Pointe au Baril, still far from the nearest settlement. Today, those islands are a busy cottage area, but in the fall of 1882, they were wilderness, a confusing maze of trees, small islands, and rocks more than twenty kilometres from anything resembling civilization. By amazing luck, the lifeboat had passed through the hazards along the shore without hitting anything.

The dawn brought clear weather and the two survivors in the boat felt their clothes drying. Tinkiss used the oar as a paddle and eased the heavy boat onto one of the islands. When they landed, Morrison sat on the rocky shore while Tinkiss unloaded the bodies of the five men. They emptied the water from the boat, launched it from shore, and began paddling toward what they thought was a lighthouse. After hours of paddling, they reached it, but the building was an empty derrick.

The trip had taken all day. Tinkiss and Morrison made beds of branches on the shore but neither of them could fall sleep. Through the night, they talked to each other. Both of the teenagers were afraid. Morrison, more than Tinkiss, wavered between believing she would be rescued and expecting to end her life in the wilderness. She fantasized about living life as a castaway or a "babe in the woods," as she later wrote. However, it seemed that Tinkiss was not her idea of a castaway companion.

Before dawn, they decided to try to find help and got back in the boat. As they drifted between the islands in those early-morning hours, they became depressed, believing they would die like the men who lay on the nearby beach. They paddled to another island, got out, and agreed they would lie down together on the shore to die.

As the sun came up, Morrison and Tinkiss slept on the rocks. They weren't really near death, even though they had gone through the melodrama of closing their eyes, never expecting to open them again. They had been sleeping a couple of hours when an Ojibwe couple who were picking blackberries in the area stumbled across them.

Morrison and Tinkiss woke up to the sight of the two native people looking down at them. Tinkiss stumbled to his feet and began pleading with the rescuers to take him to the nearest town. Parry Sound, the closest community of any size, was nearly a full day's sail in the rescuer's boat. They wanted to pick berries for the rest of the day and take the two teens to Parry Sound later, but Tinkiss offered them his gold watch if they would leave right away. They agreed but refused to carry the bodies of the *Asia*'s victims. When they sailed past the island where Captain Savage and the other four men lay, Tinkiss went ashore and jammed an oar between some rocks so searchers would have a chance of finding the island among the confusing rocks of that part of Georgian Bay.

The trip to Parry Sound lasted through Saturday night. Tinkiss slept against the side of the native couple's sailboat while Morrison lay in a bed that had been made on the floor of the boat. The next morning, they reached the Parry Sound dock and told the harbour master about the sinking of the *Asia*. Searchers left immediately but they were far too late to help.

The destruction of the *Asia* caused heartbreak in the towns that were the home to her crew and passengers. Captain Savage had spent most of his life in Goderich, and that town went into mourning when news of his death arrived. In places like Collingwood, where people knew the *Asia* well, shock was mixed with anger. The Northern Navigation Company had been criticized for years for sending overloaded ships out onto the lakes. People in Collingwood told of a Sunday-school outing on the *Northern Belle*, a sister ship of the *Asia*, that was so overbooked that crew members complained to the company's management. The *Northern Belle* was licensed for only sixty-five passengers, but more than three hundred children went aboard for a trip through the dangerous waters of eastern Georgian Bay. When the captain of the *Northern Belle* protested to the company's general manager, he was told to sell tickets to anyone who would pay.

The *Northern Belle*, and possibly the *Asia*, should never have been on Georgian Bay at all. Lloyds rated the *Northern Belle* as a riverboat and it is likely the company wouldn't have paid if she sank on the Great Lakes. In the Great Lakes ports, there was little respect for the people who worked for the Northern Navigation Company, including Captain Savage. They were considered to be washouts from better companies, unable to find work with decent ship owners.

The *Northern Belle* was one of the first ships to travel to northern Georgian Bay to look for bodies of the victims of the *Asia* disaster. Other wreckage was found nearby by the *Northern Belle* and the other ships that searched with her: a few bags of flour, timbers from the lost ship; even her piano turned up. The lake was slow to give up bodies, but a few of the ninety-five people lost on the *Asia* were recovered in those early days of the search.

Some of the searchers belonged to the families of the people who died on the *Asia*. At least ten boats carrying fathers or brothers of victims set out from the ports of Georgian Bay to search among the islands where Dunc Tinkiss and Christie Morrison had been res-cued, hoping that, by similar luck, they would find their family members. After the islands along Georgian Bay were searched, the chartered boats headed to more lonely rocks and islands near the middle of Georgian Bay.

False hope that there were more survivors was raised by a man who turned up on a train near Peterborough, telling people that he and several friends had lived through the *Asia* disaster and had been rescued by smugglers. The man later told his story to police and reporters. The press loved it. It was a far better tale than the mono-syllabic testimony of the two shocked teenagers, so it made the front page of newspapers across the continent. There was only one problem: the nattering man with his dramatic tale of storm-tossed survival and rescue by brigands was a liar. He hadn't been on the *Asia*. He concocted his story from the newspaper accounts of Tinkiss and Morrison, the only real survivors.

As for the two teens, they were becoming a problem in Parry Sound. Far from having a Hollywood ending, their story dragged on for weeks. Morrison gave a brief version of the story of her survival to authorities, then took to bed for a few weeks in the home of a charitable Parry Sound family. Tinkiss, who had arrived on the Parry Sound docks in fairly good physical shape, was expected to be the star witness at the inquest that was called into the *Asia* disaster. As soon as he was served with a subpoena, however, he left Parry Sound on the tug *Doty*. Family members of victims needed to know what had happened on the *Asia*, but the two teens weren't very helpful.

Tinkiss took the searchers aboard the *Doty* to the place where he had left the bodies of Captain Savage and the four other men in the lifeboat. They could see the oar he had used as a marker. The bodies were loaded onto the *Doty* and taken to the *Northern Belle*, which was anchored nearby. There, they were packed in ice-filled coffins.

The *Northern Belle* turned back toward Parry Sound with her grim cargo while Tinkiss and the rest of the men aboard the *Doty* sailed northward to look for wreckage. Along the way, they stopped and searched four fishing boats to see if they had found and kept anything from the *Asia* but the people in the boats were blameless.

Along the shore, some wreckage started turning up that saddened even the hardest men among the searchers. Several pieces of baggage contained pictures, and some of them matched the bodies that had been found. A child's book, given to its owner for being a good student, was pulled from among some rocks in an inhospitable part of the Georgian Bay coast. A Methodist hymnal belonging to an engaged couple was also found, along with some nautical books owned by Captain Savage.

On the third day of the search, the little fishing boat *Dreadnought* was found in the islands near Byng Inlet. After she had been cut loose from the *Asia* on the morning of the disaster, she had survived the gale and was in good shape when she was recovered. There was some water inside the *Dreadnought* but she would have made a much safer lifeboat than the ones aboard the *Asia*.

The inquest into the loss of the *Asia* was supposed to help prevent similar disasters. It opened on Wednesday, September 21, in a Parry Sound hotel. A five-man jury was sworn and taken into the hotel's dining room to see the *Northern Belle*'s grim cargo of ice-packed coffins and the men inside. Some of the bodies were identified by papers found in their wallets. Those who were crew members on the *Asia* were recognized by their colleagues on the *Northern Belle*. Once the bodies were identified, the inquest was adjourned for the day. Since Tinkiss was still on the *Doty* somewhere out on Georgian Bay and Morrison was still in bed, the coroner had no witness who was well enough to describe the *Asia*'s sinking. Forcing the young man to testify was likely to be unpopular in Parry Sound, but there were too many important questions about the *Asia*'s loss to let him leave town without giving evidence. The coroner sent a telegram to the Ontario government in Toronto, asking for instructions.

A few days later, Queen's Park wired the coroner to tell him to take his time. The teens weren't to be rushed.

Christie Morrison kept out of the public eye by simply staying in bed. Reporters had flocked to Parry Sound expecting to be thrilled by the story of the survivors. Unfortunately, they were not thrilling people, just a couple of kids who had ended up in a terrible situation and, by luck and physical strength, had managed to live through it. It was too much to ask them to become celebrities, too, and they rather quickly went back to their old lives. Eventually, the inquest fizzled out. Both teens testified. The blame was placed on the dead captain and crew members, who would never have to account for their actions or be able to pass the blame up the ladder to company management. There were stormy articles and letters in the newspapers about "coffin ships," but overcrowded, unsafe vessels kept going out in stormy weather.

The shared ordeal didn't generate any lasting bonds of affection or even friendship between the two teens. Tinkiss never went to visit Morrison while she lay in bed in Parry Sound and neither of them bothered to write. Tinkiss eventually made it to the little island town of Manitouwaning, where he ran the family hotel and died a bachelor in 1910. Morrison married a middle-class Michigan man and told her grandchildren stories of the terrible trip until she died in 1937, fifty-five years after the worst shipwreck on Georgian Bay.

Chapter Ten

The Wreck of the *Algoma*

Wreckage from the Algoma *was jammed into a cove on Isle Royale.*
(J.W. BALD/NATIONAL ARCHIVES OF CANADA)

In the summer of 1883, people living along Lake Huron and Lake Superior saw a strange glow when a certain new ship passed by. The *Algoma*, built on the Clyde River in Scotland, was illuminating her decks with electric lights, something that had never been seen on the lakes.

While the first Canadian transcontinental railway was being built along Lake Superior in the early 1880s, the Canadian Pacific

Railway Company had bought a fleet of small tugs that were used to haul logs and freight to isolated construction camps. The company soon realized that there was money to be made in Great Lakes shipping. In fact, William Cornelius Van Horne, builder of the CPR, wrote to George Stevens, its president, suggesting the $100,000 profits that the marine business earned in 1883 should be juggled onto the railway's books to make the struggling railway line look more profitable to its doubtful investors and a worried federal government. Even after the Lake Superior railway route was completed in the fall of 1885, the water route was still more efficient because of the high cost of fuel and equipment required to move people and freight over the rugged hills of northern Ontario.

In 1882, the CPR's managers looked for a Georgian Bay terminal to be the southern home of its ships. Collingwood, which was already a busy port and railway town, competed with the smaller community of Owen Sound for the prize. Owen Sound won out and served as the home port of the railway's passenger fleet until 1912, when it moved to Port McNicoll, near Midland.

Originally, there were three CPR vessels. The *Algoma*, *Alberta* and *Athabasca* were built in the Clyde River shipyards of Scotland under the supervision of Henry Beatty, manager of the shipping line. Beatty had got the job after running the company that had owned the *Waubuno*. The new ships were designed for safety. In fact, the *Algoma* had no open flames on board. Cooking was done on electric stoves, and the decks were lit with giant Edison light bulbs that were protected from water by glass domes. When a passenger wanted a match for a cigar or cigarette, a porter came to him with an electric lighter.

The three ships sailed from Scotland to Montreal and were then cut in half at a shipyard. The openings made by the dismantlers were blocked with wooden walls; then tugs pulled the new ships through the canals and small locks on the St. Lawrence River. From Kingston, they were towed across Lake Ontario to the outlet of the Welland Canal. At Buffalo, they were reassembled, and electricians from Hamilton put together the fancy new electrical system.

The *Algoma* arrived in Owen Sound on May 10, 1884, and left on her first trip to the Lakehead the next day. The other two ships that were built with the *Algoma* arrived in Owen Sound within the next four days and quickly began their Great Lakes service. When the *Algoma* arrived at Fort William, about one thousand people crowded the piers to see her. The police in the small town had to be called out to help keep order, and streets near the *Algoma*'s dock were blocked off.

The next year was interesting for Canada. The railway construction in northern Ontario and the West was finished, giving eastern Canada a link with its western provinces, and the Riel Rebellion broke out in what is now Saskatchewan and Alberta. The troops that crushed the Riel uprising travelled west on the partially completed railway, and at the gaps on the north shore of Lake Superior they walked on the ice of the frozen lake. The railway would be finished in the fall of 1885, just as the leaders of the rebellion faced death on the gallows.

The competition, companies operating ships from most of the other ports on the lakes, wasn't thrilled with the new CPR boats. The Canadian Railway's ships were faster, more comfortable, and had those modern conveniences for which passengers were willing to pay a premium. There was space for 200 people in the ship's cabins above deck and another 300 below decks. In the summer, however, when immigrants were desperate for transportation to the West, beds could be made below deck for 1,000 people.

The Toronto *Globe*'s writers were awed by the CPR ships when they arrived on the upper lakes: "No such vessels," one of the paper's reporters wrote, "have ever been seen on the Great Lakes, but their excellence lies not in gorgeousness of their furniture or the gingerbread work of decoration and equipment, but in their superiority over all other lake craft in model, construction and equipment, and in their thorough adaptability for the business in which they will engage."

The *Algoma*'s route took her along the west side of Manitoulin Island until she reached the mouth of the St. Marys River. Then she sailed among the islands below Sault Ste. Marie before passing through the Soo locks into Lake Superior. Usually, when the *Algoma* reached the Soo, the crew and passengers left the ship to stretch their legs and wander around the town.

After leaving the St. Marys River, the *Algoma* made the trip across Lake Superior, with its harsh beauty and vastness. Arriving at the Lakehead, she passed the Sleeping Giant, Pancake Island, and Silver Islet, anchoring in the shadow of Mount McKay at the mouth of the Kamanistikwia River. The dock where she berthed still lies idle near the CP Rail station in downtown Fort William, the southern part of the city of Thunder Bay.

In the staterooms, the ship's staff had hung lush ferns. The dining tables had cut flowers and the public areas were decorated with bouquets.

The cabins always had fresh linen. Each berth had a small railway reading light and the cool lake breezes were guided to passengers by little fans installed near windows.

Fortunately, the *Algoma* made her last trip in the fall when passenger traffic had dropped to a trickle. The *Algoma* left Owen Sound in fine weather and made her way up the coast of Manitoulin Island in the early evening of November 6, 1885, giving her crew and passengers a few hours in Sault Ste. Marie before they turned in for the night.

After locking through at Sault Ste. Marie, the *Algoma* spent the morning cruising through Whitefish Bay with a gentle breeze behind her. Captain Moore ordered her to run under an easy head of steam. During the noon hour, she passed the shelter of Whitefish Point and entered the main body of Lake Superior. The crew hoisted the sails, more to steady the *Algoma* in the building seas than to provide real forward power. The officers on deck failed to make proper calculations for the added velocity, however, and from the time the sails were raised, their estimates of the *Algoma*'s position were wrong. Later, they blamed the fact that a wind blowing from behind a ship is the hardest one to measure accurately and they claimed lake currents for throwing off their calculations. The *Algoma* was moving at sixteen knots, not fourteen. The wind following the *Algoma* was gale strength, not a stiff breeze. These errors would be fatal.

Through the afternoon, the winds grew stronger and snow began to fall. Shortly after 4:00 A.M., the winds shifted to the northeast and the crew of the *Algoma* finally realized they were in a full-scale storm.

"The sea was running mountains high and the boat was tossed around like a cork," Mate John Hastings said after the *Algoma* was lost. "Fifteen minutes past four o'clock [A.M.], the order was given to take in all of the sails and put the wheel hard a starboard to bring the ship about and head out on the lake again, because of the storm and the darkness. While the ship was coming about, we struck Greenstone Point, on Isle Royale, about fifty miles from Port Arthur and one mile from Passage Island Lighthouse, which has been abandoned since the first of the month. After striking the first time, the boat forged ahead, driven by the wind. A second shock occurred shortly after the first. The vessel struck the reef violently, and immediately started to break up."

The disaster happened in the pre-dawn hours of Saturday, November 7. Captain Moore thought he was about twenty-five kilometres from Isle Royale, on the U.S. side of the border line, when he decided to make a wide right turn toward Fort William. In fact, he would have seen Isle Royale if the *Algoma* hadn't been caught in the snowstorm just before the course change. The *Algoma* had almost finished the turn when her stern caught on the granite shoal of Greenstone Point.

The collision smashed the ship's rudder mechanisms, leaving her helpless in the dark. She was not twenty-five kilometres from Isle Royale; she was twenty metres away. On a warm summer day, a child could have waded from the wreck site to the rocky island shore. Certainly, a shipwreck disaster couldn't have happened any closer to land. Had the beach of this part of the island consisted of sand and not rock, the *Algoma* would simply have been grounded. Maybe her captain and bridge crew would have faced a reprimand, but the accident would now be forgotten.

In the weeks after the storm, Beatty, the shipping line's manager, said the *Algoma* could have been saved if she had begun making her turn five seconds earlier. She could have been luckier with the weather, too. The storm had grown through the night into a hurricane blizzard. Fishermen on the island, who played an important part in the rescue of the *Algoma*'s survivors, said the storm was so powerful that it tore up their deep water nets and flung them up on shore—something that had never happened before.

The gale hurled huge, cold waves at the *Algoma* and the captain knew that lifeboats couldn't safely make those few metres between the ship and Isle Royale. Once the rudder was smashed, the *Algoma* slowly pivoted in the surf until the side of her hull faced the oncoming waves. She was a well-built vessel but few ships can survive much of Lake Superior's pounding.

"Most of the passengers and a number of the crew were in bed at the time, but were awakened by the shock," Hastings told a newspaper reporter just after the accident, "and the scene that followed beggars description. Water poured in through the broken vessel and over the bulwarks, putting out the fires in the furnaces and extinguishing the electrical lights."

Realizing the ship was going to be wrecked, Hastings went below deck to wake the crew and the passengers in the steerage section. Steam and smoke poured from the boiler room as he searched in the dark. The mate found the air nearly unbreathable, but he stayed below as long as he could. One of the men he saved was John McLean, a twenty-year-old porter. After a few minutes in the dark hull of the *Algoma*, Hastings joined the crew on deck as they pounded on the doors of the more expensive cabins, trying to rouse the passengers.

In the saloon, a woman passenger was clutching her daughter and crying. They were clothed in thin night dresses which offered no protection from the blizzard outside. Hastings tried to calm them. He held hands with the woman and the child and led them along the *Algoma*'s dark deck toward the stern of the ship. As they felt their way through the gloom, a wave rolled over the *Algoma*'s deck, tearing the mother and the child from Hasting's hands. He grabbed the railing as the two people disappeared into the blackness.

"Screams of women and children were heard above the fury of the storm," Hastings said. "The crew hurried hither and thither, doing what they could in the darkness to render assistance; but their efforts were of little avail, for in less than twenty minutes, the entire forward part of the boat was carried away, together with her cargo and human freight. Several clung to the rigging and lifeline the captain had stretched along the deck, but were soon swept away and swallowed by the angry waves. The stern of the boat was steadily pushed upon the rock, and those who were not too exhausted with the fatigue and benumbed by the cold crept to the after steerage and sought its shelter. Less than an hour after striking, all was over, but fifteen of over sixty (passengers and crew) were saved."

Each time a wave rolled in, the *Algoma* was lifted off the lake bottom, then slammed down onto the rocks with hundreds of tonnes of force. The waves worked on the ship like a wrecking ball and the crew knew that she was unlikely to survive for more than a few hours. Captain Moore ordered the passengers to move to the bow of the ship. When the ship started to fall apart, however, Moore told the passengers to go back to the stern.

"Some of the men lost their reason completely and rushed into the stormy depths. About seventeen men climbed into the rigging. The terrible sea swept the boat and the masts were washed clean under the waves. Every time they came up, there were two or three forms missing. Once the mast made a dip with ten men and when it came upright again, only two persons were seen on it. The next sea swept all of the brave strugglers away.

"One man fought nobly for his life. He was washed off the boat and clung to some ropes. Slowly, inch by inch, he struggled along the ropes, hand over hand, back to the vessel. Every few seconds, a wave would dash him around like a feather, dash him up, then bury him under a mass of ice-cold water, but he struggled on, until, just a few feet from the boat, when his strength gave out and he passed away with a wild, waning appeal for aid. Many of the passengers could be seen on their knees, loudly calling for mercy and succour. The waves spared none. They dashed in and around each shrinking form and bore away as their prey each one."

William McCarter, a former Meaford resident travelling to Alberta to settle, was one of the two passengers who were saved. He described the ordeal to a journalist a few days after he was rescued:

"The *Algoma* struck about twenty minutes to five on Saturday morning. The shock was a severe one and the vessel trembled and shivered. I rushed out on deck and saw three or four deck hands rushing aft and waving like people demented. I followed the men and asked, 'What is wrong?'

"They replied that they did not know, but something terrible had happened. A stranger stopped me and said, 'There is a terrible occurrence. It is sad to think that we must die here. Let us hope that it will turn out all right.' This poor fellow was drowned less than a quarter of an hour after. The men from down below all crawled up on the higher deck and along the port side (the side facing toward the shore).

"The storm was terrible. The waves rushed in great mountains over the decks and every few minutes the despairing shriek of some unfortunate person was heard as he or she was carried out to sea and lost. The vessel lay broadside to the island and there was a dreadful

surf and a full sea pounding and beating against her side. The cabin
soon gave way and the women, children and men were then washed
off the boat, beyond all hopes of safety. A great many persons grew
almost crazy and jumped into the seas in hopes of getting ashore.

"We did not know where we were, at first, as it was quite dark and
there was a terrible storm of sleet and snow blowing in on us. The
electric lights went out a few minutes after the boat struck and the
confusion and excitement was terrible. The Captain alone remained
cool and steady. He showed what a fine man he really was and did
his duty like a man. When it seemed certain death to run a lifeline
along the deck, he seized a rope and strung out the line, telling the
people to hold onto the rope and stay calm.

"High rocks towered up in front of us and the pitiless sea tried to
snatch us in its icy clasp on every side. In this manner, we passed the
night until daylight, the waves dashing over us every few seconds
and bearing someone away from the life rope.

"I was standing between the Captain and another man when
the cabin came crashing down on the Captain and pinned him to
the ground. He cried out, 'Oh, I'm done now, but what will
become of these poor people?' The man on the other side
received a severe blow on his head and cried out, 'I'm crushed,
I'm gone.' The next great wave carried him off and he went to his
death without a groan."

Once daylight came, the survivors on the *Algoma* could see how
close to land they were. It must have been something of a shock. The
land proved to be almost a mirage, however, leading some of the
younger, stronger men to believe they could swim through the surf
to the shore. There was still no letup in the storm and anyone who
tried to leave the *Algoma* was betting long odds. Only three men

who tried their luck actually survived, and one man, who collapsed from exhaustion, nearly froze to death on shore. McCarter was no fool. He had never yet been in so much trouble, but before he went into farming, he had spent time at sea. McCarter, Hastings, and McLean, the porter, were haunted by the sounds of the women, children, and men being pulled into the darkness by the waves. All they had to eat was a small bag of apples. The rest of the food had gone off into Lake Superior with the kitchen.

"The night was terrible," McCarter said. "No one can imagine what the people have endured. Timbers were falling in every direction. The waves seemed to crush the boat like an egg shell and every once in a while a falling stick (piece of lumber from the ship) would be followed by a deep groan and we knew some brave man had given up the battle."

As he talked to a newspaper reporter, McCarter explained how he had survived, what it had taken, physically and mentally. He also credited his survival to luck.

"I was dashed several times against the bulwarks and received this cut on my left eye and on the top of my head, but in all other respects, I had a wonderful escape. Although it was madness to leap through the angry surf to dry land, several determined fellows made the attempt with life preservers. Only three landed. The others were hurled against the rocks with tremendous force and mangled beyond recognition. I had three years' experience as a sailor on the Atlantic and knew the benefit of keeping cool at such a time.

"The stern was gradually pushed up on shore until it rested solid. We huddled close together on the steerage deck with a few blankets and spent the whole day in terrible anxiety. No one felt inclined to talk, but we sat and looked with distress-filled eyes at each other, as we listened to the awful swish-swash of the merciless waves tearing along the decks and breaking the bulwarks to pieces. Before we rolled the Captain up in blankets, he said, 'Men, let us unite in prayer,' and with death staring us in the face, we knelt down, and the Captain prayed for us all."

"When night came, there seemed no hope. The sea kept bursting over the vessel. That long vigil was spent in darkness with nothing to eat or drink. During the night, we could hear the Captain inquiring from the spot where he lay, a prisoner of his injuries, 'How's the wind, mate?' and he seemed glad when he was told that it was veering around to the shore side. Sunday morning the men on the island took a life line from us and brought us ashore on a raft. We sent the Captain first and another man with him to hold him, as he was unable to stand.

"The island proved to be Isle Royale and fishermen saw and invited us to their houses and kept us very comfortable. We spent Sunday night there, and the next morning about five o'clock, the fishermen brought over their fishing tugs and asked the Captain what was best to be done. He told them to intercept the *Athabasca*. They did so, and the officers came over to the island on the tug for us about an hour after daylight."

William Mulligan, who was travelling with McCarter to settle in British Columbia, was one of the passengers who was lost.

Ironically, the day that the *Algoma* was destroyed, the last spike of the Canadian Pacific Railway was driven in at Craigellachie, British Columbia.

It took several days for the news of the loss of the *Algoma* to spread along the Great Lakes. Rumours started nearly as soon as the *Algoma* failed to sail into Fort William on time, but it took the arrival of the *Athabasca* on November 12 to confirm the worst. On board were the two rescued passengers, the bodies of two more, and some of the surviving crew members. The *Algoma*'s captain lay in a cabin, badly crushed. He would survive the ordeal and have to live with the fact that his navigation had been flawed on the night the storm began.

The two bodies were taken to the waiting room of the new CPR station and laid out in full public view. Reporters came to look at them and sent home gruesome accounts of their appearance. A tug arrived in Port Arthur the same day, carrying another two bodies. Meanwhile, on Isle Royale, searchers left behind by the *Athabasca* joined fishermen and tug operators to search through the *Algoma*'s wreckage, which was piled three metres deep in some coves.

Family members were already on their way to the lakehead to claim the bodies. Mr. Dudgeon, whose wife and two daughters had been swept from the deck of the *Algoma*, arrived in Fort William from Winnipeg on the evening of November 12. He left the next morning on the tug *Hattie Vinton* to look for their bodies.

Throughout the rest of the month, a few more bodies were found on the shore of Isle Royale or were caught in the nets of the island's fishermen. At the wreck site, photographers took pictures of the surviving stern, with its mast and shredded rigging, and then went to the coves nearby to take pictures of the heaps of lumber from the shattered cabin. Wreckage was strewn for about three kilometres along the shore: the shattered lifeboats and the life preservers, which hadn't saved anyone, the baggage of the settlers headed west, the toys of the children who had died. The steel plates of the ship's hull lay in the water near the stern of the wreck. The *Algoma* was a total loss, except for those magnificent Clyde-built engines, which were salvaged and put into a new ship, the *Manitoba*. She was built at Owen Sound in 1889, using the design of the *Algoma*.

Just over a week after the *Algoma* was lost, Louis Riel went to the gallows in Regina. The Prairies would no longer be a dangerous place for Canadian settlers. There would be almost none of the violence that was going on below the border. The settlers who had used the *Algoma* during her two seasons on the Great Lakes had helped to crush the rebellion. Within a few years, steerage passengers would no longer ride below decks on the CPR ships. The vessels would be used by travellers who appreciated luxurious, safe travel.

Through the years, some of the people who remembered the *Algoma* disaster looked for someone to blame. Westerners, even before the monopoly railway line was completed, hated the CPR and tended to blame its managers for anything that went wrong. The newspapers in Ontario, as soon as they finished hounding Riel to the gallows, began a campaign to take the blame off the railway officials and the *Algoma*'s crew and assign it to fate. The Toronto *Globe* said a miscalculation of ten miles was normal. It wasn't ten miles and it wasn't normal. If those were normal navigation procedures, precise charts of the Great Lakes would be rather pointless.

In the United States, the criticism of the ship owners was less polite. Blame was placed on Beatty, the line's manager, for relentlessly pushing the crew to follow the schedule in all kinds of weather. The criticism rings similar to the attacks on the White Star Line after the *Titanic* went down in 1912. Beatty blamed the hostile press in the United States on jealous American boat owners who had watched with envy when the three CPR ships had begun sweeping up their customers.

Some of the blame remains on Beatty to this day. The village of

Port McNicoll, on Georgian Bay, became the home of the CPR passenger fleet in 1912, just a couple of weeks after the *Titanic* went down. Many of the retired ship employees and the descendants of the *Algoma*'s crew still live there. Some of them blame Beatty for the disaster. They keep the memory of the *Algoma* tragedy alive, but they leave the blame with the line's management. They proudly point out that, except for a man who committed suicide by stepping off another ship, the CPR fleet never had another fatality in its eighty-four year history. That, say the retired sailors, proves the CPR fleet learned from the *Algoma* disaster.

That was small comfort to the families of sailors who were lost on the *Algoma*. A week after the *Algoma* was wrecked, a Toronto man, writing to the Toronto *Globe*, suggested that a fund be started for all the bereaved families who were left without support because of Great Lakes tragedies. The idea never generated any financial support. A few years after the *Algoma*'s loss, she was all but forgotten, even though her destruction was the worst passenger ship disaster in Lake Superior's history.

Chapter Eleven

Where's the Captain?

The Marquette and Bessemer No. 2 *carried railway cars
across Lake Erie. Her wreck has never been found.*
(CONTEMPORARY POSTCARD)

Lake Erie is the smallest of the Great Lakes, but it is also the most wreck-strewn. More people live on its shores than on any of the other Great Lakes coasts, working in cities where heavy industries like steel mills and car factories require the transport of millions of tonnes of raw materials and finished products. It is this shore of the Great Lakes that is the hub of the ship industry, the destination of most of the big freighters that leave the iron ore harbours of Minnesota. The tranquil Canadian coast is deceiving to people on our side of the lake. Canadians see Lake Erie as home of fishermen in small villages and farmers living along the shore. The people of Ohio think of the harbours of Cleveland and Toledo, crowded with ships that feed the factories in one of the world's greatest industrial regions.

Most of the ships that travel Lake Erie sail along the south side of the lake. There is very little international traffic. Ferry boats bring vacationers to Leamington and Sandusky, but cargo tends to go by truck or train across the bridges or through the tunnels of the Detroit River.

A century ago, however, there was money to be made hauling freight across the lake. Many Canadians depended on Ohio coal for their heat. It was loaded into rail cars in the coal fields, then trains took the coal cars to Conneaut, Ohio, where they were loaded onto ferries that carried the coal cars to Port Stanley. Steam engines waited to haul them to Ontario cities. The closer to winter, the more people were willing to pay for the coal, so the car ferries kept sailing as long as possible, even all year if the winter was mild.

John and Robert McLeod were members of a family of Great Lakes sailors from Kincardine, Ontario. Three of their five brothers were also members of ships' crews. The McLeod brothers had made their homes around the lakes. Both Robert and John were qualified captains, but John, the eldest, decided to work as his brother Robert's first mate on the *Marquette and Bessemer No. 2* car ferry in the winter of 1909. He had just been married and wanted to organize his new home in Cortright, Ontario.

The *Marquette and Bessemer No. 2* ran to Port Stanley, so he was able to get home often. If he had worked on another boat, he might have spent weeks away from his new bride.

Most of the rest of the crew were Americans living in the *Marquette and Bessemer No. 2*'s home port, Conneaut, Ohio. The chief engineer, Eugene Wood, came from a Canadian sailing family that was just recovering from the loss of Eugene's brother, George. He had been captain of the *Bannockburn* when she disappeared on Lake Superior in 1902. That ship's loss is one of the Great Lakes' ghost stories. The *Bannockburn* had been in clear sight of other ships when a snow squall enveloped her for a few minutes. Then she was gone.

Another Canadian, William Wilson, from Lindsay, Ontario, was the wheelsman. Formerly a jeweller, he was considered to be one of the better crewmen in the car ferry service.

Three men worked in the galley. George R. Smith, a tall, tough, middle-aged man from Conneaut, was the steward, head of the kitchen staff. Harry Thomas, a young man from Port Stanley, was second cook. Manuel Souars, only twenty years old, was just beginning to work his way through the ranks. In all, there were thirty-three crew members.

Most of these men had years of service to their credit. McLeod had been able to personally hire the people he wanted for his crew, and there had never been a sign of trouble among them.

The same thing could not be said for the ship. She was only four years old but there were ample signs that she was a death trap. The *Marquette and Bessemer No. 2* couldn't live up to the work demanded of her. Her fatal error was the poor design of her rear door, which allowed water into her hold if the waves came at her from behind. In addition, dynamite had often been used to free the ship from ice jams, weakening the steel in her hull.

Captain McLeod knew of the ship's problems. He had sailed her into the waves in rough weather to try to get water from piling over the stern and filling her hold. The captain had told friends that he wanted off the *Marquette and Bessemer No. 2*. While he hadn't acted on those wise thoughts, some of his crewmen had. By the time the ship made her last trip, it had become difficult for Captain McLeod to find good sailors who were willing to work on her. Captain McLeod had tried to get the ship's owners to spend the money to fix its problems, complaining the ship was dangerous, but they refused. Later, they would show the same stinginess when the families of her dead crew members were given only one month's pay to help them cope with the loss of their breadwinners.

December, 1909, had been a bad month for weather, but the *Marquette and Bessemer No. 2* followed her normal routine. Coal cars were loaded below deck by freight yard engines in Conneaut. They had to be balanced to prevent the ship from listing. Each one was held in place with blocks and chains. On Tuesday, December 7, 1909, she was filled with twenty-six carloads of coal, a carload of iron castings, and three railway flatcars of steel. A passenger, Albert Weiss, also came aboard carrying $50,000 in cash in a briefcase. He planned to use it to buy a Canadian fish company. Officially, the car ferry carried only freight, but an executive cabin was sometimes rented to friends of the *Marquette and Bessemer No. 2*'s owners. This time, the tight-fisted company's executives weren't doing any favours for Weiss.

The ship set out onto Lake Erie at 10:00 A.M., two hours late, with a southwest wind behind her.

What happened from that time on is partly a matter of speculation, but there is enough physical evidence to show that this was not to be an ordinary trip. There was the ubiquitous storm that appears in most Great Lakes shipwreck stories, but there were also other forces at work. By the time the *Marquette and Bessemer No. 2* was scheduled to reach Port Stanley, Lake Erie was being raked with 120-kilometre-an-hour winds from the north. They hammered the ports on the U.S. side of the lake, tearing up houses on the shore and flooding towns. The steamer *Clarion* was grounded and burned at the southwest end of the lake with the loss of eight men. Near Buffalo, five crewmen and a woman cook were swept off the *W.C. Richardson* when she ran aground and was chewed on by the waves.

At noon, four Conneaut fishermen saw the *Marquette and Bessemer No. 2* a few miles from the Ohio shore. Captain McLeod had come on deck wearing a fur coat, hollering through his megaphone. The men in the fishing boat couldn't make out what he was saying through the roar of the wind. After a while, the frustrated captain went back into the wheelhouse and the fishermen headed for home.

Throughout the night, the long-overdue car ferry battled the storm, searching for a safe port. It is quite likely that she crossed Lake Erie at least three times. People in several towns along the Ohio and Ontario shores said they heard the ship's whistle in the night. It called out through the blinding snow, hoping for a return blast from a harbour, as the car ferry tried to find the narrow entrances to ports along both sides of Lake Erie. The captain seemed to be sailing toward any place that offered shelter, trying at the same time to keep the waves from rolling over the *Marquette and Bessemer No. 2*'s poorly designed rear door. Each person who later claimed to have heard the ship said they could make out four wailing blasts of her whistle.

Even worse, something horrible was happening on board the ship. The evidence points toward mutiny and murder. A decent prosecutor would have no trouble piecing together the story of the ship's last hours and selling this version to a jury. The physical evidence found after the *Marquette and Bessemer No. 2*'s sinking, along with what was known of the men involved, gives us these details of the crime:

As the *Marquette and Bessemer No. 2* fought the Lake Erie storm, she began taking water over her stern car entrance. She probably listed to one side, which made it impossible to launch all four of her lifeboats. Ten members of the crew mutinied, led by Smith, the steward. The followers were galley workers Harry Thomas and Manuel Souars, along with six junior members of the crew, mostly men who worked below decks and had seen the water pouring into the back of the ship. The identity of the tenth man is a mystery but there is physical evidence that he existed.

Somewhere out in Lake Erie, after the cautious captain had turned his ship away from at least three ports, Smith had decided he was getting off the ship one way or another. He began working the crew, first among the galley staff, then among those below deck, to get support for a confrontation with the captain. Smith had access to all of the crew because they came into his galley for meals.

Any crew member with experience on the lakes knew that this was no ordinary storm. They wanted to be on land, even if the ship had to be run aground in the blizzard. Smith was able to sit with them while they griped, and then suggest that he could help them escape from the sinking which was so obviously going to happen.

Captain McLeod did not cooperate with the mutineers when they finally went to the bridge or assembled on deck near one of the lifeboats. Confronted by Smith, who wielded a knife and a meat cleaver, the captain refused to take his ship into port without knowing where the harbour entrances were or to run it up on shore. He had given up on the idea of finding some place where a ship would answer the *Marquette and Bessemer No. 2*'s whistle. Now he was making a run for the east end of the lake, where he might find shelter in Buffalo, New York.

His caution and devotion to his ship probably cost him his life. It was impossible to reason with the panic-stricken mutineers. They were making disastrous decisions, the captain argued. There was no easy way of getting the ship to a landfall without risking her being torn apart by the waves. Abandoning her was just as suicidal, since the lifeboats would be pummelled by the storm waves. His logic didn't convince the mutineers. They silenced Robert McLeod by killing him.

The forensic evidence, sparse as it is, points to Smith as the man who stabbed Captain McLeod. He was one of the largest of the mutineers and the most senior in rank. Also, the murder weapons were his. There are no clues as to whether the bridge crew, including the captain's brother, tried to save the captain. The bodies of most of the officers were never found, so we'll never know if there was just one murder victim that night. There is no indication either whether the other twenty-two men on board the *Marquette and Bessemer No. 2* struggled to get into the usable lifeboats and were beaten back by the mutineers.

Soon after the captain's murder, the ten mutineers stopped the engines of the ship and took to one of its green lifeboats in the towering seas. The men who stayed behind watched as the boat was winched toward the whitecaps and disappeared into the blackness of the stormy night. Whether the remaining crew members re-engaged the *Marquette and Bessemer No. 2*'s engines and kept trying for a safe port or just waited on the ship for the end won't be known until the ship is finally found. She probably went down somewhere near Long Point. Divers have searched for her, spurred by the money in the purser's safe, but the only clues to her resting place have been some sonar traces and a couple of collisions between ships, as well as some wreckage lying in Lake Erie's shallow waters.

The morning after the *Marquette and Bessemer No. 2* sank—it was a Wednesday—the sun came up on a green lifeboat with ten freezing, soaked men aboard. Not one of the men had thought to wear warm clothes. Nor had they even gathered up the lifeboat's oars before they launched it. Maybe they were honest or just in too much of a hurry, but no one robbed Weiss of his $50,000, a fortune in those days.

The cold winds piled water over the sides of the lifeboat, caking the little vessel with ice. Splashing water covered the hair of the men and began congealing on their clothes. Smith finally set aside his knife and cleaver, jamming them into the gunwales of the lifeboat. He sat upright, the blood on his apron mixing with the water of Lake Erie. Around him, the other mutineers huddled for warmth, groaning, complaining, crying and, perhaps, praying, as exposure and frostbite drained their life away.

We'll never know who that tenth mutineer was, because he decided that life wasn't worth the horror of that boat ride. He took off his clothes, folded them and carefully laid them over the stern of the lifeboat and jumped into Lake Erie, with no chance of survival.

In the lifeboat, the men began to die. There was no room for the bodies to fall so most of them remained upright as each man slipped away. Only Manuel Souars, the young porter, had found any kind of shelter. He hid under a seat, beneath four bodies. Eventually, despite the fading warmth of his comrades, Sonars closed his eyes and was gone, too. The lifeboat's single oar still dangled uselessly in the water, clasped by the frozen fingers of a dead crewman.

For five days, the little green boat with its cargo of death floated over Lake Erie. Smith, the lead mutineer, sat frozen upright, as if scanning for the land that they had desired so much on the *Marquette and Bessemer No. 2*'s last trip. Finally, they were spotted by a Pennsylvania state fishery inspection boat, the *Commodore Perry*.

The Pennsylvanians were horrified by the sight of the bodies frozen stiff in the *Marquette and Bessemer No. 2*'s lifeboat. Instead of taking the dead men on board their tug, the *Commodore Perry*'s crew tied a line to the boat and towed it to Erie, Pennsylvania. The tug's flag was lowered to half mast.

People already knew the *Marquette and Bessemer No. 2* was lost. A ship had seen one of her lifeboats floating empty near the middle of the lake. Whether it had held other crew members will always be a mystery. Lumber from her pilothouse had been picked up along the U.S. shore and some large pieces of wreckage washed up on the beach near Port Burwell, Ontario. The No. 4 lifeboat with her frozen sailors and kitchen workers was the first proof that the crew was dead. No one, however, suspected what had gone on in the ship's wheelhouse or boat deck on the night of the storm. People just seemed to think that Smith had a strong but not completely unnatural affection for the knife and meat cleaver found in the lifeboat. Good carving knives, after all, are hard to find and not easy to replace.

In Conneaut, the small town where most of the crew lived, people went through the sad formalities of identifying the crew members, contacting families, and holding an inquest. The bodies in the boat were thawed and laid out naked in the town morgue where they were photographed for the record. Flags in the Lake Erie towns were lowered to half mast and the local undertaker made arrangements to send the bodies of Canadians back home, this time by train along the shore of the lake.

For those families of *Marquette and Bessemer No. 2* crew members whose husbands or sons weren't among the bodies, the finding of the lifeboat was proof enough that the ship was gone. Funerals were held for all the men who had left the Ohio shore on the car ferry when she took her last run across Lake Erie. In Conneaut, hundreds of people crowded into the auditorium of a new high school to mourn all the Ohio crew members, while in Port Stanley separate funerals were held in the churches for the crew members from that town. As the weeks went by, people learned to cope with their losses and, gradually, to overcome them.

The last evidence of that terrible night on the lake was to surface nearly a year later. Many people wished it had never been found at all.

During the winter and early spring, the ship's other two lifeboats were found. One was in small fragments, with only its floatation tanks recognizable. The other was in two pieces, crushed on a rock near Buffalo. By the next summer, the bodies of four of the *Marquette and Bessemer No. 2*'s crew members had turned up. One of the dead men was mate John McLeod, whose body was found frozen in an ice flow just above Niagara Falls in April 1910.

The captain waited until the fall to give his silent testimony of the terror of the 1909 storm. On October 6, 1910, the *Marquette and*

Bessemer No. 2's replacement ship, boldly bearing the same name, made her first run across Lake Erie. That same day, Captain McLeod was found on Long Point.

The captain was in terrible shape. Deep slashes cut across his body. Those who found him realized that the meat cleaver and knife embedded in the gunwales of Lifeboat No. 4 were not the innocent tools of a ship's cook. They were murder weapons. Captain McLeod, lying on a Lake Erie beach, gave testimony about the way they had been used on the night the *Marquette and Bessemer No. 2* went down. No one was convicted of the crime, of course. The lake had meted out her own crude justice to Robert McLeod's killer and his accomplices.

Chapter Twelve

The Great Storm

*The Great Storm of 1913 sank the pride of
the Great Lakes fleet.*
(LONDON FREE PRESS)

The weather forecast on the front page of the Toronto *Globe* of Saturday, November 8, 1913, was one word: rain. If the meteorologists who had written that forecast had known of the disaster to come, the description of the weekend's weather would probably have covered the entire front page.

The Great Storm of 1913 had just about every kind of powerful atmospheric element known to the Great Lakes region: blinding

rain, hail, sleet, snow, hurricane winds. Some of the lowest baro-
metric pressures in the history of Canadian meteorology were
recorded in the midst of the storm but most barometers in the worst
of it ended up on the bottom of the Great Lakes. At the time it raged,
nobody had any idea of its severity. Communications between the
cities of the Great Lakes were knocked out on the first day of the
storm. Bits of news made it through by telegraph, when messages
were rerouted on lines away from the main blast of the storm, but
not enough information got through for people to understand the
storm's power. No one, especially along Lake Superior and in southwestern Ontario, needed news reports to realize they were in the
middle of a disaster.

Survivors who saw its fury on the open lakes talked of gigantic
waves, some as high as twenty metres. The stories sound exaggerated, except that their sources are so widespread and numerous that
it is hard to believe so many people might have fabricated their
accounts. No other tragedy on the Great Lakes has taken so many
ships. No other storm is recounted as often by the old sailors of the
lake. Fifty years after the Great Storm, its survivors were considered
to be an honoured group of Great Lakes veterans. In the 1970s, the
stories were still told by sailors who had been through many fall
gales since, but had always measured them against the fury of
November, 1913, and found them wanting.

Many fall storms pack the same powerful winds as did the Great
Storm of 1913, but those speeds are achieved in gusts, not sustained
blasts. No Great Lakes storm winds in recorded history have blown
so hard for so long. The storm lasted for four days, piling water into
gigantic waves that took a great many ships to the bottom of the
lakes. These waves rolled right along lake-freighters' decks, coating

their wheelhouses and railings with tons of ice. The storm was laced with snow that lay two and a half metres deep on the streets of Windsor, Detroit, London, and Cleveland.

In Nipigon, on Superior's north shore, people had to cope with a disastrous fire that began on the first day of the storm and nearly levelled their community. The local firefighters couldn't control the blaze, so equipment and men from Fort William and Port Arthur, one hundred kilometres away, had to come through the blizzard on a special train. The fire started on the village's main street. Backed by eighty-kilometre-an-hour winds, it tore through the business district and was about to sweep into the rest of the town when the wind suddenly changed. The sudden shift of wind in mid-storm was a relief to the firefighters who had spent nine hours fighting the Nipigon fire, but it would doom more than two hundred people on other parts of the Lakes.

The storm had raged for thirty-six hours on Lake Superior before the first word of it hit the streets of Toronto on the morning of Monday, November 10. By then, the best of the Great Lakes fleet was gone.

The *Leafield*, an English-built steamer constructed for the open sea, was the first ship to feel the blast of the hurricane blizzard. She was bound for the Canadian lakehead, loaded with steel rails from the Algoma Steel plant in Sault Ste. Marie which were destined for the Canadian Pacific Railway, when she was struck by a giant wave and a wall of snow and went to the bottom of Lake Superior. First reports of the storm said the *Leafield* was aground on Angus Island, but the hopes of the crews' families were shattered when the wreckage turned out to be pieces of the *Monkshaven*, a ship that was lost years before. Maybe the sailors who thought they had seen the

Leafield ashore had mistaken the old wreck for the missing rail carrier, or maybe they saw the *Leafield* before she slipped into deeper water after being pounded by the waves.

On the U.S. side of Lake Superior, the *Henry B. Smith* was lost with thirty men. The *Lafayette* took her crew of twelve with her. Both ships had tried to find a haven on the south shore of the lake but were wrecked when the winds suddenly changed direction.

Captain William Story of the steamer *Maricopa* barely made it into Sault Ste. Marie from Lake Superior. His crew worked feverishly to clear the ice that built up on the ship's deck and wheelhouse. It threatened to drag the ship so low into the water that the waves would flood her hold. When she did arrive at the St. Marys River, on the second day of the storm, a newspaper reporter clambered onto the icy ship to talk to the captain.

"We never had a letup from the time we left Duluth," Story told the reporter, who sent his article across what was left of the telegraph system. "The gale blew fifty miles an hour all the way down Superior. The ice gathered fast on our boat. It was necessary at times to thaw it away from the front of our wheelhouse in order to see. The furious wind, coupled with the freezing temperature, made it one of the fiercest trips I have ever seen."

Just inside Lake Superior, the ships that had passed through the Soo locks before the storm were battling to stay afloat. The steamer *Farrell* lost both her anchors in Whitefish Bay and limped back into Sault Ste. Marie. The wind was so furious that it caused the water level in the St. Marys River to fall. For lack of water, the Soo locks were barely able to work. Sensible captains found anchorage in deeper sections of the river and waited for the storm to pass.

The Canadian Pacific Railway steamer *Assiniboia*, a new sister ship of the *Algoma*, barely made it into Fort William. She was loaded down with ice as she passed the island where her older sister ship had been smashed apart in November, 1885. When the *Assiniboia*'s crew reached safety, a photographer was hired to take her picture. The wheelhouse and superstructure were caked with ice, making her look like a ghost from the lakes.

Hurricane lamps were hoisted at some ports on the U. S. side. Some sailors, such as Milton Smith, assistant purser on the *Charles S. Price*, decided to sit out the Great Storm. Smith walked off the 524-foot lake freighter at Cleveland the day before the storm lashed the lower Great Lakes. He had seen the storm warnings and heard the reports of fifty-knot winds on Lake Superior and had decided he had had enough of sailing for that year. He tried to talk his buddies into leaving, too, but they stayed with the *Price* because they needed the money.

On Lake Superior, the *Leafield* and the *Henry B. Smith* were the worst losses. Three other men died on the stranded *William Nottingham*, lost on Parisian Island. The largest of the Great Lakes claimed the lives of forty-four men during the Great Storm.

Ten lives were lost in Lake Michigan, most of them on the barge *Plymouth*, which was cut loose in the height of the storm by the boat that was supposed to be towing her. A U.S. marshall aboard the *Plymouth* damned those who had left him to die. The terrified, angry man took out a bill from a laundry and asked a more composed crew member to write a note to his wife on the back of it:

"Dear Wife and Children," the note read, "We were left up here in Lake Michigan by McKinnon, captain [of the] *J. H. Martin*, tug, at anchor. He went away and never said goodbye or anything to us. Lost one man yesterday. We have been in storm forty hours. Goodbye dear ones. I might see you in Heaven. Pray for me. Chris K.

"P.S. I felt so bad I had another man write for me. Goodbye forever."

The note washed ashore in a bottle eleven days after the storm.

On Lake Huron, the winds seemed to have a murderous intelligence to them. After two days of blowing from the northwest, they shifted to the northeast. Ships that had taken refuge near the American shore of the lake suddenly found themselves hammered by hurricane-force gusts that blew them toward shore. Along that stretch of the Lake Huron coast, there are few good ports. A harbour would only have been useful if it could have been seen, but the snow reduced visibility to zero. When the storm died out on Monday, November 10, the few ships that had survived the storm found themselves far from where their captains believed them to be. Some ships used crude soundings to test the depths of the water beneath them, hoping to match their findings with the depths marked on their charts. Others just rode the wind, hoping they wouldn't hit shore.

The last hours of the crewmen who died on Lake Huron during the Great Storm must have been terrifying. Survivors said the waves looked like great black walls that rolled out of the blizzard and washed over their ships. The *Wexford*, a 120-metre package freight carrier built in Sunderland, England, in 1883, carried a crew of eighteen. She sailed from Fort William at noon, November 6, and passed through the Soo Locks just before the storm hit Lake Superior. Aboard the *Wexford* was an English couple. George Willmott and his wife, whose name wasn't recorded by the storm's investigators, ran the *Wexford*'s kitchen. They had planned to make this their last trip and had sent money from the Soo to cover the reservation fee for their ticket back to Bristol. The *Wexford* nearly made her destination of Goderich with 96,000 bushels of wheat. No one saw the ship after she left the Soo. The first clue of her fate came when five *Wexford* crewmen washed ashore near the village of St. Joseph.

Donald Macdonald, a young Goderich man, had always wanted to ride a Great Lakes steamer. He was a brakeman on the Grant Trunk Railway in southwestern Ontario. In the months before the storm, he had completed his training to be an engineer. In early November, he took the train to Fort William and met up with a cousin who was a crewman on the *Wexford*. He got to make his trip. His body came ashore not far from his hometown.

Many of the Great Storm's wrecks still haven't been found, so the belief held at the time that some were lost in collisions has never been proven. Certainly, some of the ships foundered within sight of each other. Most of the bodies from the Lake Huron wrecks were found within a few kilometres of each other, and many of the bodies came ashore at the same time.

"Thirty ships, including the *James Carruthers*, one of the largest freighters on the Great Lakes, which was built in Collingwood for the St. Lawrence and Chicago Steamship Navigation Company, of Toronto, and launched on May 22 of this year, have foundered with their crews or have been dashed to pieces on shoals, islands or the mainland," the *London Free Press* told its readers on Wednesday afternoon.

"The horrible experiences of helpless men aboard the big lake carriers will never be related. The frozen bodies, kept afloat by lifebelts bearing the names of half a dozen well-known steamers, and cast up on the shore from Port Franks to St. Joseph and Goderich, furnish evidence for the most terrifying conjectures.

"Boat owners are hoping against hope that some encouragement may come, but every hour brings further news of death and disaster."

Great Lakes skippers were shocked that the *Carruthers* was lost. Here was the largest freighter on the Great Lakes, just out of the shipyards, lost on her third trip. Her captain, H.H. Wright, was said to be one of the best on the lakes. Later, there was speculation that the grain aboard the *Carruthers* had left her riding too high in the water. She had been built to carry cargos of iron ore, which would have made her more stable.

Here is an example of how powerful the storm was. On November 9, the lake freighter *Matao* left Sarnia, headed for Fort William. Once the ship entered Lake Huron, ten-metre high waves poured over the *Matao*'s deck. The boiler room began to fill with water but the coal shovellers worked fiercely, knowing the ship's survival depended on them. Captain Hugh McLeod managed to turn the ship around without losing her in the troughs of the waves. He raced toward shore, hoping he could ground the ship before her engines failed and she went under. Finally, at Point Aux Barques, Michigan, the crew felt the welcome shudder of the ship ploughing onto the rocky shore. The crew couldn't see land but they knew it was there. They stayed on the *Matao* until the storm was over. When Lake Huron finally calmed, the *Matao* was on land, more than three hundred metres from shore. It took more than a year to get her back to Lake Huron.

The *Argus*, a coal carrier, wasn't as lucky. Waves lifted her bow and stern. The midsection of the ship wasn't strong enough to support her load of coal. Captain Iler of the *Crawford*, sailing near the

Argus just off Kincardine, watched her crumple "like an egg shell."

In the midst of the storm, reports came in from a surviving ship that a lake freighter was floating upside down north of Sarnia. Never, in the history of the Great Lakes, had a full-sized grain or ore carrier been known to have turned turtle. Even more of a mystery was the identity of the ship. In the first couple of days after the storm, as the overturned hulk drifted southward on Lake Huron, most marine experts believed the ship was the 120-metre steamer *Regina*. The last time the *Regina* had been seen, she was heavily loaded with steel gas pipes. On November 11, the day after the storm finally ended, the Lake Carriers' Association chartered the tug *Sarnia City* to go out to the floating wreck to learn its name. The captain of the *Sarnia City* didn't stay at the wreck site long, but he probably never forgot what he saw.

The wreck's bow was thrust ten metres from the water's surface, and her stern lay under the water. The wreck had settled nearly a metre since she was first seen. The waves were still high, and the ship's name couldn't be seen because it was under water. For an hour or so, the men of the *Sarnia City* stood on the bobbing deck of their tug, marvelling at the sight of the great black hull as waves rolled up its sides. The captain of the tug said he thought the hull was too big to be the *Regina*, but land-bound ship owners and coast guard officials didn't believe him. No one thought the lake was capable of flipping a larger, more modern lake boat.

On the Sunday after the storm, a diver crawled down the side of the mystery wreck and identified it as the *Price*.

Then, as word spread of the identity of the mystery ship, an even greater puzzle cropped up at the makeshift morgue in Thedford, Ontario. Members of the *Price*'s crew were washing ashore wearing life jackets from the *Regina*. The first strange corpse was identified as John Groundwater, chief engineer of the *Price*. He was found with *Regina* life jackets strapped all over his body. Three other *Price* crew members were found carrying *Regina* life jackets. Two men, one from each ship, were found on the beach, clasping each other's arms, frozen solid.

How did the *Price*'s crew get the *Regina*'s life preservers? The two ships were last seen fifteen miles from each other, travelling in opposite directions. Some of the freighters that had survived the storm had made course changes to keep their bows into the wind, so it is possible that the *Regina* and *Price* had hit each other. The diver who looked over the mystery hull saw no sign, however, of damaged plates. Perhaps the crew of the *Price* had gone into the water in the wreckage field of the *Regina* and had found some of her life jackets to wear. Or was the storm even more cruel, allowing some of the crew of the *Price* to be rescued by the *Regina*, only to lose their lives when the second ship went under the mountainous black waves?

In July 1986, divers Wayne Brusate, Gary Biniecki and John Severance used sonar to find the *Regina* in the southern part of Lake Huron. Brusate, the first diver on the wreck, identified her by finding the ship's brass bell. The hull was almost totally overturned, and surrounded by wreckage. For six months, the divers surveyed the wreck, finding no sign that she had been in a collision. Her rudder was set hard to starboard and the cladburn in the bridge, the mechanism the captain used to set the engine speed, registered "All stop." Most of the cargo of pipe that had been stacked on her decks was gone, probably jettisoned during the storm. Around the wreck lay cases of canned food, cargo from inside the ship's hold. The divers believe the *Regina* was abandoned. This would explain why the engine was stopped. Only the engine room workers had actually succeeded in launching a lifeboat, since the boat that washed up at Point Franks just held people who worked below deck. The captain had gone down with the ship, and his body washed up at Port Sanilac, Michigan, in 1914.

The divers maintain that the *Price* entered the *Regina*'s wreckage field soon after the *Regina* sank and tried to rescue the men in the lifeboat. When the *Price* turned to pick them up, she was caught in the troughs of the waves and capsized about twenty-five kilometres from the place where the *Regina* went down. According to their theory, the men in the *Regina*'s lifeboat were thrown life preservers by their would-be rescuers on the *Price*. Later, they may have tried to save *Price* crewmen by helping them into their lifeboat and throwing them *Regina* life preservers.

Another theory holds that the life jackets were switched after the bodies came ashore by looters who plundered the bodies. No one would have gained anything by doing so, however, and many of the life jackets were frozen in place.

The first bodies started coming ashore at Grand Bend the day after the mystery ship was found. Searchers found the corpse of a man wearing a life jacket from the freighter *Wexford*. He was frozen in a grotesque position, as though he were pleading for help. Two fellow crewmen were found the same day. The local coroner set up a morgue in the nearby village of Thedford and waited as the lake began to give up its grim fall harvest. The next flurry of wreckage came from the *Carruthers*, the largest and newest ship on the Great Lakes. Thedford's hardware store was soon full of bodies wrapped in newspapers, so two warehouses had to be pressed into service.

Ten frozen bodies washed up on November 11 on the Canadian

shore. Seven bore life jackets stencilled with the name *Charles S. Price*. Three wore life jackets from the *Regina*. The same day, two bodies in a lifeboat were found. Lifeboat and oars were stencilled with the name *Regina*. The *Regina*'s owners visited the scene later that day, however, and said their boat's hull was painted green, not white. On Wednesday, a lifeboat carrying eight frozen corpses rolled ashore at Port Franks. On Thursday, November 14, the entire south-eastern shore of Lake Huron seemed to be a jumble of bodies and wreckage coming from the *Price, Carruthers, Regina, Wexford, Argus,* and *Turret King*.

Ghouls from nearby towns and farms made money by going through the pockets of the dead men, taking their season's earnings. Many of the bodies that were washed ashore on Lake Huron were never identified because their wallets were stolen. Also, looters combed the wreckage, looking for things of value from the ships. Their thefts made it harder for investigators to piece together the story of the catastrophe.

"Terrible as has been the greatest of the Great Lakes tragedies, with the disappearance of scores of vessels and the loss of perhaps 200 men," the Toronto *Globe* reported, "it has been left to man to make the horror more horrible. Tonight, steamboat officials returned from Port Franks with information that will be placed into the hands of the Attorney General's department of a nature that casts a reflection upon this province. Not only have they the names of men they found carting wreckage away from the death-strewn shore, but they also have under surveillance one man who is said to have in his possession $800 taken from a foreigner's belt found on shore, and the names of men who have even gone so far as to rob the dead.

"The ghouls found three victims of the storm in or near a lifeboat of the *Regina*. Two of the men were visible, but one body lay in the bottom of the boat under water, and this fact saved his body from being desecrated… The work of the body looters was limited by a creek, for they could not get across this, and it was on the other side of the creek that the other eight bodies [of *Regina* crewmen] were found. On one of the other bodies was found $113, while all the others had money on them. The victims who were washed up west of the creek had their pockets rifled, the perpetrators of this vile crime not even leaving anything by which the men might be identified. Those who are stealing wreckage are making it more difficult for the steamship men and the county officers to identify the dead, as lifebuoys have been taken off victims and mixed up, and the names on boats taken away. It is therefore hard to locate the boats from which the wreckage comes."

On November 13, four patrols of armed men were dispatched to stop the looting and to search the countryside near the Lake Huron shore for stashes of wreckage.

The shoreline search lasted for weeks. Hundreds of people, spurred by an offer of a twenty-five-dollar reward for each body that was found, walked the beaches of Lake Huron every day until winter set in, then resumed the search the following spring. They were so thorough that they found a body from the tug *Searchlight*, which had sunk five years earlier.

Ten days after the mysterious overturned hull was first spotted, it was finally laid to rest. The *Price* lost enough air to allow it to settle to the bottom of Lake Huron, taking her secrets with her. By then, the grieving people on shore had realized that not one person survived from the eight lake freighters that had gone down on Lake

Huron. More than forty ships had been wrecked, stranded, or sunk. Among the mourners were the wife and family of Howard Mackley, the *Price*'s second mate. As his ship had passed by the Mackley home on Lake St. Clair, his wife had stood on their dock and waved good-bye. He signalled to her with two blasts of the ship's horn. When the roads were finally opened in the week after the storm died out, a mailman came to the Mackley's home, delivering a love letter that Howard Mackley had mailed to his wife from Detroit.

At least one Lake Huron search party found a clump of sailors frozen together, encased in chunks of ice. The cook on the *Argus* came ashore wrapped in the heavy coat of the ship's engineer and she was wearing the captain's life jacket. The steward of the *Charles S. Price*, Herbert Jones, was still wearing his apron when his body was found on a sandy Lake Huron beach. Eight lake freighters had gone to the bottom of Lake Huron: The *Carruthers*, *Price*, *Hydrus*, *Argus*, *Regina*, *Isaac M. Scott*, *John A. McGean*, and the *Wexford*. The best estimates place the loss of life on Lake Huron at 178 sailors. Overall, the death toll on the Great Lakes reached 248.

The little towns along the lakes that supplied the crews for the Lake Huron steamships were places of horror and mourning. Officials hiring new crew members often selected people the sailors already knew. Brothers and cousins worked together on the ships, so that, when a ship went down, extended families lost their wage earners. Eighteen sailors on the *Price* were from Collingwood. Seven crew members of the *Wexford*, including its captain and most of its officers, were also from Collingwood, where many of the big ships had been built. Captain Bruce Cameron had been only twenty-six years old when he was lost with the *Wexford*. His father, Alex, had been a lakes captain, and Bruce had gone out on the boats when he was sixteen. He had been a good enough hockey player to make it to one of the fledgling professional teams but had stayed on the ships because they paid more. Cameron was one of the five crewmen whose bodies were washed ashore at St. Joseph. In his pocket was the bill of lading for the grain he was supposed to have brought into Goderich. Nine crew members of the *Leafield* were also from Collingwood, as was a sailor on the *Carruthers*.

Sailors on the lower lakes suffered less than their friends farther north. Lake Erie took the lives of six men who were aboard the U.S. light ship *No. 12*, which was torn from her anchorage twenty-five kilometres west of Buffalo. Early Monday morning, the storm hurled the *No. 12* against the Buffalo harbour breakwall, tearing her to pieces. Its flotsam was tossed into Buffalo harbour as a sort of insult to the U.S. Coast Guard.

Along the shores of the lakes, cities were paralysed by one-metre snowfalls. Huge waves washed away a long stretch of Chicago's beautiful waterfront parks. When telegraph and telephone lines were restored after four days of pummelling, stories drifted into the cities along the lakes of people freezing to death on farms, being stranded on lonely roads for days, or trapped in wilderness areas by the thick blanket of snow and house-high drifts left by the storm. It took nearly a week just to clear the snow off the railway lines which were the main land link in southern Ontario. Just outside London, blinding snow caused a rear-end collision between two freight trains, killing five railway workers. The rail lines were re-opened and the trains started running just in time to carry the corpses of dead sailors from the makeshift morgues in the small towns along

Lake Huron to their families in the ports along both sides of the Great Lakes.

In all, the estimated value of the lost ships and cargo was $3,500,000 in the money of the time—probably fifty times that in today's currency. Many of the lost vessels weren't insured or carried policies for far less than their real value. The men on board weren't covered at all, unless they paid high premiums for private insurance. Their families were left to fend for themselves.

For many years, sailors visiting the ports around the lakes could earn themselves a drink by telling a story of terror in the Great Storm of 1913. Hundreds of men could, without exaggeration, tell of being stranded for days on some god-forsaken shoal or island while ten-metre waves, driven by 120-kilometre-an-hour winds, clawed at their ships. More than sixty ships were destroyed on shoals or run aground without loss of life to their crews, but the survivors often earned their lives by spending days huddled in the high end of a wreck or by praying that their ship would outlast the boiling, grinding seas spawned by the storm.

For example, the crew of the U.S. ore carrier *L. C. Waldo* were trapped without food or dry clothes in the battered wreck of their ship on Manitou Island in Lake Superior. The wind and waves swept away the ship's cabin, its masts and smokestack. Only an auxiliary steering system was left. Captain J. W. Duddleson used it to steer the hulk toward shore, navigating with a pocket compass illuminated by a lantern. Duddleson tried to steer between Gull Rock and Manitou Island by listening to the sound of the waves crashing on the rocks, but after eighteen hours his luck ran out. The twenty-six men and two women aboard the *Waldo* huddled on the deck of the fore section for ninety hours, waiting for help. At night, they had no lights.

There was no radio on board and the ship's flares were lost. As the waves washed over their ship's decks, the crew tied themselves to the *Waldo*'s railings and hatch covers.

Finally, the steamer *Stephenson* tried to come to the aid of the *Waldo* but couldn't get close enough to take the crew off. For seven hours, the *Stephenson* approached the wreck and tried to manoeuvre so that her boats could be lowered to rescue the *Waldo*'s crew. The rocks nearly got the *Stephenson* several times, so, finally, her captain gave up. She backed away and called for help from the Portage lifesaving crew, which worked out of the upper peninsula of Michigan with small boats. With the help of the tug *Hubbard*, the volunteer Portage lifesavers rescued all of the *Waldo*'s crew.

Could anything have saved the sailors who died in the Great Storm? At the time, mariners said wireless radios, which were just coming into use, would have been of little help since most of the sinkings occurred in hurricane conditions far out on the lakes. The weather forecasts issued to the major ports were fairly accurate but they didn't predict the great shift in wind direction that happened midway through the storm. That freak wind shift was probably responsible for more death and destruction than the two days of steady gales. Today's technology could have tracked the storm more accurately. Ships on the Great Lakes are usually better built than most of the ships that went down in the Great Storm. A hurricane blizzard with the power of the 1913 storm, however, would still take many lives along the Great Lakes. Today's covered life rafts and thermal suits might help crews survive the loss of their ships, but a storm that powerful could still take vessels to the bottom of the lakes to join the *Carruthers*, *Regina*, *Leafield* and *Wexford*.

In Goderich, which felt the full force of the storm and mourned

the loss of several local people who worked on the boats, the parish-
ioners of Knox Presbyterian Church have held a service every year
for the mariners of the Great Lakes. A plaque in a small park at the
west end of Cobourg Street commemorates the storm and the people who lost their lives. A monument in the United Church cemetery,
not far away, receives fewer visitors. A grave holds the bodies of
several men who washed ashore nearby. No relatives were able to
claim them, and they weren't identified. A fine granite tombstone
marks their grave, inscribed with just one word: "Sailors."

Chapter Thirteen

The *Inkerman* and
the *Cerisoles*

The Inkerman *and the* Cerisoles *are probably the
two most mysterious shipwrecks on the Great Lakes.*
(Thunder Bay Historical Society)

In the summer of 1918, the dark night of World War I was finally
starting to show the glimmers of dawn. After four years of trench
warfare, which turned northern France and Belgium into one
large killing field, the Allied armies were finally starting to move
forward. Year after year, the newspapers had claimed that the stale-

mate on the western front was about to break. The French, British, Canadians and, after 1917, Americans, were supposed to be leaving the trenches and were fighting their way toward Germany. Headlines, most of them premature, blared that the kaiser was soon to be brought to justice and the world would be made safe from "the Hun."

For much of that time, on the Western Front, there was only the meat grinder of attrition in which attacking soldiers, usually the Allies, suffered more than defenders. Modern technology had created weapons that favoured well-entrenched defenders: the machine gun, long-range artillery, poison gas, barbed wire. Canadian soldiers were among the attackers. Casualty lists grew until the very last days of the war, in the cold fall of 1918. Only the development of tanks and airplanes could shift the advantage to the attacker. While these machines had been invented, soldiers would have to wait until the next war to realize their possibilities.

After all the years of propaganda and wartime censorship, the news stories of breakthroughs began to be true as the summer days of 1918 shortened. The kaiser's army started to collapse after years of useless fighting. One after another of the smaller countries that supported Germany began asking for truces, beginning with the Bulgarians, in the summer, and continuing on until German generals began secretly negotiating with their Allied counterparts in October. By the first week of November, the kaiser was a fugitive in Holland, the ancient Hapsburg monarchy was finished in Austria, and flag makers in the Allied countries were gearing up for the street celebrations that everyone knew would take place within the next few weeks.

On the Great Lakes, the war had been considered won and peacetime attitudes were already settling in by the summer of 1918.

Workers who had lived with wartime austerity were demanding more money. In Britain, during the last months of the war, a railway strike had shut down the transportation system, paving the way for a wave of strikes in all the victorious countries. At the Canadian lakehead cities of Port Arthur and Fort William, workers at the city's grain elevators had gone on strike, causing a slowdown in food exports to Canada's allies. Both strikes would not have been tolerated two years before, when the Allies were losing the war. The walkouts were just a taste of the labour troubles that were to come in the next three years, as Canada entered a period of union radicalism and post-war industrial decline.

Hard times were still in the future. The grim recession wasn't to begin until 1919. Some workers still put in long days at weapons factories, even after the Armistice. Contracts for munitions, guns, and ships had been awarded to factories along the Great Lakes when the Allies were still struggling to break out of Flanders, and they had work to finish, even if the weapons were headed straight for the scrap heap. It takes months to gear a country up for war, and almost as long to wind down the war effort. Entire economies in North America and Europe had to be reinvented before things returned to normal and the factories would be converted to more peaceful work.

All these munitions plants operated as though the streets of Canada were filled with lurking saboteurs. The secrecy that cloaked Canada's war effort, backed by the draconian rules of the Official Secrets Act, was supported by the wartime fears of the nation. People still believed the 1916 fire that destroyed the Parliament building in Ottawa was the work of foreign agents. Armed guards patrolled bridges and railway trestles, looking for enemy spies. Citizens with German names were hounded, no matter where they were born or how many generations of their families had lived in Canada before them. Canadians had memories of street fights in Berlin, Ontario. These had broken out just after the beginning of the war, in response to the idea of civic leaders to rename the city Kitchener after the field marshal who had been chief of the British general staff. He had died in the early months of the war when the ship on which he was travelling hit a mine in the North Sea.

Kitchener's death had been far from an isolated incident. The war at sea was vicious. During the war, 3,622 British ships had been sunk. Among the Allies, shipping losses were 15,000,000 tons, while shipyards on the Allied side had only been able to build 10,000,000 tons. Between 1915 and 1917, German submarines and mines had come close to starving Britain and France into asking for peace terms, so the construction of defensive naval vessels was given the highest strategic priority.

The official secrecy shrouded the construction of a small fleet of French minesweepers in Fort William, Ontario, built to help clear the coast of northwestern Europe of the thousands of mines that were laid by both sides in order to blockade each other's ports. The mines were still taking their toll on shipping, even after the Armistice. Actually, some of these powerful explosives would still be a menace nearly a decade after the end of the war; so, despite the dawn of peace, the three minesweepers built in 1918 in Fort William had a useful, if probably short, career ahead of them.

In hindsight, however, the efforts to keep the Lake Superior minesweeper construction project secret seem rather bizarre. Secrets are only valuable if someone wants to know them. The enemy countries had enough troubles without worrying about little warships taking shape in the middle of Canada. Perhaps the secrecy was simply a diplomatic courtesy to France, which had suffered so horribly in the war and was paying for the new minesweepers.

The ships were built at the Canada Car and Foundry Company's Fort William shipyard near the mouth of the Kamanistikwia River. They were Navarin-type minesweepers, forty-seven metres long, seven metres wide, and divided into four watertight compartments. Each was armed with ten-centimetre guns in the bow and stern. The artillery had a range of about twenty kilometres. The ships looked like a cross between a navy patrol boat and a fishing trawler, with a single funnel and masts fore and aft. In all, the Fort William shipyard was contracted to build twelve of the ships. The minesweepers were built to be manned by a crew of thirty-six.

Even shipyard executives were later to admit the minesweepers were built in a hurry, without frills, but they denied the ships were so badly constructed that they couldn't handle the Great Lakes. Four French officers supervised their construction. Employees of the Canada Car and Foundry Company worked in secrecy, with orders not to tell anyone about the three ships. Wartime paranoia was high, whipped up by the news media, which was under direct government control. In the local papers, advertisements asked if there were "traitors in our midst?" Reading the smaller print, worried citizens found that the ads were asking about joyriders, who were accused of wasting gasoline needed for the war effort.

The minesweepers' crews, members of the French navy, arrived in the Canadian lakehead in the fall, coming by steamship from the Georgian Bay village of Port McNicoll. They had travelled from Montreal to the Great Lakes by train. The vastness of Canada's forests must have amazed the French sailors, who had spent the last four years combing their country's coastline for German mines and submarines. The Great Lakes journey should have given the crews some idea of the vastness of Lake Superior, which, to them, had probably been just a blue spot on a globe until they made this trip.

Three of the new minesweepers were named the *Inkerman*, *Cerisoles* and *Sebastopol*, after battles in the Crimean War in which the French and British had fought together as allies. Conditions aboard the ships were cramped and spartan. In their haste to finish the ships, the Canadian workers had built only the minimum comforts into them. There was no fanfare at their christening. After the launch, the ships were given short trial runs on Lake Superior, on the far side of the lakehead harbour's protective peninsula and islands. The minesweepers seemed to perform up to the standards set in their construction contracts, developing speeds of about twelve knots, and were said to handle well in rough water.

When the ships left Fort William on Saturday, November 23, 1918, they had Canadian lake pilots helping them to navigate Lake Superior. Each of the pilots was a seasoned Great Lakes skipper. The minesweepers steamed out of the harbour together, the *Inkerman* under the command of Captain Mezou, the *Sebastopol* skippered by Captain Leclerc and the *Cerisoles* with Captain Deude at the helm. Captain Leclerc was the overall commander of the small fleet. Before the ships left port, a member of the four-man commission who had supervised the construction handed each of the captains an envelope containing sealed orders, which were to be read once the ships were out of the harbour.

The small French fleet sailed out into Lake Superior at the worst possible time of the year. The fall gales were especially fierce in 1918. Making matters worse, the wind was blowing hard from the southwest, across the long bay of Lake Superior that ends at Duluth,

Minnesota. That meant the ships were buffeted along their sides as they sailed toward Sault Ste. Marie. If there was trouble, there would be little hope of rescue for the crew. Most Great Lakes ships had finished their sailing season and were tied up for the winter; their crews had headed home, where they would stay until Easter. The inshore areas of the lake were about to be locked in by winter's ice, making a search difficult in those days before long-range aircraft. Even potentially more dangerous was the fact that the wireless operators on the three ships spoke only French and used a code that was unfamiliar to Canadian seamen. Henri Jacobs, the wireless operator on the *Inkerman*, had installed a wireless system that conformed to the standards of the French navy. The three ships could communicate with each other but with no one else on the Great Lakes.

Within a few hours of clearing the Sleeping Giant, the long peninsula that shelters Thunder Bay behind the image of the Ojibwe hero Nanibojo, the fleet of minesweepers began to be lashed by Superior's gales. Midway across the lake, a day's sailing from Fort William, the fleet fought its way through a blizzard that blew from the southwest and was fed by the open waters of the lake. The minesweepers, on unfamiliar waters, had no way of getting their bearings in the hurricane blizzard that enveloped them.

The *Sebastopol*, sailing ahead, emerged from the blizzard on the American side of the border line. She barely made it. Marius Mallor, a French sailor on the *Sebastopol*, later wrote from Port Stanley on Lake Huron: "Here I am after leaving Port Arthur, but you can believe me that I would have preferred to have remained there, because on the first night of our voyage, our boat nearly sank, and we had to get out the life boats and put on life belts—but that is all in a sailor's life. Three minutes afterwards the boat almost sank with all on board—and it was nearly 'goodbye' to anyone hearing from us again... You can believe me, I will always remember that day. I can tell you that I had already given myself up to God."

Officially, no one ever saw the *Cerisoles* and the *Inkerman* again. The two ships may have tried to reach shelter on the south side of the lake. Stories circulated in northern Michigan that the ships were spotted just off one of the American islands. Conventional wisdom holds today that they were lost on the Superior shoals, a shallow region near the middle of the lake which wasn't properly charted until after the loss of the two minesweepers. If the two minesweepers hit the shoal, their bottoms could have been torn out and the crew would have quickly succumbed in the lake's frigid water.

The ships, although officially declared seaworthy, could have been swamped by the storm. They may have lost their bearings in the blizzard and collided. All these scenarios call for the lake to have somehow breached the four watertight compartments of each ship. The destruction of the minesweepers happened quickly, since the *Sebastopol*'s wireless never received messages from the stricken ships. Whatever caused the loss of the *Inkerman* and the *Cerisoles* must have been horrifically powerful and terrifying to the men who sailed from Fort William believing they were on their way to France, but who, instead, died together in a blizzard on an inland sea seven thousand kilometres from home.

For two more days, the *Sebastopol* struggled through the gale, finally reaching Sault Ste. Marie. Captain Leclerc later said he took the *Sebastopol* into the Soo locks believing the other two ships would arrive in a few hours and join him in the St. Marys River. On Sunday, December 1, Lieutenant Garreau, the French officer in charge of overseeing the construction of the three ships in Fort

William, received a telegram from Captain Leclerc, saying the *Sebastopol* had arrived in Port Colborne. Mysteriously, there was nothing in the message about the *Inkerman* and the *Cerisoles*.

The first public news of the possible loss of the ships arrived in Fort William on December 3, ten days after the two ships had left the city bound for Sault Ste. Marie. A vessel agent, J.W. Wolwin, received a telegram from the U.S. Hydrographic Office in Duluth, Minnesota, asking whether the ships had turned back to Fort William. Within a couple of hours, the probable loss of the two ships was reported to the city's newspapers and a search began on Lake Superior. Still, city officials, including Fort William mayor Hy Murphy, hinted that the two ships may still have been sailing somewhere on the Great Lakes, under a shroud of censorship and official secrecy. Days before the loss of the ships was reported to the newspapers, he had been told that the *Inkerman* and the *Cerisoles* had not officially arrived at Sault Ste. Marie. Instead of beginning a search, the mayor and other officials in the city sat on the news and waited.

In the next few days, rumours swept Fort William that the ships could have secretly locked through at Sault Ste. Marie without being registered because they were naval vessels. Stories that the two lost ships had been seen together at Whitefish Bay by the crew of the steamer *Osler* also spread along the city's waterfront. Surely, people said, the lack of communication about the two ships was just part of the news blackout that surrounded their construction and marine trials. Maybe they were on Lake Huron or Erie, headed for the Welland Canal. The stories were wishful thinking. The *Inkerman* and *Cerisoles* were probably lost long before the *Sebastopol* made the comparative shelter of Whitefish Bay.

The day after the first alert of the sinking was issued in Fort William, tug boats began searching the shoreline and islands of Lake Superior to see if the two minesweepers had taken shelter to wait out the storm or had run aground. The tugs themselves were taking a risk. The storms hammering the Fort William area in early December were almost as bad as the blizzard that sank the two minesweepers. Temperatures remained below freezing and near-gale winds were blowing from the northeast. From the U.S. side of the lake came reports of wreckage but the flotsam turned out to be pieces of the cabin of another unlucky vessel.

Experienced sailors said the only hope for the ships was that they had been beached on an isolated part of Superior's shore, where no one had been able to find them. In the week after the ships disappeared, such a hope wasn't too far-fetched. The Canadian Pacific Railway line and a few fishing villages were the only break in the forest north of Lake Superior. The coves and natural harbours of thousands of islands along both sides of the coast had been used by ships in trouble for years, but they had also been the scene of some of the lake's worst wrecks. By the middle of December, even the hope that the two ships had been stranded on some distant island had died away and no one doubted they were lost.

An inspector for Lloyds, the company by which the two minesweepers were insured until they were to have reached France, said he had watched as the ships were built and that faulty workmanship was not the cause of their loss.

"The French minesweepers built at the Canadian Car and Foundry Company's shipyards were structurally strong and seaworthy, and as perfect a type of boat that I have ever inspected," Peter Corkindale told a newspaper reporter.

"As well as myself, there were four inspectors from the French commission present while those boats were building. Lt. Garreau was one of them, and he will back up my statement that the minesweepers built at the Car Works were of the most seaworthy type and perfectly strong. Yes, it is true that there have been all kinds of rumours—false and malicious, most of them—about the efficiency of the minesweepers, especially since the *Inkerman* and *Cerisoles* have been feared lost, but there seems to be no one to trace them down to except people who know nothing about boats and their construction.

"These boats, on account of the speed with which they had to be delivered, were completed without much of the extra finish put on boats in peace time, but that had nothing whatever to do with their strength or seaworthiness. Some of the best boats ever built have been sunk in storms, and in this case it would only be fair for people to wait for the facts before rushing out with injurious rumours which are not backed by anybody in a position to know what they are talking about."

The *Inkerman* and the *Cerisoles* are almost forgotten now, but the seventy-eight French sailors and two Canadian skippers who went down with them represent the largest unexplained loss of life on the Great Lakes.

Officially, no bodies ever came ashore and the wrecks have never been found. A year after the ships went down, however, Charles Davieaux, the lighthouse keeper on Michipicoten Island, found a body washed up on the beach. He buried it without the kind of official inquiry and forensic testing we have today, and no one knows whether it came from the two French ships. A skeleton found years later near the little fishing village of Coldwell, on the north shore of

Lake Superior, was buried in an unmarked grave. Some people in Coldwell thought the bones may have belonged to one of the unfortunate French sailors, but Lake Superior takes many lives every year.

In Toronto, the newspapers' fingers of blame were pointed toward port authorities in Fort William, who were accused of allowing the ships to leave their cities without an experienced Great Lakes mariner on board. The *Cerisoles* and the *Inkerman*, however, each had a licensed Great Lakes skipper on their bridge. Eventually, blame conveniently settled on the lake itself, which had taken so many ships and lives in the past century. Within a few weeks, public attention shifted to the arrival in Canada of the Spanish flu virus, which killed, within a few months, more people than all the battles of World War I.

Seven years after the loss of the *Inkerman* and the *Cerisoles*, the Superior Shoal was finally charted near the main steamship course on Lake Superior. It is the peak of an old volcanic hill. Fishermen knew it was there, although the lake trout they brought in from the shoal were strange-looking and had a terrible taste. Speculation has continued since the shoal was found that the two minesweepers were lost on it, although there is no more evidence pointing to Superior Shoal than there is to any other spot on the Great Lakes.

The disappearance of the two minesweepers is still shrouded in mystery. The cause of their loss can only be known if the wrecks are found. Until then, the secrecy of wartime hampers normal speculation. Conspiracy theorists in Thunder Bay have believed for years that the ships steamed straight to the United States as part of some secret wartime deal. That theory borders on paranoia, since the crews were never seen again. Even stranger than the actual sinkings, perhaps, was the behaviour of Leclerc, captain of the *Sebastopol*.

Why hadn't he reported the loss of the *Inkerman* and the *Cerisoles* when he locked through at Sault Ste. Marie? If he believed the two ships were still afloat and thought the fleet had simply been separated, why didn't he wait for the other two minesweepers under his command before heading down Lake Huron? Or, if he suspected the loss of the two ships while he was still on Lake Superior, why didn't he begin a search? And why did his telegram from Port Colborne to Fort William, sent at least a week after the loss of the *Inkerman* and *Cerisoles*, not even mention the two lost ships and the eighty men aboard them? Wartime haste may have been a factor in Leclerc's behaviour. His actions may have been the deeds of a man who had not yet gained respect for the Great Lakes. After all, he may have believed, ocean warships built with watertight compartments could not possibly be threatened by a storm on an inland lake, hundreds of miles from the sea.

Even more strange, perhaps, is the hand-written entry in the old, worn leather-and-corduroy-bound ledger book used in those days by the government of Canada to record the nation's shipwrecks. Each wreck is listed alphabetically, by year, with a few details of the wreck, the name of the investigator who led the inquiry into the sinking, and the crewman, if any, who could be blamed for the loss. There are no details about the sinking of the *Inkerman* and the *Cerisoles*. Their loss is simply recorded. And the grim ledger, now kept in a National Archives of Canada warehouse outside of Ottawa, says they sank on Lake Ontario.

Chapter Fourteen

Alone on the
Bridge

The captain of the Arlington *went down with his ship. Crewmen
later debated whether he really wanted to or not.*
(BOWLING GREEN UNIVERSITY ARCHIVES)

O nly Fred Burke knows why he's on the bottom of Lake
Superior—and he's not talking. His tomb is the *Arlington*,
a 244-foot steel screw steamer weighing 1,870 gross
tonnes. She was about half the size of a typical lake freighter, a boat
that was small enough to fit through the Welland Canal in the days

before the construction of the St. Lawrence Seaway. These canal-sized freighters carried a relatively small load but could transport grain from the head of Lake Superior to the flour mills on the Toronto waterfront. The Burke brothers, three captains from Midland, Ontario, bought the *Arlington* from Canada Steamship Lines in 1939 and put her to work carrying western grain to the ports on Georgian Bay. The Burkes, like their ship, were formerly part of the CSL fleet, but, as the Depression waned, they had organized Burke Salvage and Towing, buying up surplus boats and fitting them into niche opportunities that arose for short-haul and smaller ships. Captain Fred Burke, a large, gruff man who lived in a charming old house just off Midland's main street, was sixty-two and had taken command of the *Arlington* after a full career as a CSL skipper.

While the *Arlington* was almost thirty years old, there was no reason for her owners and crew to suspect the ship was unseaworthy. The hull, boiler, and equipment of the *Arlington* was inspected by Henry Morris, surveyor for the American Bureau of Shipping, who found the vessel in good shape just two weeks before she sank.

The spring of 1940 was a turning point in history. The "Phoney War" that had settled in along the Western front in the previous fall was about to end. As the *Arlington* prepared to sail from the lakehead, Hitler's panzer armies were gassing up for their drive across Holland, Belgium and northern France. Great Lakes sailors were shipping out for the convoys that dodged the German U-boat wolf packs to supply Britain. In early May 1940, the strange loss of one man on the Great Lakes was news. A year later, after the German navy had built submarine pens along the French coast, the deaths of hundreds of sailors became a grim routine.

First mate Junius Macksey supervised the loading of 98,700

bushels of No. 1 northern wheat at Port Arthur the morning of Tuesday, April 30, 1940. The *Arlington* was so heavily loaded that she drew 17'5" and had only three feet of her hull above the water-line. The ship's hold was divided into two large compartments, each with three big hatches covered with timber and protected by canvas tarpaulins tied to the deck. At about noon the *Arlington* left for Owen Sound.

Along with Captain Burke and first mate Macksey, who also had his captain's papers and had worked as a Great Lakes skipper, there were fifteen sailors from Midland and the towns nearby. Most of these men were very young and lacking in experience or were near-ing retirement and considered too old by the bigger, better-paying companies. They worked at the stern of the ship, which housed the engine room, the galley and most of the crew sleeping quarters.

When the *Arlington* left Port Arthur pier, the larger steamer *Collingwood*, also carrying wheat to Georgian Bay, was immedi-ately ahead of her. The two vessels maintained these relative positions for about four hours, until the ships reached Passage Island near the entrance of Thunder Bay. It was still daylight, but snow squalls blew across the lake from the northeast. The captain of the *Collingwood* couldn't see Passage Island or hear its foghorn, so he reduced speed to let the *Arlington* pass. That ship had a wireless direction finder that allowed it to take bearings from the radio beam transmitted from the Passage Island stations.

The captain of the *Collingwood*, Tom Carson, was worried about the weather and later said if he had been travelling alone he would have followed the sheltered route along the North shore, rather than head out across the middle of Lake Superior. He counted on Captain Burke's skill and experience. It was a bad choice. Captain Burke, like many old-time Great Lakes skippers—even survivors of the Great Storm of 1913—had no use for weather reports and, in fact, had forbidden his wireless operator to bring them to the bridge. The weather forecast issued at Port Arthur was not particularly alarming, but a more prudent man would have at least taken a look at it.

Wireless operator William Lee did not report the weather warning to anyone. "The captain never seemed to be interested in weather reports, and I had other duties to attend to," he said.

The ships were far south of the Slate Islands and far out of sight of land, when the weather turned nasty. By midnight, waves were washing over the ship, spraying foam into the windows of the pilot-house at the front of the ship and the engine room and galley at the stern. Macksey suggested to Burke they head toward the shelter of the north shore, but Burke insisted on holding his course.

Between nightfall and dawn, discipline on the *Arlington* broke down, and the chain of events that sent the ship to the bottom of Lake Superior began to take shape. From 11 P.M., three hours after dark, the waves were large enough to roll right over the *Arlington*'s deck. Each wave pried at the ship's hatches and tossed the *Arlington* into a wide roll. A little after midnight, when Macksey went on watch, there were signs that water was somehow seeping into the hold. But since the ship had no lifeline, it was too dangerous to send a sailor onto the decks to check the hatches. Macksey sent a crewman to tell the captain, but Burke came into the wheelhouse from his cabin, looked around, and went back to his bed. As the storm battered and tore at his ship, Burke was called back to the bridge again and again, but each time he disregarded the advice that Macksey offered.

By the early morning, sailors at both ends of the ship could see that some of the tarpaulins covering the hatches had been torn apart, and water was pouring into the hold, soaking the grain. The wheat, immersed in water, began to expand. The *Arlington*'s cargo began swelling, pressing on the steel wall between the grain holds and the engine room.

Just before dawn, the bridge crew noticed the ship was listing slightly. Macksey wanted to turn the ship so her stern took the brunt of the waves. Doing so would point the ship southwards, costing time. But Burke insisted on keeping the ship's bow to the waves. Macksey, the younger captain, traded harsh words with Burke, believing his plan was the only way to ensure that a crewman could examine and fix the damaged hatches.

"You'll never get anywhere like that," Burke replied. Then he ordered the wheelsman to turn the bow into the waves. Macksey blew the ship's whistle four times to summon the *Collingwood* to come closer, then went out to try to supervise the repairs to the hatches. He ordered a crewman to try to jerry-rig a new hatch cover. At the same time, power to the ship's wheel was cut. The *Arlington* was caught in the trough of the waves. Burke could no longer steer his ship.

By then, the dawn was beginning to break and the men on the bridge at the bow of the ship could see that some of the crew at the stern were trying to swing out the starboard lifeboat. Macksey went down to the deck to join them. He worked his way to the lifeboat, climbed into the stern, and took command. Burke was left on the bridge with just his wheelsman, Elmer Callan, but soon he, too, would leave.

"I stayed at the wheel until the steam went off and the wheel was useless," Callan later said in testimony. "I think I'll go too, Cap," he claims to have said. To this, the kindly captain is alleged to have replied, "All right my boy, go ahead. Be careful." Callan asked if the captain would leave too. "Aren't you coming?" Callan asked. The captain didn't answer.

It was now 4:45 A.M. The engine room was rudely disturbed by loud creakings, popping rivets, and a flood of water that rose to the knees of Dan Quesnelle, the man who laboured to keep the coal fires burning. Quesnelle could see water seeping in through plate seams high up in the bulkhead.

As soon as he saw the water coming through the bulkhead, Quesnelle ran into the engine room and told the second engineer that he had better call the chief engineer very quickly. There was no telephone between the bow and stern of the ship, so, other than risk a man's life on the wave-washed deck, there was no way to tell the captain this serious news. The chief engineer was lying, fully-dressed, on his bed, trying to get a bit of sleep, when the second engineer arrived.

By the time the chief engineer arrived in the engine room, Quesnelle realized the water was about to put out the fire. Along with the two engineers, he climbed from the engine room to the deck and ran to the lifeboat. While helping launch the boat, Quesnelle caught his hand in a pulley, losing part of a little finger.

Still, it seems, Captain Burke would not admit his ship was lost. Even as his men left the bridge and worked their way along the now-tilting deck to a lifeboat, he stayed at his post. The ship's wheel would not turn, the stern was settling into the lake, but still Burke would not leave.

Most of the crew climbed into the lifeboat on the starboard side. It was then pulled by ropes to the stern, where the last four or five men got in. Rather than rescue the captain, the men in the lifeboat chose to save the cook. Testimony at the inquiry into the *Arlington*'s loss gently touched on the fact that this lifeboat was the only means of escape left to the crew. All the survivors later agreed that the ship was settling very quickly to port. In fact, some stated that when they pushed away from the stern of the ship the port lifeboat in its chocks was already touching the water. The fact that this lifeboat was taken to the stern of the ship to rescue the cook, rather than to the bow to save the captain, did not help Fred Burke's chances of survival.

Once the cook and the rest of the sailors were aboard the small boat, Macksey took hold of the tiller and told the men to row away from the *Arlington* to prevent the lifeboat from being pulled under when the ship went down. The crew of the *Collingwood*, now drifting close by, watched while the *Arlington*'s men rowed toward them.

Captain Burke stepped out of the bridge, looked at his men rowing away, made a gesture that was later interpreted as a wave, then went back inside and shut the door. A moment later, the *Arlington* rolled over and sank stern-first. She was near the middle of Lake Superior, about ten miles east of Superior Shoal.

Francis "Fat" Swales, 17, a local hockey star who was hired by Captain Burke because the older man was a big fan of the local team, later testified that Captain Burke died a hero. Swales slept through most of the drama and was awakened by a watchman yelling, "Wake up! She's sinking!"

He told reporters that "Captain Burke would have had great trouble getting off the ship, as he stayed in the wheelhouse until the last man jack of us was in the lifeboat. He stuck in the wheelhouse, guiding the ship while the rest of us took to the lifeboats. He couldn't have had much chance to save himself, for the ship went down within 20 minutes of the time I was roused and told to get in the boat."

As the *Arlington* sank, the *Collingwood* came in closer. "First thing I could see was the men trying to launch a boat," Captain Tom Carson said. "I made as close for her as I could without endangering my own ship. I called through my megaphone to ask if everyone had got off, and the reply came that Captain Burke was still aboard the *Arlington*. I thought the first officer was Captain Burke, and I yelled from the pilothouse through the megaphone to ask if every member of the crew was aboard, and I was astonished when the first mate hollered 'I have everybody but Captain Burke.'"

Days later, at the inquiry into the *Arlington*'s sinking, wheelsman Elmer Callan was asked if the captain knew the ship was sinking.

"That is a pretty hard question to answer. Sometimes I do not think that he did. At other times he must have. Everyone else on the ship realized it. I know I did."

William Lee, the young wireless operator who had tossed away the weather report, entered the bridge just as Callan was heading out. "Captain Burke told me to go at once with the other men to the lifeboats astern," he claimed. "There was no time for me to go to the wireless cabin in the forecastle because the ship could not stay afloat more than a few minutes. The captain said, 'Stand by the *Collingwood*.' Those were the last words I heard him say."

Ted Brodeur, 19, making his first trip as a deckhand, believed Burke wanted to go down with the ship: "The captain, it seemed to me, had time to get off, but instead just waved to us with his hat from the wheelhouse and then went down to his cabin and closed the door. A few minutes earlier he had ordered us to the lifeboats while he stood at the wheelhouse door. I had been sleeping soundly when the watchman called out, 'Get up! She's sinking!' When I got to the deck I looked over and saw the *Collingwood* standing by in heavy seas about 250 yards away. I went back, got my wallet and watch and went on deck again. I remember, before getting in the lifeboat, the captain yelled from the wheelhouse: 'Stand by the *Collingwood*!' About seventeen minutes later, the *Arlington* went down. We were about fifteen minutes in open water before reaching the *Collingwood*."

Marine investigator Fred Slocombe, who took the testimony of the *Arlington*'s crew, believed Burke didn't know his ship was sinking.

"Captain Burke had absolutely no knowledge of the fact that the bulkhead had burst and that water was pouring into the stokehold in great volume. He no doubt realized that water must be entering the vessel, but probably thought it was only through the torn tarpaulin of Hatch #5. He had thus no reason to suppose that the vessel would so suddenly increase her list and founder. It seems feasible that the meaning of the wave of the hand was that he would join his men in a moment, and that he entered his room to get the ship's papers or some private possession. Captain Burke was a stout, heavy man, no longer young, and it is quite likely that if the list to port increased suddenly after he had entered his room he would find it impossible to climb up again to the door, which was on the high side."

His death, Slocombe believed, was an accident. Burke had made mistakes all through the night, but Slocombe did not believe he should be censured for the loss of the *Arlington*. "In any case, Captain Burke paid with his life for any error he may have committed, and was the only one of the ship's company to be lost."

After picking up the *Arlington*'s lifeboat, the *Collingwood* then drifted right through the wreckage. "I could see oil spots and wreckage along side—cabin doors and hatch covers were along my port side, and I was looking for Captain Burke," Captain Carson told Slocombe's inquiry, "but no sign of Captain Burke was seen." In about half an hour the *Collingwood* engaged her engines and made for the north shore near Michipicoten Island.

Later, Captain Ed Burke said that the idea that his brother chose to go down with his ship was "nonsense, nothing but poppycock. He did what any other captain would do. He waited until all his men were off the boat. He had no lifebelt and naturally would try to get one before leaving. We have no doubt that he must have been injured in some way to make him unable to leave the boat before it sank.

"He had more courage than most men on the lakes. He wasn't the kind of man who would throw his life away if there was any chance of him getting off the boat. Even if the boat sank with him on it, he would have been able to jump into the water if he was not hurt. We don't know what my brother was doing when he apparently waved his hand. Some people say he was waving goodbye, but that is just silly. He may have put his hand up to hold on to his hat or he may have put his arm up and shouted 'hold on there' or something to that effect. Whatever was the reason for his not leaving the ship, it certainly has nothing to do with tradition or any other such silly tripe."

About 500 people waited at Midland's dock when the *Collingwood* arrived with the survivors. They were waving arms from portholes. Captain Carson stepped off the gangplank, his collar pulled up and his hat over his eyes, and walked to Captain Ed Burke and shook his hand. Ship inspector J.T. Mackenzie went aboard the *Collingwood*, met the *Arlington*'s crew, and told them not to talk to anyone, an order they broke as soon as they met the reporters waiting on the pier. He then escorted them off the ship and took them through the crowd to waiting cars. The little procession

ALONE ON THE BRIDGE   193

went up the main street to the town hall, where they began testifying in a preliminary inquiry. Captain Carson testified, then went back to the *Collingwood*.

On May 26, the *Collingwood* ran aground on a clay bank near Sarnia when Captain Carson had a stroke at the wheel of his ship.

The Burke Company collected insurance on the *Arlington*, but the owners of the wheat received nothing for their uninsured grain. Burke Salvage and Towing could not be successfully sued, since the loss of their ship was chalked up to an act of God.

The inquiry never came up with a convincing reason as to why Captain Burke decided to ride the *Arlington* to the bottom of Lake Superior. All of the witnesses and the officials who took their testimony pussy-footed around the obvious answer. On a cold spring morning, an overweight 62-year-old man had little chance of survival, even for a few minutes, in the icy, grey waves of a Lake Superior storm. Seeing his ship listing and its stern settling under the waves and watching his men row away in the last serviceable lifeboat, it's doubtful that hand gesture was a wave. If Captain Fred Burke, master mariner, said anything to his men as they left him to share the fate of his ship, it probably wasn't goodbye.

Chapter Fifteen

Always Trust Your Accountant

The invitation read:

To all employees,

You are invited to attend a stag party aboard my boat on September 21 at 4 P.M. for a buffet lunch and refreshments.
Come one, come all. Prizes will be awarded to the best fishermen.

Plant superintendent,
B. Corbeau (signed)

John Parker, the accountant at the Midland Foundry and Machine Company, typed up the notice, and, in the second week of September 1942, tacked it up on the company bulletin board. The company had finished a wartime contract, and the workers at the factory were invited to celebrate. Company executives had suggested a party at one of the local hotels or at a cottage, but the workers on that hot, dirty foundry floor had something else in mind: a trip on the yacht owned by plant manager Bert Corbeau.

Corbeau was one of the more interesting men in the southern

Georgian Bay area. Born in Penetanguishene, he had made his name as a player in the NHL for the Montreal Canadiens. In his best year, he scored a respectable eight goals in a twenty-game season. In 1918-19, he came within a game of winning the Stanley Cup. Montreal was tied with Seattle 2-2-1 in the series when it was called off because of a vicious outbreak of Spanish influenza. It was the only year that the cup was not awarded. He played a few years in the minors, then returned to his hometown to work for a living.

Corbeau built a cottage at Honey Harbour and dabbled in boats, eventually buying the 25-metre yacht *Wawinet* from a widow in Collingwood. The *Wawinet* was a pretty motor launch, one of the better boats in the Midland area. Corbeau had trouble paying for the boat. In fact, he'd missed so many instalments that the former owner hired a lawyer to recover the boat or the money. By the spring of 1941, Corbeau had the debt under control and was making payments on the boat's lapsed insurance policy. He came up with the cash by taking fishing charters onto Georgian Bay.

Corbeau took the yacht out of the water in the summer of 1942 to install two eight-cylinder Rolls Royce engines in her hold. Then Corbeau had the boat painted by Stanley Leclair, one of his employees, before it was put back in the water.

Most of the workers of the company accepted the invitation. Of the 45 workers at the plant, 42 men were on the yacht as it sailed from Penetanguishene dock for an afternoon and evening of fishing. Another employee was running down the Penetanguishene main street hill to catch the *Wawinet*, but the boat was already moving up the 10-kilometre bay, headed for the Severn Sound "gap" and Honey Harbour. It was wartime, but beer, cigars and cigarettes, which were rationed, were served to the men. Stanley Leclair had brought his own cigars. He didn't want to share them, so he went into the engine room and stashed them.

The yacht left Penetanguishene at 4 P.M. It anchored off Corbeau's cottage for a few hours while the men fished and went inside to have dinner at a little buffet. After dinner, the *Wawinet* sailed across a small bay to Honey Harbour. A few men got off and walked around the little town. By dark, the *Wawinet* was moving among the southern Thirty Thousand Islands, and by about 9:30 P.M., headed back into the open bay toward Penetanguishene.

Despite the *Wawinet*'s gorgeous turn-of-the-century lines, she was a boat with problems. First, the Polson Iron Works in Toronto had built her with a very rounded bottom. There was no place for ballast. Second, the new engines made the yacht over-powered. Corbeau did not understand that the large engines changed the dynamics of his yacht. Third, the yacht had no life preservers or lifeboats, just two small boats pulled behind, used for fishing in shallow water.

The *Wawinet*'s portholes were about a metre above the waterline, when the yacht wasn't heavily loaded. These windows were rectangular, and, even if closed, were not water-tight. Because most of the men below deck were smoking, these windows were wide open.

Elmer Shaw, president of Midland foundry, hadn't wanted to make the trip. He was one of the people who wanted to have the celebration at a hotel or a cottage, but gave in when the foundry employees insisted on the boat. Shaw paid for all the food. Unlike most of his employees, men who had grown up along Georgian Bay, Shaw couldn't swim.

Even though it was planned as a stag party, the men on the *Wawinet* were fairly sober. Corbeau rationed the company's beer carefully and didn't touch it himself. One man sang Scottish songs, and another was playing a mouth organ, while a third man step danced. Below decks, a few of the men played cards and swapped dirty jokes.

No one knows what happened in the wheelhouse at 9:50 that night. At least three men were there: Corbeau, Rudy Ellery, and Charlie Rankin. Of the three, only Rankin survived, and, though he told me the story of the yacht's sinking, he never explained why, all of a sudden, Corbeau sharply turned the wheel of the boat.

"Suddenly the boat swerved to the left, and water started coming in through the portholes. The boat then righted itself and suddenly sank. I would say within a couple of minutes of the sharp turn that it had made. I was warmly dressed but managed to throw off my leather windbreaker before jumping into the water and starting to swim," Rankin said after the accident. Corbeau said, "Stand where you are, boys, there's not much water here. She will settle." But, within three minutes, the yacht sank in six metres of water.

Tom Davidson was sleeping on deck, under a canvas awning, when "suddenly I rolled onto the floor when the boat listed to one side. Then the boat rolled the other way. I know that the boat did not turn over because I got up on the canopy over the deck and stood there 'til the water came right up."

Machinist Harry Lavinge was toppled over by several men who pushed to the stern of the yacht, hoping to get into one of the launches that was trailing. "We all got pretty excited, I guess. The men were scrambling for the boats. Corbeau said, 'Keep quiet, fellows. The boat is just going to settle.' But the fellows were pretty excited and capsized one of the boats by jumping into it, instead of into the water first and clinging to the side of the boat.

"I had all of my clothes on when I went into the water. I had to swim half a mile and waded for a quarter of a mile as there is quite a shoal there. The boat sank in about twenty-five feet of water. The water was quite calm at the time, but about half an hour after it happened, a wind came up."

Like Lavinge, most of the men set out for land, either toward Beausoliel Island or Present Island. Both were about three kilometres away. Their choice tended to determine who lived and who died. Most of the men knew that part of the bay very well, and people like Parker, the accountant, tried to convince them all to find the sandbar that runs south from the island. For only 20 metres away from the shipwreck, the lake was just one metre deep. Anyone who found that sandbar could walk those three kilometres to Beausoliel Island.

"If you went one way, you lived," Charlie Rankin told me in the early 1980s. "If you went the other way, you died." Corbeau must have gone the wrong way. None of the survivors saw him once he went into the water. Two days after the yacht sank, his body was found near the wreck, and Corbeau's clothes washed up on an island nearby.

With Corbeau gone, Parker tried to lead the men: "After a little while I said, 'Fellows, if we swim this way, we will hit Beausoliel Island.' Well, some of them thought Present Island was closer. So we struck off for Beausoliel Island and I said, 'We will let ourselves go with this wind, it is easier than swimming.' Well, if we had just swum fifty feet that way, we would have hit bottom; if we had just swum off starboard we would have hit the sandbar. But we swam the whole length of one sandbar, about a mile, and I said, 'We want to make sure that we don't drift past the end of this island.' After we got back our senses, and started to go down that way, we kept turning a little bit. One fellow, Stan Leclair, yelled, 'I'm all through, I'm all through!' And he put his foot down and said, 'Bottom! Bottom!' Well, we put our feet down and we were up to our knees. We were only in about two and a half feet of water."

Leclair says, "When I felt the sandbar, I yelled so much my throat got stuck and I could hardly breathe." He had taken his sweater off at the boat, dropped his trousers soon afterwards, and stripped off his socks along the way. By the time Leclair made it to shore, he was wearing just his underwear.

Thomas Garratt, a labourer at the plant, had worked as a guide for eight years along the east shore. He led a smaller group towards the sandbar. "I told them, 'If you fellows will all swim now, I will get you ashore in a very short time.' Well, it was only few minutes after that, perhaps two or three minutes after that, that I hit something. At first I thought it was the other boys' legs and, after I hit upon it a couple of times, I stuck my foot down and was in the water about three inches over my knees, and I had been swimming at least two or three hundred yards when I could have been walking. About 150 feet from where the boat sank, you can stand in the water without being over your head."

Stewart Cheetham was one of the few men who survived without finding the sandbar. Instead, he unknowingly swam parallel to it. "In the moonlight I could see an island ahead of me. The water was much warmer than the air and was calm, so I knew I could make it if I took my time and didn't get excited. I finally reached the shore and made my way to the end of the island where I knew there was a guard's cabin. I found it and woke him up, and later he took me across to Beausoliel Island, where I joined the other sixteen. I did not hear or see any of the others from the time I started swimming."

Charlie Rankin had, in the meantime, tried to prevent panic at dinghies. One was already under the water. It would be recovered by police a few days later. Some men tried to climb into the remaining small boat but it capsized at least twice before Rankin's good sense prevailed. He helped non-swimmers like Shaw, the plant manager, get a hand-hold on the boat. "Finally we all stayed in the water, most of them hanging onto the boat and pushing it toward land. I didn't go near it but swam for Beausoliel Island and reached land at about the same time as three others. It was terrible. I could hear the cries of the men behind me as they gave up the struggle and sank. The four of us made for the YMCA camp, broke in and lit a fire. Later, we were joined by the other twelve."

Albert Perrault, a labourer, was lucky to find space in the little boat. "There were several of us in it: Orvil McClung, Mort Garrett, Joseph Porter, Ken Lowes and myself. We had a long, hard paddle. I myself can't swim a stroke. I guess we must have waded about half a mile because we left the boat as soon as we could touch the bottom with our feet. When we reached shore, we threw ourselves into the bushes and cuddled up to keep warm. Some of the men had shed all their clothing. Then someone yelled, 'There's a cabin,' so we got shelter there. Henry Deschamps got the caretaker on the island, an Ojibway Indian, Peter Tonch, who brought a priest, Father Collins, with him. The priest was wonderful. He brought coffee and cigarettes, and he took off his clothing and wrapped it around the men. He went back into the bush and chopped wood for a fire."

Perrault's father-in-law was lost in the wreck.

Albert Miller, another plant employee, also found his way to the small boat: "I was sitting at the stern of the boat, talking to Laurie Gouette. Suddenly the boat gave a sharp turn and a list. It went over so far that Gouette and I were thrown out of our seats and slid across the deck until the rail stopped us. We hung on, almost like hanging onto the side of a wall until the boat righted herself and threw us back into the middle of the deck again. Then she went down like a stone.

"There was a bright moon, and when I got to the top I looked around. I could see them in the water, all the men who had been on the trip. There was shouting and yelling. Some of them couldn't swim, and were doing their best to hang onto the cushions. I got rid of my pants and shirt but couldn't get rid of my shoes. The water wasn't very cold. Laurie Gouette was away off somewhere. I seemed to be striking off all by myself. They were all shouting for help, but there didn't seem to be much sense to it. I was saving my breath. I wasn't doing any shouting.

"I had never swum more than half a mile in my life but on that night I outdid myself. I wasn't tired. I just kept on swimming. Finally I got into something. It was a dinghy from the yacht, turned upside down with some of the party hanging onto it. One was Elmer Shaw, our president. How he got there, I'll never know. He couldn't swim a stroke. He'd told us this before the boat went down. He'd been laughing about it. Ernie Robinson was holding onto the dinghy with him and there was someone I didn't recognize. We righted the dinghy and bailed it with our hands until it was floating enough to hold us. Mr. Shaw and Robinson got in and hung onto the side. Just then, there was a voice from off to our right. It said, 'I can't hold on any longer.' And this was followed by a yell. It was Stan Leclair. He had come in near us and thought he was a goner. He let down his feet when he couldn't swim anymore and they touched bottom. We were on the shoal that sticks out from Beausoliel Island. Leclair came over to the dinghy and hung on. I walked beside it and pushed it towards shore. We landed and made for the YMCA camp. It's closed for the season but we broke into the main hut, found matches and started a fire. There were five of us at first, but others staggered in, in ones and twos. No one said very much. We were dog tired, damp and cold."

Henry Deschamps gave up his seat in the boat to Albert Perrault. He swam half a kilometre, found the sandbar, and waded in the rest of the way. He helped break into the YMCA camp. "I took Stanley Leclair with me and covered him with one of the mattresses. Then I went back for the other fourteen who had landed. When the boys were settled, I went to the end of the island and got Peter Tonch, the caretaker. He brought clothes with him. Then I walked down the beach and swam about 200 feet in hopes of finding some of the other fellows. The caretaker took us to the mainland at about 3:30 A.M. and I arrived back in Midland at about 8:30 A.M., barefoot, I might add."

By dawn, the seventeen survivors knew they were in the minority. "Twenty-five of my pals are gone and I don't feel too good today. I'm glad to be alive, but it's something I certainly never will forget," Albert Miller told a newspaper reporter the day after the disaster.

The day after the yacht sank, a storm blew through southern Georgian Bay, making recovery of the bodies more difficult. Corbeau's body was found on the first day of the search. An inquest that began as soon as Corbeau's body was brought in determined drowning was the cause of his death. Then the hearing adjourned for a week while police searched the lakeshore for bodies, and divers probed the wreck.

At the end of September, the coroner's jury tried to determine why the yacht sank. Henry Deschamps, one of the survivors and a man who knew boats very well, said the yacht was top heavy. The bottom was almost rounded, drawing four feet of water, while the top of the superstructure was fourteen feet above. There were no life jackets, just flotation cushions and two small yawls with oars that were towed behind the yacht. One of those little boats capsized and sank as soon as some of the men tried to climb in.

William Mackenzie, the government inspector based in Midland, said boats were required to carry a lifebelt for every passenger. But he would not stop a boat from going out "unless I knew he was breaking the law." Two months later, F.A. Willsher, chairman of the board of Steamship Inspection, found that Corbeau used the yacht as a charter boat, and, according to Canadian law, it should have been inspected every year.

"The law provides protection for all persons carried on ships— passengers and crew—but it is the onus of the owner to have a ship comply with the provisions of the Act, and, whether or not this ship was subject to inspection, it would appear that on the voyage in question the equipment required by law was not on board, and to this may be attributed in a great measure the loss of life. It would seem that there is indifference on the part of owners of vessels of this type to comply with the requirements of the law as far as concerns with inspections and the carrying of equipment."

John Lawson, the coroner, said: "It seems like a lack of protection to the public. The system seems to be bad." He found, based on autopsy reports, that Corbeau was not impaired. Since the captain was dead and no witnesses had offered a reasonable explanation for his decision to suddenly turn the wheel, the inquest did not lay blame. The coroner and the jury donated all their inquest fees to the fund set up to help the families of the victims.

Now, as pleasure boaters make holiday runs on the Great Lakes, they're often stopped by police patrols and checked for safety equipment and life jackets. That turned out to be the legacy of the loss of Corbeau's yacht. The Corbeau family decided the *Wawinet*, which could easily have been salvaged, should be left in the Georgian Bay forever. The Corbeau family was too busy with funerals to think of the yacht. Jack Corbeau, Bert's 18-year-old cousin, drowned in Lake Michigan the same night the *Wawinet* was lost. He was swept overboard from the Canada Steamship Lines lake freighter *Collingwood*. Two other sailors drowned with him that night.

Chapter Sixteen

The *Noronic*

As firefighters pumped water into the Noronic, *the ship settled
onto the bottom of Toronto Harbour.*
(NATIONAL ARCHIVES OF CANADA)

These days, only a few afternoon cruise ships and short-distance ferries sail the Great Lakes. They are only faint reminders of a time when the Canadian Lakehead and the cities of southern Ontario were linked by fleets of ships in fierce competition to carry people to the west. Two generations ago, big passenger ships carried thousands of people and their cars to Fort William and Port Arthur, where they caught trains for the Prairies and British Columbia. Canada may have had a national railway system a century ago, but the Trans-Canada Highway system wasn't finished until after World War II.

Other passenger boats took people from Ontario to Buffalo. Detroit, Chicago and Milwaukee, giving Canadians a link with the U.S. cities that have been so important in the development of the lakes. The traffic wasn't one-way, of course. Thousands of U.S. visitors stopped in Canadian ports every year. Perhaps more people travel across Ontario and into the United States by car every year than they did by ship in those days, but car traffic often cuts people off from the world. It is life in a bubble, with a radio soundtrack. You don't hear waves, see stars, or talk to too many strangers. A Canadian transport minister recently said passenger trains didn't make his heart go "pitty pat." If he travelled on them, he must have missed the opportunity to learn about the rest of Canada from his fellow passengers. The same kind of education occurred on Great Lakes ships, and it was good for Canada.

Sadly, the age of the passenger ship didn't end gently or gracefully. While aircraft and cars began draining away business in the 1930s and early 1940s, the end of the ships really can be traced to one terrible night in Toronto harbour.

On a July evening in 1945, the Canada Steamship Lines passenger ship *Hamonic* lay quietly at her anchor on the St. Clair River at Port Edwards, near Sarnia, when a fire began at a freight shed nearby. Within minutes, it spread to the cruise boat. The *Hamonic*, like her sister ship, the *Noronic*, was a steel-hulled vessel. Her cabins were made of wood. The partition walls inside her hull were dry timber; the staircase walls were made of pine; hardwood panelling covered the walls of the ship's lounge. The *Hamonic* had no sprinkler system or fireproof bulkheads. Nearly every year, the *Hamonic*'s interior had been spruced up with a new coat of oil-based paint. The *Hamonic* was allowed to breach the lax fire codes at the time because of a grandfather clause in the laws which protected the owners of older vessels from paying for expensive refits. Quite simply, she was a fire trap.

The *Hamonic* burned quickly, but the wind was on the side of the three hundred people who were on board. All of them escaped. One man, a freight handler, drowned when he dove into the river to escape the flames.

The damage to the ship was $1 million. The *Hamonic*'s wreck was towed to the scrap heap, and the relatively cheap lesson she offered went unheeded. Four years later, in Toronto harbour, no one would be able to ignore the *Hamonic*'s message. The *Noronic* was built and maintained exactly the same way as the *Hamonic*, and nothing had been done to make her any less of a menace since the 1945 fire. To make matters worse, her crew had no training in fire fighting and evacuation.

Late September can be the best time of the year along the Great Lakes. Soft warm days give way to pleasant evenings. If fall is a bit early, the leaves are changing colour. Summer crowds leave the beaches to go back to work or school. Hotels cut their rates to attract business, and people trying to squeeze in a last bit of summer take to the road.

The Canada Steamship Lines steamer *Noronic*, a 6,800-tonne ship built in Port Arthur in 1913, spent September 1949 catering to late-season travellers. The *Noronic* was the largest cruise ship on the lakes, a rather dowdy floating hotel. She had ended her regular passenger runs to Lake Superior and was put to work as a cruise ship, taking people from Cleveland and Detroit to the Thousand Islands, the spectacular Canadian Shield country where Lake Ontario empties into the St. Lawrence River. Almost all of the 171-member crew and about twenty of the 524 passengers were Canadian.

The *Noronic* arrived at Pier 9 at 7:00 P.M. on the night of Friday, September 17, a calm, warm day. A light southerly breeze brought warm Gulf of Mexico air to Toronto, making a stroll in the city tempting to passengers and crew. The staff of the *Noronic* was given shore leave and the captain went into the city to visit friends.

It was a normal cruise-ship evening. Some of the younger passengers spent the time drinking, listening to music, and talking. By midnight, people who had been crawling through the city's bars had started to make their way back. No one knew that a disastrous fire was about to destroy the *Noronic* and take with her the glory days of ship travel on the lakes.

The fire started in a closet next to cabin 462, a small stateroom near the rear of the promenade deck, at about 1:00 A.M. The cause was probably careless smoking by cleaners who dumped their cigarette butts into a garbage can in the closet. Gordon Churche, a Chicago jeweller out for a walk on C deck, one of five decks on the ship, saw a strange glow through the window of the cabin. He called for help. A couple of crew members saw smoke and went into the empty stateroom. Smoke puffed from the closet. The heat was beginning to bake the paint on the outside of the door. When one of the crewmen touched the door handle, he burned his hand.

Instead of leaving the fire alone until they were armed with fire extinguishers, one of the men grabbed a cloth and wrapped it around the doorknob. Then he twisted it open. Given this fresh breath of oxygen, the fire shot out of the closet door and began burning the paint on the cabin wall. The crewmen raced down the hall and grabbed a fire extinguisher. It didn't work. They ran for a fire hose but they didn't know how to turn it on. It was probably too late anyway.

Members of the skeleton crew left on board the *Noronic* started yelling that the ship was on fire. A few tired and drunk passengers opened the doors of their rooms and stared into the corridors. When they saw the smoke, they either joined the small knot of men trying to fight the blaze or gathered up their belongings and headed toward the gangways. Those who fought the fire were in a state of panic. If a piece of equipment was complicated, they insisted it didn't work and threw it away. At this time, most of the people on the *Noronic* were still unaware of the danger. Four men from Cleveland, playing poker in the *Noronic*'s spectacular observation lounge on the top deck, saw the glow of the fire reflected on the freight shed next to Pier 9.

"Cripes, that building's on fire," one of them said.

Within a few minutes, the fire was spreading in sheets along the starboard side, the side of the ship that faced the pier. Luck had conspired against the people on the *Noronic*. The fire started in a place that was perfect for the wind. Then it blew down the only side of the ship that offered an easy escape. As it spread, it blocked most of the stairwells from the decks below and above. Crew members could simply walk out a door from the engine room to the pier, but passengers would have to fight for space on the two gangways or take their chances jumping into Toronto harbour. The only piece of luck they had was that the water was still fairly warm.

Many passengers trapped by the fire stopped resisting quickly. On C deck, searchers later found an elderly woman sitting on a chesterfield, untouched by the fire. She had a look of peace on her face. The fire had robbed her of oxygen and she had suffocated.

In the days following the disaster, the crew members who had been aboard the ship found various reasons why the fire alarm on the pier hadn't been pulled when the blaze was found. The switch wasn't used until twenty minutes after the red-hot closet door had been opened. If the fire department had been given a chance, many more of the *Noronic*'s passengers could have been saved.

After the alarm was finally set off, city firefighters raced to the scene. Eighteen fire trucks and a fire-fighting boat were at Pier 9 within a matter of minutes. Next came fleets of police and ambulances. Then hearses.

Chief engineer Fred Bonnell was sleeping in his cabin when one of the crew called into the room that the ship was on fire. Bonnell pulled on his pants and went to the fire-alarm indicator board to see how far the blaze had spread. By the time he reached the indicator, he couldn't see it for the smoke. The chief engineer went back to his cabin to try to retrieve the ship's log and some other important papers, but his way was blocked by smoke and flames.

There was panic as passengers realized the *Noronic* was doomed. People trampled each other in stairwells, only to make it to the top and find them blocked by fire. Luck, not ship-board disaster preparation or fire-fighting skill, would determine who survived. Able-bodied people had a good chance to get off the *Noronic* if they were prepared to jump about four metres into the lake. Many of the passengers, however, were older people. The tiny crew had no idea what to do. For a moment, Bonnell paced the deck, trying to find ways to help people off. The fire spread toward the bow, where Bonnell was, and people on the dock called to the chief engineer to climb off the ship. After a minute or so, he left the *Noronic*. Most of the rest of the crew didn't even stay on the ship as long as that.

One witness said the *Noronic* "went up like a paint factory." It was a fitting analogy: much of the fire's fuel was the thick paint that covered all of the exposed wood and steel on the *Noronic*. Sometimes, the paint was more than thirty layers thick.

Mildred Biggs, a Detroit woman who had made the trip to the Thousand Islands every fall for the past thirteen years, thought the shouts of fire were a hoax, a prank by some of the young people who had spent the evening drinking.

"I knew there was sometimes a little rowdyism on board, but I couldn't figure out how somebody could be so stupid. The fire just welled up along the corridors and spread faster than I've ever seen," she said. Biggs was one of the first people down the gangway.

Captain William Taylor, who, at the age of sixty-five, was just about to retire, arrived back at the ship at about the same time that Biggs made it to the pier. Like most of the crew, Taylor had spent the evening in the city's bars. Later, he was faulted for being drunk when he got back to the *Noronic*, but by the time he arrived at Pier 9 there was nothing he could have done to change what was to happen. He was no more than a bystander.

He went back to the stern to see if there was a chance that the fire could be put out with the equipment on the ship. Already, though, the flames were far out of control and moving forward, toward the bow of the ship.

"I hollered 'fire' to people on the dock as I proceeded through the ship," he said the night of the disaster, in a somewhat self-serving interview with Canadian Press reporter Forbes Knude. "I cut over to the port side and went down on deck and pulled down a fire hose and opened it.

"I threw water and made as much noise as possible to arouse people, and one of the crew and several other people came and helped me. We broke open windows but there were no passengers in those rooms. We found a woman who had fainted and carried her to the deck below so that she could be carried out through the gangway from the engine room.

"The fire at this time was aft to the midships door and we did our best to put out the fire in that section. But a room could go 'pfft,' like that, and the windows would blow out, and the whole thing would be ablaze. I ran forward to the bow, where Mate Gerry Wood was putting people over the side with a rope. I went back and fought as long as I could on that side and then went down to D deck. The rooms of the crew and passengers were open with no one in them.

"Members of the crew kept hollering for me to get out of there, as the fire was coming down. I visited the crew's quarters aft and went down through the engine room and from there out to the dock. I asked people there, 'Are you sure everyone is out?' and decided that they could not be. I went back to C deck and it was ablaze all the way through. It was hot there. I went a second time to D deck and used the hose again. Water was, by that time, up to the door jamb. A stout kid was with me and we walked in water up to our knees. We had to hold our breaths to keep from getting smothered and we came out on the dock again through the engine room. I went along the dock to the bow to see whether I could see anyone on board, and tried to get back, but people on the dock tried to stop me. I guess I wasn't polite to them."

For most of the rest of the night, the shattered captain was crumpled on the dock, watching the misery on board his ship. Just before dawn, he was taken to the *Kingston*, a passenger ship near the *Noronic*'s dock, and was put to bed in one of its cabins.

Toronto Star reporter James Hunt, who lived on Toronto Island, had been out on the town that Friday night. At about 2:00 A.M., he had driven by the *Noronic*. Everything seemed fine. He parked his car and went into a lakefront restaurant to wait for the water taxi to take him back to the island.

While he ate, he thought of the times when he had seen the *Noronic* in his hometown of Sarnia. As kids, he and his friends had chased pennies that passengers tossed off the ship at her berth on the St. Clair River. When Hunt was six years old, he had taken his first lake cruise on the *Noronic*. In the middle of Lake Huron, the captain had let him take the wheel. As a teenager, he had worked as a bellhop on the *Noronic*, catering to the whims of passengers who appreciated the comfort and style of the old Great Lakes ships.

After a couple of drinks, Hunt left the restaurant to meet the water taxi.

When he came out, the sky was glowing with flames from the *Noronic*.

"I ran to the scene. Neither firemen nor police had yet arrived. The top deck of the ship was enveloped in flames. The scene was one of bedlam. People were running about, shouting. 'Where is my husband?' one woman was shouting hysterically while police tried to restrain her as she fought to get back on board the ship. Literally hundreds seemed to be clambering on ropes from the blazing ship. The flames were spreading more rapidly now, but figures that appeared to be men could still be seen on the decks. Some dived over the side and swam to safety.

"Minutes later, they started to bring out the injured. Some appeared to be very badly burned and were writhing with pain as they were put in ambulances and rushed to hospital. Others huddled in blankets in the Canada Steamship Lines offices. Most of them seemed shocked, as if they didn't realize what had happened. There was an old man with his arm tightly around his wife, who was quietly sobbing. Others, though not burned, were running wildly around, looking for relatives and friends. A good half hour after I arrived, two men could be seen at the bow of the ship. They appeared to be surrounded by flames. Then the firemen put up their ladder and, showing incredible courage, clambered up to reach them. The men were helped to safety, though one of them, Captain William Taylor, fell into the bay when the ladder broke. He was rescued by firemen and taken to the enclosure.

"By this time, the ship was a mass of flames. Certainly no one could remain alive who was still aboard the inferno. You could feel the heat when you got close to the ship and the scores of fire hoses that were pouring on it seemed to have no effect."

The water taxi that Hunt had been waiting for was one of the boats that scoured the bay looking for *Noronic* passengers who had jumped from the ship. Jacqueline Turner, a young woman who had been returning to the city from Toronto Island, saved at least six people who floated, dazed, among the embers and wreckage.

"One woman dropped like a stone into the water near us. I saw many people clambering down the ladders and ropes. We would pick up one victim from the bay at a time and rush them to the dock or the life-saving cruiser and go back for another. Someone warned us to get away from the fire at the stern where we were because it was getting worse."

Ross Leitch, the driver of another water taxi, helped save more than one hundred people. He had seen the fire from Toronto Island, gone to the fire station there, and wakened the men on duty. Then he scooted across the harbour.

When he arrived, he found absolute mayhem. People were pouring over the side of the ship in a mad scramble to survive. The first person he saved was a woman, suspended halfway between the *Noronic*'s deck and the water. Leitch helped her into his boat. Then he turned to the mass of people in the boat channel. As he pulled people from the water and drove them to the dock or the life-saving boat, his boat filled with bloody clothes. Sometimes, people in the water grabbed the side of his small boat, nearly capsizing it. With the help of two other men, he managed to haul people into the water taxi and steer it to shore, even when people were still hanging onto the boat. All the while, he could hear the terrible noise from the *Noronic*, the screams, the shouts, and the steady wail of the ship's siren.

Leo Kari, an eighteen-year-old busboy, was sleeping in his cabin near the stern of the boat when the fire broke out. The mayhem on deck woke him up. Pushing through the passengers, he found a lifeboat. Somehow, he and several other crewmen were able to launch it. None of the *Noronic*'s other boats left the ship that night.

"We couldn't get the lifeboat free because the ropes were stuck. I remember struggling back to my cabin through the smoke. I tried to find a jackknife to cut the rope. I couldn't see a thing."

216 TRUE CANADIAN STORIES OF THE GREAT LAKES

Once he got back to the lifeboat, he saw that none of the passengers seemed to want to go in it. Three women passengers were panicking. Kari helped to grab them and shove them into the lifeboat. By then, most of the other passengers were gone.

"We looked for other passengers but they were at the front. We could hear them shouting. But it was useless to try and go through that fire. We had to shove off with an almost empty boat or we wouldn't have got away at all."

Kari's friend, Jack Brough, an eighteen-year-old bellhop from Sarnia, used a fire axe to smash windows on the promenade deck to get to passengers who were trapped in their cabins. Some of the people in the cabins were unconscious. Brough pulled a man and a woman from one cabin and rescued another woman who lay in a pool of water that had been blasted into her cabin by the firefighters.

Some of the people in the cabins were in shock. They seemed to have no idea what was going on around them. Others were so weak from smoke inhalation that they had to be dragged to the *Noronic*'s deck. André Cinq-Mars and André Charron, teenaged carnival workers from Montreal, were walking near the *Noronic* when the fire broke out. They heard the frantic blast of the ship's whistle and ran toward Pier 9. As they got closer, they could see the flames shooting from the stern of the ship. When they reached the pier, Cinq-Mars helped people to get down the gangway but Charron couldn't stand and watch. He climbed a rope and went onto the burning deck, looking for people to help. Cinq-Mars helped a couple of elderly people to a police car. When he got back to the *Noronic*, police wouldn't let him go to the side of the ship. He stood watching for hours for Charron, but the young man never came back from the fire.

Fire ladders were run up the side of the ship but they were almost useless. So many people tried to get down ladders at the bow that they broke and the passengers tumbled into Lake Ontario. Even so, more than four hundred people were rescued. The people most in danger were on the upper decks, cut off by clogged stairwells and flames from the decks below. A crane took some of these passengers off the ship, but most of the casualties occurred in the higher parts of the *Noronic*. One man looked down at the firefighters ten metres below, raised a glass, and stepped into the flames.

Fire hoses poured water into the ship from the pier. By the time the first water hit the *Noronic*, there was no hope of saving it. Firefighters wanted to protect the pier and prevent the fire from spreading to nearby ships and buildings. The heat was so strong that the *Noronic*'s steel lifeboats melted. Windows exploded from the heat and trapped air in the hull, showering fleeing passengers with glass. Firemen worked in terrible conditions, covered with water and scorched by the flames. At its height, the fire was so hot that an unused hose on one of the fire trucks ignited. For a second, fire hoses were turned toward the truck, then were directed back toward the *Noronic*.

Not all the men on board the *Noronic* were as gallant as Brough. Ten young people were drinking and singing in a galley on C deck, one of the highest parts of the ship. One of them went outside and saw the smoke and fire. He then ran back into the galley. "No kidding, gang, the ship is on fire," he told them. Sylvia Carpenter, one of the women at the party, ran out the door, to the dock-side rail. However, her way was blocked by men trying to escape.

"Someone had thrown a rope ladder over the side," she later said, "but it was all tangled up. I put a hitch knot on it to hold it to the stanchion. As I did so, three men pushed in front of me and shoved some screaming women out of the way. They went down the rope."

Alberta Agla, another woman at the party, went down to A deck. It was a scene of panic.

"There was a mob. People were pushing back and forth. Men were pushing women around and many were knocked to the floor. The screaming filled the air. There was so much panic that I don't know how these people got segregated to find a way to safety. I slid down a rope."

Along the ship's deck and on the gangplank, many of the passengers were carrying trunks and suitcases. Not satisfied with saving themselves, they were trying to save their luggage, too. The suitcases broke open as people pushed against each other, showering clothes into the harbour and onto the pier. People trying to hold onto their luggage clogged the two gangplanks, at a terrible cost to the people who were trying to get off the *Noronic*.

In the water below, a man swam alongside the ship. Joyce Baxter, who had arrived at the scene of the disaster at about the same time as Hunt, saw the swimming man. He moved among several other passengers who needed to be rescued. Baxter helped to pull out a couple of dazed women but the man said he wanted to stay in the lake. Baxter wanted to know why.

"I don't have any pants on," said the man, who was wearing a flannel pyjama top.

"Don't be silly," said Baxter, who was surrounded by firemen, injured people, and shocked survivors. She took his hand and pulled him out, turning her head discreetly until a firefighter wrapped a blanket around the man and took him away.

A priest, Charles Wigglesworth, walked along the dock, giving the last rites to the people who lay on the firefighters' stretchers. By dawn, after five hours of consoling the fire's victims, he had lost count of the number of people who had been anointed.

Some of the uninjured passengers were led down the dock to the steamer *Cayuga* and put into beds in that ship's cabins. No one remembers any of them balking at the idea. Other people with minor burns or who hadn't been hurt wandered through the crowd of firefighters and spectators, looking for lost family. Wives and husbands were often separated and taken to different hospitals and first-aid stations, so many people didn't know if their spouses were alive or dead, injured or safe. The din was frightful: the people aboard the *Noronic* shouted and screamed, as did the horrified people on the dock. Sirens of fire engines and ambulances howled through the night. The noise could easily be heard a kilometre away, and, except for the terrible sounds made by the trapped passengers, it didn't stop until morning.

A steady stream of police cars and ambulances took away the survivors. By the end of the night, the seats of the cruisers were covered with blood from passengers who had smashed windows to escape. On their way to the hospitals and first-aid centres, the stricken passengers and police officers had to endure the stares of the mass of people who watched the ship burn. Most were held back by police at Queen's Quay, the road that runs along Toronto's waterfront. Curious people stood on the street all night, finally dispersing after seeing the ship in the early-morning daylight. As they left, people who had heard about the disaster that morning crowded into their places.

About 190 people who were injured were taken to Toronto hospitals and to first-aid centres in the Royal York and King Edward hotels. Many of them quickly left the first-aid centres, despite terrible burns, to go back to the *Noronic* to look for family and friends. The city morgue had been filled before the fire was out. By early morning, 150 bodies had been taken to the Horticulture Building of the Canadian National Exhibition. A few weeks before, the stately old pavilion had been the site of the country's largest flower-judging competitions. Now it was a scene of horror.

Two hours after the firefighters started pouring water into the ship, the *Noronic*'s stern settled on the bottom of Toronto harbour. A few minutes later, the bow sank. The *Noronic* straightened, ending a dangerous list that worried firefighters. Part of the stern was submerged. By then, the ship was a total loss.

For the rest of the night, fire hoses played over the hulk, but by then all the damage was done. Once in a while, they saw a bit of fire but it was quickly extinguished. People waited for the dawn, helped the living and covered up the dead. News of the disaster spread to the outskirts of the city and across North America. It was the worst peacetime disaster in Toronto's history. Only the explosion of a powder magazine during a War of 1812 battle had caused more carnage. In 1949, Toronto was the prosperous financial capital of Canada, a metropolis that had never witnessed this kind of suffering. All the facts of the disaster were reported by the competitive local press in depressing detail.

Still, it would be another day before the false rumours were cleared up.

Ed Feeny, a *Toronto Star* reporter, was allowed onto the ship the morning after the fire, while rescue workers still searched for victims.

"It was a horrible picture of charred remains amid foot-deep embers and melted glass. I saw the blackened bits that were once people. There was a young woman clutching her baby. The remains crumpled when picked up by firemen. There wasn't a wooden partition standing. There was no wooden furniture or upholstery unburned. No stairways remained except one on the bow of the ship. Every pane of glass had been melted by the intense heat.

The decks, crumpled and buckled from the heat, made progress hazardous for the firefighters seeking the dead."

As Feeny picked his way through the hulk, he interviewed firefighters as they carried dead passengers, wrapped in tarpaulins, on steel stretchers. They were sickened by their work and angry at the crew of the *Noronic*. Firefighters blamed the crew for not calling them as soon as the fire broke out.

"Amid the odour of charred wood inside the burned-out hull was that sickly smell of burned bodies, hundreds of them. What first appeared to be embers of burned furniture turned out to be the bones and blackened flesh of victims."

Firefighters told Feeny they had found the bodies of many couples in a last embrace. They had died quickly. The fire had been so hot that the wood of the ship's deck had burned away, exposing the steel of the ship's hull.

As Feeny worked his way toward the stern of the ship, he met George Beatty, a captain at the Dundas Street West firehall. The officer had even more reason to be sickened by the carnage. His son had been at a party on the *Noronic* the night before. As he talked to Feeny, a member of his fire brigade came aboard to let him know that his son had left the ship before the fire broke out.

That morning, authorities could still only guess at the death toll. Not knowing that most of the crew had been off the ship, visiting the city's bars, firefighters believed there were at least forty sailors trapped in the *Noronic*'s hull. Divers who answered the city's call for volunteers searched the ship that afternoon and found no crewmen. Most were staying with friends in Toronto, away from the ship and the troubling questions that they knew were coming.

While Feeny watched the firemen do their grisly work, bodies were taken down the *Noronic*'s two gangplanks and loaded into a string of hearses that waited on Pier 9. There weren't enough of them, so Red Cross vans and a truck from the Salvation Army joined the waiting line. The city administration asked funeral home operators to donate their work as a public service, and many of them did. The bodies, sometimes eight at a time, came down the gangplanks in tarpaulins. Firefighters working below deck struggled to make out bodies in the gloom. Most were so cremated that they broke when they were touched. At about 10:00 A.M., one fireman, who had tried to gather up a body in front of the wheelhouse, staggered to the ship's rail, leaned over and cried.

In the boat slip around the *Noronic*, chairs, furniture, and luggage were mingled with life jackets. Among the debris, men in rowboats probed the water with grappling hooks, looking for the bodies of people who had jumped overboard and drowned.

Captain Taylor spent the first few days after the fire at the home of another Great Lakes captain. His hands were bandaged, and his face, scorched by the flames, was covered with salve. He told visitors that he had wanted to finish his career without loss of life. The Canada Steamship Lines publicly insisted that none of its employees had been negligent but it later settled $3 million worth of damage claims. The *Noronic* fire spelled the end of the Great Lakes passenger ship business.

In the days after the disaster, the shattered relatives of the *Noronic*'s dead passengers arrived in the city. Most of them carried some hope that the first reports were wrong, that somehow their kin were safe. Sometimes, the dead were recognizable only from a piece of jewellery or unusual buttons on their clothes. Sometimes, the initial reports had been wrong and people went back to their homes in the United States, accompanied by people reported to have been killed. The most relieved family members were those who were related to the *Noronic*'s crew. The first newspaper stories put the number of the dead among the ship's crew at sixty, which left little hope for families. During the first day after the fire, that casualty list shrank, until, finally, the divers who had searched the hold found no one belonging to the *Noronic*'s crew. All had either been off the ship or had been saved.

The city rallied to help the *Noronic*'s survivors with donations of clothes, cash, blood, work, anything they might need. Someone came forward and volunteered to wash dishes at one of the makeshift hospitals. Ten hours later, she was still there, still washing dishes. Several volunteer secretaries stayed up all night typing lists of survivors and of people known to have died. Clergy consoled anyone who needed them.

Some Toronto residents were not showing much generosity of spirit to the families of the dead. A twenty-five-year-old ghoul who showed up at the makeshift morgue at the exhibition grounds wouldn't leave when constable Ed Williams told him to. An argument broke out.

"I know my rights," the man said. As the police officer shoved him, the man retaliated by swearing.

Then the cop punched the gawker and handcuffed him. On

Monday morning, a judge sentenced the man to twenty-one days in jail for obstructing a police officer. People like this mouthy spectator added to the grief of the families of the *Noronic* victims.

The inside of the building smelled like embalming fluid. X-ray technicians carrying charts from the most badly burned bodies mingled among doctors, nurses, and the shocked relatives. Some of the victims were identified from such odd things as a personalized shaving brush or a book of matches from Duffy's Tavern in Harrison, Montana. The meagre forensic evidence made it hard for some families to ever accept they had lost a loved one.

Twenty American passengers returned to Detroit a few days after the fire, using free train tickets given to them by the Red Cross. On board the train, other passengers pestered them about the *Noronic* fire. Most didn't want to talk about it. Instead, they talked to each other or looked out the window. Most had lost their luggage and all of their money and felt uncomfortable in the used clothes they had been given. When they ate in the train's dining car, the meals were free. Six Detroit girls who had travelled together on the *Noronic* sat in one group of seats. Only one of them could swim, but they had all made it safely to the pier. Nearby was an eighty-year-old man who had been saved by one of the girls. The man's hands were bandaged but otherwise he was alright. He was wearing a grey suit over his pyjamas.

A few talked about how lucky they had been: they had gone into the city or were visiting friends on a part of the ship near the bow, which the fire reached last. Some had burns. One man wore a sling that held his dislocated shoulder, which he had injured when he had rescued his wife. Jim Condon, a cigar-smoking Texan lawyer, sat in his seat, scoffing at a reporter's suggestion that he had been one of the fire's heros.

"I didn't do anything but help a couple of people off the boat," he said.

Irene Pavey, the last person to leave the bow of the ship, praised the *Noronic*'s captain for trying to save passengers from the cabins on the main deck. She pointed to Condon, who had helped the captain to smash the windows, and insisted he was, indeed, a hero. Condon had stayed on the ship for half an hour, finally leaving with Pavey. In one last gallant gesture, he carried the woman's purse as she climbed down a ladder.

"There was no sense in getting ruffled," the lawyer said as he took another puff from his cigar and settled back into his seat.

Relatives of the *Noronic*'s passengers waited at the Detroit railway station, frustrated at the time it took for the train to get across the Detroit River. When the train's passengers finally got off, most of the people on the platform were in tears. Very quickly, the passengers left the old train station, going their separate ways. Their trip had ended without drama. There would be no meeting of *Noronic* survivors, no special therapy for those who had to live with the memories of that dreadful night. They would deal with the *Noronic* disaster as best they could, on their own.

The fire claimed 118 lives.

Two days after the fire, the Canadian government ordered an inquiry. The hearing gave the passengers of the *Noronic* a chance to air their anger at the crew and captain. The commission's report blamed the crew but also criticized the ship's owners for not installing proper safety equipment. Captain Taylor was given a three-month suspension of his master's license by a naval tribunal. His reputation was ruined.

Rather than incurring the expense of upgrading their ships, most of the owners of Canadian Great Lakes passenger boats sold them for scrap. For another fifteen years, a couple of old liners, sister ships of the *Algoma*, which was lost back in 1885, made runs on Lake Huron and Lake Superior, but by the mid-1960s, they were sold off for the value of their steel.

Chapter Seventeen

The *Edmund Fitzgerald*

The Edmund Fitzgerald *is the most famous*
wreck on the Great Lakes.
(OGLEBAY NORTON)

On a warm July morning in 1994, the mini-sub *Clelia* was gently lowered from the research ship *Edwin Link* into the calm waters of Lake Superior. Three men were aboard the sub as it blew its air tanks and began to sink down to the wreck of the *Edmund Fitzgerald*, ninety fathoms below the surface. At that time of year, the lake was gentle enough to be a playground for boaters and fishermen. It was far different from the maelstrom that stole twenty-nine men from their families. For Tom Farnquist, the only member of the sub's crew to have been to the *Fitzgerald*'s wreck site before, the trip was to be another chance to finally answer the riddles of this famous Great Lakes tragedy.

It took five minutes for the *Clelia* to make the trip from the surface to the Great Lakes' most famous wreck. Farnquist watched the sunlight disappear. As the sub drifted gently down, its powerful searchlights were switched on and the cameras aboard started to roll. The *Clelia*'s lights shone aimlessly into the blackness of Superior until, at last, a beam hit the twisted steel of the *Edmund Fitzgerald*.

Even after seeing the wreck twice, once through the stereoscopic eyes of a robot and another time from the windows of a submarine, Farnquist was still amazed by the wreck. It lay on a bed of clay, surrounded by seven-metre chunks of lake bottom that had been ploughed up when the *Fitzgerald* slammed into it.

"There's nothing around the ship except flat bottom, but when you get close to the site, there are those big chunks of clay. You can tell that the *Fitzgerald* rammed into the bottom with its full weight. It didn't stop until it hit solid bottom, twenty-five feet down in the clay," Farnquist said.

The *Clelia* was the fourth submarine to visit the wreck site. In 1976, the summer after the *Edmund Fitzgerald* sank, the U.S. Coast Guard sent an unmanned submersible to the *Fitzgerald* to gather information that was to be used in the official inquiry into the *Fitzgerald*'s sinking. The sub had scanned the *Fitzgerald*'s bridge and photographed the lettering on her bow, providing proof to the ship's insurers that she, indeed, did rest at the southeast end of Lake Superior, near the entrance to Whitefish Bay. Then it had scanned the long deck of the freighter, photographing the huge steel covers of the ship's hatches.

The Coast Guard had used the photographs of the deck to try to prove its theory that the hatch covers had given way and allowed in water from eleven-metre waves which pounded the *Fitzgerald* on the night of Monday, November 10, 1975. Since then, most shipwreck experts who studied the *Fitzgerald*'s sinking had rejected the Coast Guard's verdict. A second theory, that the *Fitzgerald* had been slammed onto a shoal, was backed by ship owners and still hadn't been proven. By the summer of 1994, a third theory was being tested, that the *Fitzgerald* had developed a structural crack in her hull which caused her to take on water and nose-dive to the bottom.

Four years after the Coast Guard's scan of the wreck, a famous group of marine explorers paid a short visit to the grave of the *Fitzgerald*. In late September, 1980, an expedition from Jacques Cousteau's ship, the *Calypso*, filmed the *Edmund Fitzgerald* for a television special on the Great Lakes. At a Sault Ste. Marie press conference, at the end of the month, Yves Cousteau said he believed the *Edmund Fitzgerald* had broken into pieces before she sank. This opinion conflicts with the Coast Guard's conclusion that the ship went down because water had poured into her hold through deck hatches and two torn-off vent covers. *Fitzgerald* fanatics were disappointed with both Cousteau's dive and his conclusions. The divers had visited only the photogenic wheelhouse area of the ship, leaving with a few minutes of marketable film but no evidence to back their verdict on the sinking's cause.

There was some irony to the *Calypso*'s down-bound trip on Lake Huron. She almost foundered in a fall gale. The Cousteau crew got some of the best Great Lakes storm film ever shot, but they earned it the hard way. If they knew about their countrymen on the lost minesweepers, they might have approached the lakes with a little more care and caution.

For nearly nine years, the *Edmund Fitzgerald* was left alone, the untouched grave of the men who are imprisoned inside her. The wreck is much too far below the surface of Lake Superior to be disturbed by the hoards of recreational divers who visit wrecks and who, too often, break Ontario's heritage laws and pick clean the hulks in shallower parts of the Great Lakes. In late August 1989, researchers lowered a small submersible robot carrying video cameras to the wreck of the *Edmund Fitzgerald*.

Farnquist took part in that expedition, which produced the best pictures yet of the wreck. Over the years, interest in the sinking seemed to be growing, rather than waning. People wanted answers to the riddle of the *Fitzgerald*'s loss, but there were still no answers, only a few more clues.

When the *Edmund Fitzgerald* was launched, in 1958, she was the largest ship on the Great Lakes. Overall, her length was 729 feet, with a gross weight of 13,632 tons. Full, she weighed just over 40,000 tons. By comparison, the *Titanic* was 882 feet long and weighed 45,320 tons. Her maximum speed was 28 kilometres an hour, fully loaded.

Hull 301 was launched at the Rouge River, Michigan, shipyard of the Great Lakes Engineering works. Like most other ships built on the Great Lakes, she slipped into the water sideways off the cradle that supported her steel hull when it was under construction. The wave created by the launch nearly swamped the little tugboat *Maryland*, which anchored about a city block's distance from the launch.

Once she was in the Detroit River, steelworkers, pipefitters, boilermakers, and electricians did the finishing work on her. The *Edmund Fitzgerald* was named after the chairman of the Northwestern Mutual Life Insurance Company of Milwaukee, which owned the ship. Edmund Fitzgerald's grandfather and five of his great-uncles had been Great Lakes ship captains. At the time the *Edmund Fitzgerald* was launched, the *W.E. Fitzgerald*, built in 1907 and named after Edmund's father, still plied the lakes.

Northwestern Mutual Life Insurance had built the ship as an investment. It was leased to Oglebay Norton for twenty-five years, to be used in the iron-ore trade between the Lake Superior ports that handle Messabi Range ore and the cities on the Detroit River and Lake Superior that make the ore into steel. As an added perk for Oglebay executives, a passenger suite had been built on the *Fitzgerald*. It was last used in October 1975, just before the *Edmund Fitzgerald* sank.

The *Edmund Fitzgerald* looked like a larger version of most of the lake freighters that can be seen on the waterfronts of Toronto, Hamilton, Windsor-Detroit and Sault Ste. Marie. Crew members lived on the bow and stern of the ship. The long deck in between had two tunnels that connected the bridge and fore deck with the main living and eating quarters at the stern. The tunnels were designed to protect the men who worked the ship from the storm waves that sometimes splashed over the *Edmund Fitzgerald*'s deck. In theory, once the ore was loaded and the steel covers were bolted down over the cargo hatches, there was little need to leave the comfort and warmth of the living quarters and foredeck.

The *Edmund Fitzgerald* had eight ballast tanks that were used to keep her stable. As water was let into her, air rushed out through fifteen-centimetre vents on her deck. Mushroom-shaped steel vent caps prevented water from pouring back down through the vents when the ship passed through storm waves. These tanks were drained by six huge electric pumps. She was outfitted with some of the most modern communications systems available at the time, including several radios (working on AM and FM, and able to transmit on citizen-band frequencies) and three radio-telephones. She was also equipped with two radars that were able to identify nearby ships and shoreline. Unlike a well-equipped weekend sportsman's fishing boat, she didn't have a depth finder. The *Fitzgerald* may have sunk because of the lack of this relatively inexpensive piece of equipment.

Her seventeen-year career on the Great Lakes was uneventful. There were a couple of minor mishaps, but no accident had delayed her for more than a few days. The *Fitzgerald*'s years on the lakes had, by no means, made her an old ship. Some freighters that work the lakes are more than half a century old. In 1972, however, she lost the distinction of being the longest ship on the Great Lakes.

The *Edmund Fitzgerald* was still considered to be one of the best lake boats on which to work. Her bridge crew had the most senior-ity of any of the officers in the Oglebay Norton fleet. Other ships belonging to the company dipped their pennants when the *Fitzgerald* passed by.

Several captains had skippered the *Fitzgerald* before Ernie McSorley took over. McSorley was born in Ogdensburg, New York, just across the St. Lawrence River from Prescott, Ontario. He spent his boyhood on one of the busiest waterways in the world. During the Depression, he signed up as an eighteen-year-old deckhand, steadily rising through the ranks until he became, at thirty-seven, the youngest captain on the Great Lakes. McSorley's first assignments weren't exactly choice ones. He skippered small freighters and barges and was then given command of mid-sized lake boats, before finally getting the plum job of captain of the *Edmund Fitzgerald*. By the fall of 1975, he had been captain of the *Fitzgerald* for just over three years. He was due to retire in 1978.

Later, McSorley's decisions on the afternoon and early evening of Monday, November 10, 1975, would be scrutinized far more than McSorley may have ever wanted them to be. Did McSorley and Oglebay Norton allow an overloaded ship with improperly fastened hatch covers to go out into Lake Superior at the most dangerous time of the shipping season? Did McSorley wander too closely toward a notoriously hazardous area, Six Fathom Shoal, between Michipicoten Island and Caribou Island? Did he know he was in trouble and not ask for help, allowing his pride and sense of author-ity to get between him and the possibility of rescue for his crew? And was McSorley lax when it came to safety?

If McSorley passed all these tests, then he was later falsely accused by the U.S. Coast Guard and by some of the researchers who studied the wreck site on the bottom of Lake Superior. The blame could lie with the ship itself, which, after seventeen years of carrying heavy cargos of iron ore, may have been vulnerable to storms because the hull had become brittle from metal fatigue. The tangled, twisted hull plates that lie around the wreck site testify to the ship's inability to survive the power of a mid-sized gale that didn't take any other lake freighters. The steel had crumpled in the impact of collision with the soft, muddy lake bottom. The heart of the storm appears to have tracked over northern Lake Michigan, not Lake Superior, but no ships were lost on the former lake. The waves at the wreck site ranged to about ten metres, but until about two hours before she sank, the *Edmund Fitzgerald* had sailed through seas that were relatively calm for November on the Great Lakes.

The trip should have been uneventful.

On the afternoon of Sunday, November 9, 1975, the *Fitzgerald* left the Burlington Northern Railroad dock in Superior, Wisconsin, at the extreme southwestern end of Lake Superior. She was loaded with just over 26,000 tons of taconite pellets, semi-refined iron ore which is mined in Minnesota and shipped to the steel mills of Indiana, Michigan, and Ohio. Her destination was a steel mill in Detroit, just a few kilometres from the place where she was built. At least one letter sent by crew members from Wisconsin suggests the men aboard the ship were eager to get under way, since this was to be the last trip of the season. The *Fitzgerald*, in fact, left Superior a day late.

When she got under way, McSorley and the members of the crew knew that a gale was moving toward Lake Superior from the U.S. Southwest. An official gale warning for all the Great Lakes was issued on Sunday night at 7:00 P.M. by the U.S. National Weather Service. By then, the *Edmund Fitzgerald* was steaming up the Minnesota shore of Lake Superior in the company of the *Arthur M. Anderson*, another ore freighter with which the *Fitzgerald*'s crew had rendezvoused as she left Two Harbours, Minnesota.

At about 2:00 A.M., McSorley and Jesse Cooper, the captain of the *Anderson*, talked by radio telephone. They decided the storm was becoming potentially dangerous and that they should take the north fall shipping route, in the lee of Superior's north shore.

During that Sunday night, the two ships travelled parallel to Lake Superior's Canadian shore, past Thunder Bay, Nipigon, and Schreiber. They were too far from shore to be seen. By then, the U.S. Weather Service had upgraded the gale to a full-fledged storm, with the potential for fifty-knot winds; so McSorley had been wise to follow the longer, more protected route on the Canadian side of the border. Early Monday, a camper on the Slate Islands, off Terrace Bay on the north shore of Lake Superior, saw the *Fitzgerald* and *Anderson* pass by.

The winds were beginning to increase but weren't yet gale-force. Not far from the Slate Islands, the two ships began moving southeast, past Marathon, Heron Bay, and the desolate shore of Pukaskwa National Park. In the twilight, they passed by the last haven before reaching the Soo: Michipicoten Island and the harbour it shelters. Then they turned almost due south toward the St. Marys River. Throughout the trip, the *Fitzgerald*, the faster of the two ships, had been steadily pulling out in front of the *Anderson*. Around noon, the winds were about thirty-five knots from the northeast but they had begun to die down. McSorley knew the calm was the prelude to a wind shift.

At Michipicoten came the first hint of trouble. Although the waves were still only three to four metres high and the winds were nearly calm, McSorley reported to Cooper that his ship was "rolling some." An hour south of Michipicoten, McSorley asked the *Anderson*'s captain to help him navigate, since the *Fitzgerald*'s radar wasn't working. The failure of the radar probably contributed as much to the loss of the *Fitzgerald* as any other single factor. Without it, the crew had no way of making out the shoreline and being sure of their position. Lacking both depth finders and radar, the *Edmund*

Fitzgerald was practically blind. By then, the winds were still about thirty-five knots and heavy snow had begun to fall.

At Caribou Island, about thirty kilometres from the entrance to Whitefish Bay, the *Anderson* stayed far from shore while the *Fitzgerald* sailed toward the lee of the island. The snow and darkness kept the bridge officers of the *Anderson* from seeing the *Fitzgerald*. Both ships planned to sail between Caribou Island and the Canadian shore. Copper steered a little to the east to miss Six Fathom Shoal, but after the *Fitzgerald*'s loss, he reported to his head office that the *Fitzgerald* didn't make a course correction. On the *Anderson*'s bridge, Caribou Island and the *Fitzgerald* appeared on the radar screen simultaneously. The *Anderson*'s bridge crew knew that the *Fitzgerald* could have been slammed onto Six Fathom Shoal. A few minutes later, McSorley radioed the *Anderson* to say the *Fitzgerald* had developed a list.

Also, McSorley's ship had lost part of its deck rail and two of the covers of the ballast tank vents. For the first time, McSorley seemed worried about the fate of his ship. He cut his speed so the *Anderson* could keep up and turned on both of the *Fitzgerald*'s huge ballast pumps. By then, the waves were building quickly, high enough to roll over the decks of both ships. Cooper later said the waves rolling over his deck were three to four metres high. The force of the water crumpled several of the *Anderson*'s life boats.

The two freighters were steering directly for the centre of the low pressure area. There is no evidence that anyone in authority on either ship thought the *Fitzgerald* was in danger of sinking, but Cooper believes there was a trace of fear in McSorley's voice.

Just as the *Anderson*'s first officer finished recording the *Fitzgerald*'s damage in the *Anderson*'s log book, a warning was issued by the U.S. Coast guard that the Soo locks had been closed because of high water. The storm was now passing just south of Sault Ste. Marie, and the best protection for ships on Lake Superior was in Whitefish Bay, at the entrance to the St. Marys River. Already, several lake boats and ocean freighters had steamed there for protection.

At 6:00 P.M., half an hour after nightfall, the waves had risen to nearly ten metres. McSorley ordered his crew not to go on deck. The *Anderson* and *Fitzgerald* were now in dangerous waters. Still, unless McSorley had begun to realize just how bad his situation was, there was no concern about the possibility of either the *Anderson* or *Fitzgerald* being lost in the storm. Cooper left the bridge of his ship. An hour later, the *Anderson* called the *Fitzgerald* with some navigational information. Then, ten minutes later, this conversation occurred:

Anderson (First Mate): There is a target nineteen miles ahead of us, so the target is nine miles on ahead.

Fitzgerald (McSorley): Well, am I going to clear?

Anderson: Yes, he is going to pass west of you.

Fitzgerald: Well, fine.

Anderson: Oh, by the way, how are you making out with your problem?

Fitzgerald: We are holding our own.

Those were the last words that were transmitted from the *Edmund Fitzgerald*, a modern ship with excellent communications equipment, travelling in one of the busiest waterways on earth. If she had sent a distress call, someone would have heard it.

Cooper returned to the bridge just as the conversation was wrapping up and noticed that the *Fitzgerald* was shown on radar to be about nine miles away, just approaching Whitefish Point. No one glanced at the radar again. When they did, the *Fitzgerald* was gone.

As the *Anderson* entered Whitefish Bay, the storm let up. Crew members could see lights on shore and could make out some of the freighters that had taken shelter. The *Fitzgerald* wasn't among them.

The *Anderson*'s crew began searching around their ship with radar but found nothing. They tried calling for the lost ship on different radio frequencies but the *Fitzgerald* didn't answer. Then Cooper called the U.S. Coast Guard.

At first, the response was non-committal. Instead of springing into action, the Coast Guard told the *Anderson*'s bridge crew to watch for a missing pleasure boat that was lost in Whitefish Bay. The *Anderson*'s bridge crew fumed for about ten minutes, then called the Coast Guard back. This time, there was a more desperate tone in Cooper's voice.

Logs of the call, introduced as evidence at the inquiry into the loss of the *Fitzgerald*, show the desperation:

"I am very concerned with the welfare of the steamer *Edmund Fitzgerald*. He was right in front of us experiencing a little difficulty. He was taking on a small amount of water and most of the upbound ships have passed him. I can see no lights as before, and I don't have him on radar. I just hope he hasn't taken a nose dive," Cooper told the Coast Guard radio operator at 8:25 P.M.

By then, everyone on the *Fitzgerald* had probably been dead for at least half an hour. Fifteen minutes after Cooper's conversation with the Coast Guard, a call went out for Canadian and U.S. military search planes.

Later, the U.S. Coast Guard would be criticized by people on the Michigan shore of Lake Superior for not having the equipment necessary to mount a rescue. On the night the *Fitzgerald* was lost, the question was a moot point, although, of course, of considerable importance to the people who still sail the Great Lakes. Maybe crews' lives were at risk because, in the fall of 1975, there was no rescue ship stationed on the Upper Great Lakes large enough to be able to challenge the gales of Lake Superior. There is no evidence anywhere that the crew of the *Fitzgerald* ever had a chance of being rescued. The ship literally disappeared from the surface. She was gone so fast that the crew never even began trying to escape.

Testimony at the U.S. Coast Guard inquiry into the *Fitzgerald* sinking showed the crew of a lake freighter needs about ten minutes to launch a lifeboat in good weather, about thirty minutes in storm seas. Inflatable boats and survival suits are probably more useful than old-style lifeboats in a fast sinking, but the lack of a distress signal and the fact that bodies were never found strongly suggests the *Fitzgerald* went to the bottom before any crew members had a chance to move from their stations, if they were on duty, or their berths.

About midnight, five hours after the loss of the *Fitzgerald*, the crew of the *Anderson* had returned to the area of the big ship's sinking and began finding wreckage. Through the night, a shattered lifeboat, an oar, and some life jackets were taken aboard the *Anderson*. Five vessels and three aircraft, including a Canadian Forces Hercules aircraft carrying two twenty-man dinghies, searched in the darkness, but there was never much chance that members of the *Fitzgerald* crew would be found alive.

Probably, when the ship began her dive, the crew of the *Fitzgerald* knew they were doomed, but there was no time to react.

The bow of the boat plunged into the water so fast that no distress signal was sent. The force of the water crashed through the pilot house. Within seconds, the bow of the ship was far enough down in the water that the pressure of Superior's depths would have smashed every window, forced water into the forward cabins, and drowned or crushed the men inside. The stern cabin, where most of the crew was, followed within a few seconds. The *Fitzgerald* was actually longer than the depth of the water. Her bow, with the weight of the fully loaded ship behind her and the stern still out of the water, hit the bottom within a few seconds from the time it disappeared from the surface.

Even though the lake bottom was soft, it did little to cushion the impact of the *Fitzgerald*'s sinking. A huge slash was torn in the *Fitzgerald*'s bow and some of the thick steel plates of her hull were buckled.

The *Fitzgerald* tore in half about midway along her cargo deck, and part of the hull disintegrated into a flutter of crumpled, torn plates which quickly plunged to the lake bottom. The stern of the *Fitzgerald* rolled as it fell toward the lake bottom and landed upside down. It is likely that the crew members in the stern had died before they were crushed in the impact. The pattern of the sinking accounts for the fact that only one body has been seen at the wreck site. Only the body of McSorley and his officers in the wheelhouse had a reasonable chance of floating free from the sunken ship. The rest are either trapped in the wreck or have settled in the mud of the lake.

All that was left of the *Edmund Fitzgerald* was some debris that had broken loose from the deck as the ship went down or had floated to the surface when the *Fitzgerald* reached the lake bottom. Gone were twenty-nine men whose families would have to live with the emptiness of having suddenly lost husbands, sons, and brothers. The *Fitzgerald*, a ship that, with better luck, would have anonymously sailed the lakes for another generation before being cut up for scrap, entered the historical mythology of North America. No one aboard her would have chosen to become a symbol of the dangers of the Great Lakes, but the ship's fate was a reminder that the inland seas are far from tamed.

Tuesday morning, two more freighters heading down Lake Superior joined the *Anderson* in the search. Surprisingly, three ocean-going ships that had been taking shelter in Whitefish Bay refused to help. Their assistance wasn't needed, but exhausted crew members of the *Anderson* cursed them anyway. By then, eight ships, including the *Anderson*, were travelling in a line, searching for wreckage, bodies, or boats from the *Fitzgerald*. Nine Ontario Provincial Police officers walked the rugged Ontario coastline, down wind from the wreck site. They found some of the *Fitzgerald*'s life belts and other small pieces of battered debris from the wreck.

Some false hopes were raised the day after the sinking when someone on the Canadian shore called the U.S. Coast Guard to say there was a man clinging to a log just offshore. The call turned out to be a hoax. In the ten-degree Celsius water, there was no chance of surviving long. By Tuesday morning, Coast Guard captain Charles Millradt was telling reporters that "any hope we had is very dim now."

Finally, Cooper ordered his ship into the Soo. On the way, it stopped to drop off the battered debris from the *Fitzgerald*. The *Anderson*'s captain was so shaken by the ordeal of losing the

Fitzgerald and spending the night searching for her that he went into seclusion on Tuesday, November 11. By then a full day had passed and every important clue to the *Fitzgerald*'s sinking that could be found on the surface of the lake was already in the hands of the Coast Guard. New evidence for the Coast Guard inquiry would have to come from the wreck itself, but no survey would be made until the next spring.

Meanwhile, the storm that sank the *Edmund Fitzgerald* continued to damage and kill as it swept southward across the lakes. A sailor, Leonard Alexander Martin, died on Lake Erie when the fishing tug *Southside* capsized off Port Burwell that Monday night. At Crystal Beach, an old two-storey hotel collapsed when storm waves undercut its foundation. Port Dover's main street was under water, and a third of the town's houses were flooded. Winds on the shore of Lake Ontario were clocked at one hundred kilometres an hour. Parts of Toronto were blacked out because trees were blown onto power lines.

Finally, a few weeks after the *Fitzgerald*'s loss, the shipping season ended. A Coast Guard survey of eastern Lake Superior at the end of November located the *Fitzgerald*'s wreckage, and plans were made to photograph the ship the next spring. Remembrance services were held in the home ports of the ship's crew members and at Detroit's old Maritime Sailor's Church, now nearly hidden by the giant skyscrapers that were going up on the river's shore. A haunting song by Gordon Lightfoot ignited the public's imagination about the Great Lakes' last big wreck, and people who had never seen the fury of a Great Lakes storm started arguing about the causes of the *Fitzgerald*'s sinking.

In the summer of 1995, the bell of the *Fitzgerald* was raised and placed on display in a memorial at Whitefish Point, Michigan. It was replaced on the wreck by a bell inscribed with the names of the lost crewmen, a fitting grave marker to the men who went down on one of the lakes' most famous ships.

Tom Farnquist sees Great Lakes storms just about every year from his home on Whitefish Point. As the *Clelia* drew near the *Fitzgerald*'s pilot house on that day in July 1994, the marine explorer and historian was close enough to be able to see that the *Fitzgerald*'s telegraph was set for "full ahead." Gone was the trapped, floating life jacket that could be seen in earlier Coast Guard pictures. The clay was already beginning to cover parts of the ship.

The *Clelia* took Farnquist to the twisted deck of the *Fitzgerald* and then into the mass of buckled plates that had folded when the *Fitzgerald* accordioned into the lake. Off to the side was the *Fitzgerald*'s stern section, with its huge propeller. It had kept turning even as the ship plunged to the lake.

"It's a powerful feeling to see the *Fitzgerald*, to be just inches from the bridge," Farnquist said. Just out of reach, this time, was the ship's bell, which the families of the *Fitzgerald*'s crew wanted recovered for the monument at Farnquist's museum on Whitefish Point.

"After all of these years, there's no gravestone, no memorial for the men on the *Edmund Fitzgerald*. We're going to try to get that bell back so they will have a place to lay their flowers," he said.

Something Farnquist didn't see on this trip was the one body that has been located. The *Fitzgerald* crewman, who was spotted by a commercial diving expedition a month after the *Clelia*'s dive, lay silently a few hundred metres from the wreck as the *Clelia*'s small engines manoeuvred the submarine along the shattered windows of the bridge. Before he died, he may have known the reason for the *Fitzgerald*'s loss. Like the ship, he is a silent part of the mythology of the Great Lakes. Perhaps he should be allowed to remain shrouded in mystery.

Bibliography & Notes

The Little Boat of Charity

The study of native history is fascinating, made all the more inter-esting these days by high-quality studies that have been published in the past two decades. See Jennings, Francis. *The Ambiguous Iroquois Empire*. New York: W.W. Norton & Co., 1984. For a description of the goals of the Iroquoian Jesuit missions by one of their supporters, see Parkman, Francis. *The Jesuits in North America in the Seventeenth Century*. Part II. Boston: Little, Brown and Co., 1925. The authoritative historian of the Hurons, written somewhat from the perspective of the natives, is Bruce G. Trigger. *The Children of Aataentsic*. Montreal: McGill-Queen's University Press, 1976. A shorter work of Trigger's that provides insight into Huron life is *The Huron, Farmers of the North*. Toronto: Holt, Rinehart and Winston, 1969. A recent and easily obtained book that provoked an important debate on the ravages of colonization is Wright, Ronald. *Stolen Continents*. Toronto: Viking/Penguin 1992.

The *Griffin*

Most good Canadian histories have an account of the *Griffin*. Several 19th and 20th century printings of Louis Hennepin's *A New Discovery of a Vast Country in America*. (London: 1698) were pub-lished. For LaSalle's version of events, see Cox, Isaac Joslin, ed.

"The Journeys of Rene Robert Cavelier." New York: Allerton Book Co., 1922. [New York: AMS Press, 1973]

Revenge of the *Nancy*

The loss of the *Nancy* and subsequent naval action are described in *Ontario Historical Society Papers and Records*, Vol. 9 (1910). These papers include all the correspondence used in this chapter. The *Nancy*'s salvaging is described in *Canadian Magazine*, May, 1926. For a description of the loss of the *Nancy*'s figurehead, see "Found—Man Who Set Eyes on Figurehead of the *Nancy*." *Toronto Evening Telegram*, June 12, 1930. Anyone interested in ships of this period should visit the Nancy Island Historic Site at Wasaga Beach and Discovery Harbour in Penetanguishene. Both are open in the summer tourism season.

The "Coffin Ship" *Atlantic*

Writers seem to have taken sides over the issue of who was entitled to the money recovered from the *Atlantic* in the 1850s. See *Inland Seas* 14:4 and 19:3. For information about the latest salvaging effort, see *Buffalo News*, May 5, 1994, B6; *Financial Post*, May 6, 1994, p. 39; *Los Angeles Times*, June 6-7, 1994, Metro section p.1; *Los Angeles Times*, June 26, 1994, Metro p. 1; *Mesa Tribune*, Mesa, AZ. Aug. 2, 1992, P. B1; Press Release "Canadian actions to preserve historic shipwreck supported by New York State and Pennsylvania officials." Carried by *Business Wire* (BRW), July 16, 1991.

The Heroine of Long Point

The only complete contemporary account of Abigail Becker's life is "The story of Abigail Becker, the Heroine of Long Point: as told by her step-daughter, Mrs. Henry Wheeler" [edited] by R. Calvert. Toronto: W. Briggs, 1899. The Norfolk Historical Society in Simcoe, Ont., has some documentary material as well as photographs of Ms. Becker. There is surprisingly little material available from the period of the loss of the *Conductor*.

Politicians in Peril

Since the *Speedy* had no survivors and there were no witnesses to the sinking, the story of her loss has been put together from physical evidence from the wreck. See Palmer, Richard. "The Wreck of the *Speedy*" in *Inland Seas* 42:1. The *Ploughboy*'s near-loss is briefly mentioned in most biographies of Sir. John A. Macdonald. See Adam, G. Mercer. *Canada's Patriot Statesman. The Life of the Rt. Hon. Sir John A. Macdonald.* Toronto: C.R. Parish and Co., 1891; Pope, Sir Joseph. *Memoirs of the Rt. Hon. Sir John Alexander Macdonald.* Toronto: Musson Book Co., 1896. The *Ploughboy* mishap is mentioned briefly in Creighton, Donald. *John A. Macdonald, the Young Politician*, Toronto: Macmillan, 1952, which remains the definitive modern biography of Canada's first prime minister. See also Barrie, James. *Georgian Bay, the Sixth Great Lake.* Toronto: Clarke, Irwin and Co., 1968, to see the *Ploughboy* mishap within the context of Georgian Bay's history.

Spies and Rebels on the Lakes

The Toronto *Globe* covered the U.S. court cases that arose from the *Philo Parsons* incident and the other Lake Erie raids. In late 1864, stories appeared under the heading "Lake Erie Pirates." For more information on Denison and the *Georgian*, see Denison, George Jr. *The Petition of George Taylor Denison Jr. to the Honourable House of Assembly Praying to Redress the Matter of the Seizure of the Steamer "Georgian."* Toronto: Leader and Patriot Steam Press Establishment, 1865. See also MacLean, Guy. "The *Georgian* Affair" in *Canadian Historical Review* 52:2. Thompson's activities became public when the Union Republican Congressional Committee reprinted his reports in 1868, possibly to strengthen the hand of Radical Republicans in the congressional elections that year. A copy of the report is on file in Canada's National Library in Ottawa. The best book on Canadian-U.S. relations during the Civil War is Winks, Robin W. *Canada and the United States: the Civil War Years*. Baltimore: Johns Hopkins University Press, 1960. For succinct discussions of the political and propaganda value of the Beall-Thompson activities, see *Inland Seas* 5:1, 5:2, 45:1, 45:2 and 45:3. For more information on Great Lakes ships involved in the Civil War, see *Inland Seas* 15:4. For overviews of the political craftsmanship of Canada's first prime minister, see Adam, G. Mercer. *Canada's Patriot Statesman. The Life of the Rt. Hon. Sir John A. Macdonald*. Toronto: C.R Parish and Co., 1891; Creighton, Donald. *John A. Macdonald, the Young Politician*. Toronto: Macmillan, 1952; Pope, Sir Joseph. *Memoirs of the Rt. Hon. Sir John Alexander Macdonald*. Toronto: Musson Book Co., 1896. For more information about Bennett Burleigh and his fantastic generation of war correspondents, see Knightley, Phillip. *The First Casualty*. New York: Harcourt Brace Jovanovich, 1975.

Georgian Bay Ghost Ships

See Barrie, James. *Georgian Bay, the Sixth Great Lake*. Toronto: Clarke, Irwin and Co., 1968; Boyer, Dwight. *Ghost Ships of the Great Lakes*. New York: Dodd Mead, 1968; Marsh, E.L. *A History of the County of Grey*. Owen Sound: Grey County Council, 1931. For descriptions of the wreck sites, see Amos, Art, and Patrick Folkes. *A Diver's Guide to Georgian Bay*. Willowdale: Ontario Underwater Council, 1979.

The *Asia*

See Toronto *Globe*, Sept. 18-24, 1882. The *Globe* covered the sinking and the inquest. It also carried the story about the fake survivor. See *Mer Douce* (November-December 1921), for a description of the wreck and the survival of Morrison and Tinkiss. See also: Bowen, Dana Thomas. *Memories of the Great Lakes*. Cleveland: Freshwater Press, 1946; Boyer, Dwight. *Ghost Ships of the Great Lakes*. New York: Dodd Mead, 1968.

The Wreck of the *Algoma*

Eyewitnesses and survivors of the *Algoma* disaster gave accounts of the wreck within a few days of the ship's loss. See Toronto *Globe*, Nov. 13, 1885 and subsequent issues. Reporters at the *Weekly Sentinel*, Port Arthur, filed reports of the arrival of survivors in the

Nov. 13, 1885 edition and subsequent issues. See also Wrigley, Ronald. *Shipwrecked: Vessels that Met Tragedy on Northern Lake Superior*. Cobalt: Highway Book Store, 1985.

Where's the Captain?

Dwight Boyer's *Ghost Ships of the Great Lakes* gives a full account of the loss of the *Marquette and Bessemer No. 2*, which he wrote with the help of crew family members. It was published in New York by Dodd Mead, 1968. Boyer's account carries some suggestion of foul play. See also Hepburn, Agnes M. *Historical Sketch of the Village of Port Stanley*. Port Stanley: Port Stanley Historical Society, 1952; Hilton, George Woodman. *The Great Lakes Car Ferries*. Berkley: Howell-North, 1962. Newspaper accounts of the sinking of the ship and the retrieval of bodies were somewhat sparse after the initial loss. The best coverage of the sinking was in the Cleveland newspapers.

The Great Storm

Frank Barcus wrote the definitive account of the Great Storm. *Freshwater Fury* (Detroit: Wayne State University Press, 1960) is out of print but may be found in research libraries. The Great Storm is standard fare for Great Lakes shipwreck books. See works by Bowen, Boyer, and Ratigan. The best material on the storm can be found in newspapers of the time. The *Toronto Star*, Toronto *Globe* and the *London Free Press* did excellent reporting on the disaster and stayed on the story through the inquests in the winter of 1913-1914. *Inland Seas* 27:3 contains an overview of the Great Storm. For a description of the discovery of the *Charles S. Price*, see *Inland Seas* 42:2. The discovery of the wreck of the *Regina* is described in *Inland Seas* 43:2.

The *Inkerman* and the *Cerisoles*

Most material for this chapter comes from coverage in the *Thunder Bay Chronicle* and the Toronto *Globe*. For a description of the loss of the two minesweepers, see Wrigley, R. *Shipwrecked*. Cobalt: Highway Book Store, 1985. See also Mauro, Joseph R. *A History of Thunder Bay*. Thunder Bay: City of Thunder Bay, 1981.

Alone on the Bridge

Reporters from the *Globe and Mail* and the *Toronto Star* covered the return of the crew of the *Arlington*. Stories ran daily in both papers in the first week of May. The National Archives of Canada has the report of the hearings held into the loss of the *Arlington*, including verbatim transcripts of testimony of the *Arlington* and *Collingwood*'s crew, the official report into the wreck, and correspondence about subsequent litigation regarding the lost cargo.

Always Trust Your Accountant

Charlie Rankin was a friend of my grandfather's and told me, several times, the story of the loss of the *Wawinet*, which was known generally in the Midland area as "Corbeau's Yacht." Soon after the sinking, the federal government conducted an inquiry into the loss of the ship, with testimony taken from all of the survivors, plus the people who maintained and inspected the ship. These transcripts, some 200 pages, are in the National Archives of Canada. In the same file are the report of the commissioner of wrecks, newspaper clippings from the disaster, and the correspondence regarding Corbeau's difficulties paying for and insuring the *Wawinet*.

The *Noronic*

For a brief description of the *Noronic*, see *Inland Seas* 5:1. The *Noronic* fire is mentioned in most Great Lakes steamship books. A chilling account of the fire is in Vol. 1, No 1 (1994) of *Perils of the Deep*, a magazine published in Canoga Park, Ca., by Challenge Publications Ltd. It may be difficult to find in Ontario. Quite explicit reportage of the fire was in the *Toronto Star*, whose coverage by Ed Feeny was stellar. Mr. Feeny died in March, 1995. His work is used with permission of the *Toronto Star* Syndicate. Jim Hunt's reporting on the fire in the *Toronto Telegram* was solid eye-witness work by a top journalist.

The *Edmund Fitzgerald*

For a photograph of her launch and background on the ship and the Fitzgerald family, see *Inland Seas* 14:2. Robert Hemming's *Gales of November* (Chicago: Contemporary Books, 1981) was written with the cooperation of family members of the *Fitzgerald*'s crew. It is the definitive work on the disaster. Frederick Stonehouse's *The Wreck of the Edmund Fitzgerald* (AuTrain, Mich.: Avery Color Studios, 1977), contains considerable material from the official inquiry into the *Fitzgerald* disaster. See also: Ratigan, William. *Great*

Lakes Shipwrecks and Survivals. Grand Rapids, Mich.: Wm. B. Eerdsmans, 1977 edition.

It is surprising how poorly the story of the loss of the *Edmund Fitzgerald* was covered by Canadian media at the time. The first story on the loss of the ship appeared on p. 2 of the Nov. 11, 1975, *Globe and Mail*. The *Toronto Star* similarly underplayed the story. Much better work came from reportage of the U.S. Coast Guard inquiry into the loss of the *Fitzgerald*.

Acknowledgements

It's not very often that a Canadian writer gets the chance to write an acknowledgement to a second edition of a non-academic historical work. This piece of good fortune would have eluded me if my publisher, Anna Porter, and my editor, Michael Mouland, hadn't gone far beyond the call and put this project together. Special thanks to Tony Hawke, who originally published this book under the Hounslow imprint. Tony loves books and writers and gave me a break that has dramatically changed my life. Special thanks, too, to the publishing people at Prospero who believe Canadian books should get new life when there's a market for them.

This book wouldn't have been written, illustrated, or published without the help and support of a small navy of friends, family, colleagues, and researchers. The most important debt is owed to the editor of the first edition, Liedewy Hawke, who caught such beauties as "pothead plots" when I meant to say Irish "potato plots." Spell-check systems are marvellous, but nothing replaces the human touch.

Special thanks to my wife, Marion, and my aunt, Dawn Varney, who encouraged me to write books rather than find a paying job. My father, Paul Bourrie, and my grandfather, the late Ernie Bourrie, worked on the sister ships of the *Algoma* when they were high school students and gave me details about life on Great Lakes boats. My mother, Peggy Scott, and her husband, Mike, did valuable research for me in Thunder Bay, especially for the chapter dealing with the loss of the two French World War I minesweepers. Debbie Levy, a bookstore owner and journalist in Penetanguishene, steered hard-to-get marine books my way and was a source of support. The late Marlene Pruesse, friend and mentor, encouraged this project.

Among my colleagues, author and journalist Mick Lowe of Sudbury, Mike Tenszen of Saint John, New Brunswick, Linda Richardson of the *Sault Star*, John Ferri and Kate Harries of the *Toronto Star*, and Mike Seudfeld, formerly of the *Midland Free Press*, have either contributed ideas or have helped shape this book. The late Robert Vezina, retired city editor of the *Toronto Sun* and one of Canada's best newspaper stylists, gave valuable writing advice while I worked for him in the last years of his life.

Staff of the Library of Parliament, the National Library, the Public Archives of Canada, the Ontario Archives, the Thunder Bay Historical Museum, Ste. Marie Among the Hurons in Midland, Discovery Harbour in Penetanguishene, the Nancy Island Historic Site, the Port McNicoll Historic Society, the New York State Historical Commission, the Canadian Pacific archives (Steve Lyon), the Canada Steamship Lines archives (Kim Bailey), and the Great Lakes Historical Society have generously contributed their time and ideas. So, too, have Jan van de Wetering, my father-in-law, and his wife, Dr. Marie Francoise Guedon. Reverend Ria van Holten, my mother-in-law and an author in her own right, helped maintain the atmosphere of support that every writer needs to see a project through with enthusiasm.

For the second edition, no list of thanks would be complete without Rosa Harris-Adler, Michael Fitz-James, Gail Cohen, and Maxine Corea at the Leonard Shore Memorial Library in